How to Use this Interactive Text

D1797690

To provide the knowledge and practice to help you succeed in the examination for Paper 2 *Information for management control.*

To pass the examination you need a thorough understanding in all areas covered by the syllabus and teaching guide.

Recommended approach

(a) To pass you need to be able to answer questions on **everything** specified by the syllabus and teaching guide. Read the text very carefully and do not skip any of it.

(b) Learning is an **active** process. Do **all** the questions as you work through the text so you can be sure you really understand what you have read.

(c) After you have covered the material in the Interactive Text, work through the Pilot paper **Question Bank**, checking your answers carefully against the **Answer Bank**.

(d) Before you take the exam, check that you still remember the material using the following quick revision plan.

    (i) Read through the **chapter topic list** at the beginning of each chapter. Are there any gaps in your knowledge? If so, study the section again.

    (ii) Read and learn the **key terms**.

    (iii) Look at the **exam focus points**. These show the ways in which topics might be examined.

    (iv) Read the **chapter roundups**, which are a summary of the **fast forwards** in each chapter.

    (v) Do the **quick quizzes** again. If you know what you're doing, they shouldn't take long.

This approach is only a suggestion. You or your college may well adapt it to suit your needs.
Remember this is a **practical** course.

(a) Try to relate the material to your experience in the workplace or any other work experience you may have had.

(b) Try to make as many links as you can to other papers at the Introductory and Intermediate levels.

Approach to examining the syllabus

Paper 2 is a two-hour computer based examination.

The examination currently consists of one section as follows:

	Marks
50 multiple choice questions of 2 marks each	100

See page (vii) for how **to** tackle multiple choice questions.

Important note on terminology for future sittings of CAT 2

The IASB issued a revised IAS 1 *Presentation of Financial Statements* in September 2007. This will become effective for periods ending on or after 1 January 2009. What this means for your CAT 2 exam is that a balance sheet will (with immediate effect) be called a statement of financial position and a cash flow statement will be called a statement of cash flows. The examiner will continue to use the term income statement in your exams until June 2009. After that, the examiner may choose to use the term 'statement of comprehensive income', although 'income statement' is more likely.

Terminology for exams before Jun 08	Terminology for exams from Jun 08 to May 09	Terminology for exams from Jun 09 onwards
Income statement	Income statement	Income statement or statement of comprehensive income.
Balance sheet	Statement of financial position	Statement of financial position
Cash flow statement	Statement of cash flows	Statement of cash flows

CAT

INTRODUCTORY
PAPER 2
INFORMATION FOR MANAGEMENT CONTROL

INTERACTIVE TEXT

BPP is the **official provider** of training materials for the ACCA's CAT qualification. This Interactive Text forms part of a suite of learning tools, which also includes CD-ROMs for tuition and computer based assessment, and the innovative, internet-based Learn Online.

This text has been specifically written to the **current syllabus** and Teaching Guide.

- Clear language and presentation

- Plenty of questions, examples and quizzes to demonstrate and practise techniques

- Pilot paper for Paper 2 *Information for Management Control* with suggested solutions prepared by BPP Learning Media authors

FOR EXAMS IN DECEMBER 2008 AND JUNE 2009

LEARNING MEDIA

First edition 2003

Sixth edition June 2008

ISBN 9780 7517 4821 5
(Previous ISBN 9780 7517 3569 7)

British Library Cataloguing-in-Publication Data
A catalogue record for this book
is available from the British Library

Published by

BPP Learning Media Ltd
BPP House, Aldine Place
London W12 8AA

www.bpp.com/learningmedia

Printed in Great Britain by

WM Print
45-47 Frederick Street
Walsall
West Midlands
WS2 9NE

We are grateful to the Association of Chartered Certified
Accountants for permission to reproduce past
examination questions. The suggested solutions in the
exam answer bank have been prepared by BPP Learning
Media Ltd, except where otherwise stated.

Contents

The Computer Based Examination

The ACCA has introduced a computer based examination (CBE) for CAT Papers 1–4 (in addition to the conventional paper based examination for papers 3 and 4).

Computer based examinations must be taken at an ACCA CBE Licensed Centre.

How does CBE work?

- Questions are displayed on a monitor
- Candidates enter their answer directly onto the computer
- Candidates have two hours to complete the examination
- When the candidate has completed their examination, the computer automatically marks the file containing the candidate's answers
- Candidates are provided with a certificate showing their results before leaving the examination room
- The CBE Licensed Centre uploads the results to the ACCA (as proof of the candidate's performance) within 48 hours

Benefits

- **Flexibility** as a CBE can be sat at any time.
- **Resits** can also be taken at any time and there is no restriction on the number of times a candidate can sit a CBE.
- **Instant feedback** as the computer displays the results at the end of the CBE.
- Results are notified to ACCA **within 48 hours**.
- **Extended closing date periods** (see ACCA website for further information)

CBE question types

- Multiple choice – choose one answer from four options
- Multiple response 1 – select more than one response by clicking the appropriate tick boxes
- Multiple response 2 – select a response to a number of related part questions by choosing one option from a number of drop down menus
- Number entry – key in a numerical response to a question

CAT CBE

You will have two hours in which to answer a number of questions, which are worth a total of 100 marks. See the ACCA website for a demonstration and up to date information (www.acca.org.uk/colleges/cbe_demo).

Tackling Multiple Choice Questions

MCQ's are now part of all CAT exams. Papers 1 and 2 are examined by CBE, Papers 3 and 4 can be taken by CBE or by a written paper which is 40% MCQs. Paper 5 is now 50% MCQ's and Papers 6-10 are 20% MCQs. All MCQs carry 2 marks.

The MCQs in your exam contain four possible answers. You have to **choose the option that best answers the question**. The three incorrect options are called distracters. There is a skill in answering MCQs quickly and correctly. By practising MCQs you can develop this skill, giving you a better chance of passing the exam.

You may wish to follow the approach outlined below, or you may prefer to adapt it.

Step 1 Skim read all the MCQs and identify what appear to be the easier questions.

Step 2 Attempt each question – **starting with the easier questions** identified in Step 1. Read the question **thoroughly**. You may prefer to work out the answer before looking at the options, or you may prefer to look at the options at the beginning. Adopt the method that works best for you.

Step 3 Read the four options and see if one matches your own answer. Be careful with numerical questions as the distracters are designed to match answers that incorporate common errors. Check that your calculation is correct. Have you followed the requirement exactly? Have you included every stage of the calculation?

Step 4 You may find that none of the options matches your answer.

- Re-read the question to ensure that you understand it and are answering the requirement
- Eliminate any obviously wrong answers
- Consider which of the remaining answers is the most likely to be correct and select the option

Step 5 If you are still unsure make a note and continue to the next question

Step 6 Revisit unanswered questions. When you come back to a question after a break you often find you are able to answer it correctly straight away. If you are still unsure have a guess. You are not penalised for incorrect answers, so **never leave a question unanswered!**

After extensive practice and revision of MCQs, you may find that you recognise a question when you sit the exam. Be aware that the detail and/or requirement may be different. If the question seems familiar read the requirement and options carefully – do not assume that it is identical.

P
A
R
T

A

Computer systems

Computer hardware and software

1

Study guide

			Syllabus reference
1	(a)	Describe the different types of hardware configuration: stand alone PC, networked system, mainframe with terminals.	1(b)
	(b)	Explain where the different types of hardware configuration may be used.	1(b)
	(c)	Describe the hardware and software components of a computer system.	1(b), 3(b)(iii)

1 Introduction

Accounting staff do not need to have expert knowledge of computer hardware, software and networks to perform their roles effectively. However, since so much accounting work is now performed using computers, it is useful to have a working knowledge of the **tools of your trade**.

This paper, Information for Management Control, covers the basic techniques required to use a computer system safely and to effectively recognise, provide and maintain management information.

Part A of this book (chapters 1-5) covers **computer systems**, Part B (chapters 6-16) focuses on **management information**.

2 Hardware

2.1 A computer

FAST FORWARD

> A computer may be defined as a device which will accept **input** data, **process** it according to certain rules and stores or **outputs** data.
>
> Computers have traditionally been classified as supercomputers, mainframes, minicomputers and microcomputers (or **PC**s), but the distinctions are less distinct with modern systems.

Key term

> A **computer** is a device which will accept input data, process it, and store or output the results.

Let's look more closely at the definition above.

(a) The **device** is actually a group of mechanical and electronic devices working together to accept **inputs**, **process** them and produce **output**.

(b) A computer processes data according to **rules**.

(c) A computer's operations are performed 'according to programmed **logical** and **arithmetic** rules.' The **arithmetic** element might be as simple as $x + y = z$. An example of a **logical rule** is 'if x does not contain a value then display an error message'.

A **computer** is therefore a mixture of physical, **tangible** things like keyboards, screens, circuits and cables (**hardware**) and **intangible** arithmetic and logical rules (**software**). Using electrical impulses, the two are connected and communicate with each other. A **peripheral** is a piece of equipment, such as a printer, that can be connected to a computer.

2.2 Computer hardware

Key term

> **Hardware** means the various physical components which comprise a computer system, as opposed to the non-tangible software elements.

2.3 Types of computer

Computers can be **classified** as follows, starting with the most powerful.

- Supercomputers
- Mainframe computers, now sometimes called 'enterprise servers'
- Minicomputers, now often called 'mid-range' computers
- Microcomputers, now commonly called Personal Computers (PCs)

Question   Computer systems experience

If you are studying at a college, discuss the types of computer systems fellow students have encountered. Most will probably use PCs but there may be some who have experience of larger systems.

Answer

There are a vast range of software products available. Fellow students may have experience of systems they have found to be particularly good, or particularly bad. Discussing system qualities and types should help your overall systems knowledge, and may prove useful when system purchases are being considered.

2.3.1 Supercomputers

Supercomputers are the most powerful computers. They are quite rare, and are not used in business. Supercomputers are able to process very **large amounts** of **data** very quickly. They are used for very complex calculations, for example by astronomers tracking the movement of objects in outer space. Manufacturers of supercomputers include Cray and Fujitsu.

2.3.2 Mainframes

After supercomputers, the next most powerful computers are mainframes. A mainframe is a **very powerful** computer often used at the centre of a large computer system. The mainframe is linked by cable or other telecommunications links to a number of terminals. A mainframe has significantly **more processing power than a PC** and offers very **extensive data storage** facilities. Some people now refer to mainframes as 'Enterprise servers'. Manufacturers include IBM and HP.

2.3.3 Minicomputers

The term 'minicomputer' is sometimes used to describe a computer that has **more processing power than a PC**, but **less than a mainframe**.

The term isn't used very often now, as with the development of more powerful PCs and physically smaller mainframes, it is difficult to define exactly what a minicomputer is. Price, power and number of users supported are sometimes used as distinguishing features. Manufacturers of minicomputers include IBM, ICL and DEC.

2.3.4 Personal computers (PCs)

The most common type of computer is the **Personal Computer** or PC. A PC is a general-purpose, single-user computer designed to be operated by one person at a time. The technical name for a PC is a **microcomputer**.

PCs are now the norm for small to medium-sized business computing and for home computing. Often they are linked together in a **network** to enable **sharing** of information between users.

The **physical components** of a typical Personal Computer (PC) are shown in the following diagram.

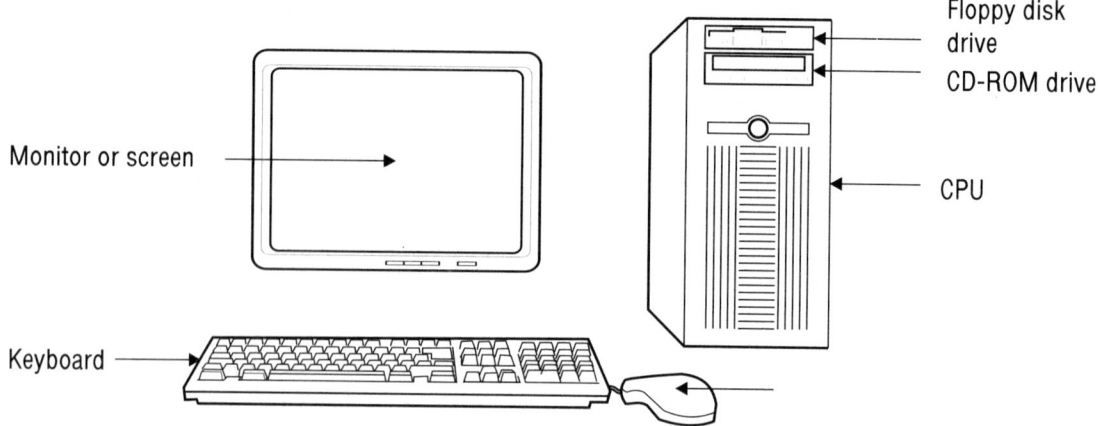

Monitor or screen

Floppy disk drive

CD-ROM drive

CPU

Keyboard

2.4 Other common descriptions of computers

We have described the four main categories of computers. You may also hear other descriptions of computers that relate to their role or some other characteristic. Some common example are:

- File servers
- Portables (or laptops)
- Macs
- Workstations

2.4.1 File servers

A file server is more powerful than the average desktop PC, although many file servers are in fact very powerful PCs. The file server provides **additional services** for users of networked PCs. We shall discuss these in more detail later in this chapter.

A very large network is likely to use a 'mainframe' computer as its server. Many mainframes are now often referred to as **'enterprise servers'**.

2.4.2 Portables (or laptops)

Laptop computers are popular as they are easy to transport, and therefore allow people to use their computer on the move or in a number of **different locations**. They also save desk **space**.

Laptops, also referred to as notebooks, are powered either from the mains electricity supply or through the use of a rechargeable battery. Laptops now offer full functionality – top models include all the features of desktop PCs.

Handheld computers (or palmtops) range from machines which are little more than electronic diaries, to relatively powerful processors with PC compatibility and communications features.

While portable PCs are becoming extremely popular (even in the office, as they save precious space on crowded desks), they have some disadvantages, such as the following.

- Keyboard **ergonomics** (ie keys which are too small, or too close together for quick typing).
- **Battery power** is often limited.

2.4.3 Workstations

The term workstation is sometimes used to describe a high performance personal computer used for a specialised purpose. However, the term is also now also often used to describe a person's desk, chair and computer – their immediate **working environment**.

2.4.4 Macs (Apple Macintosh computers)

Computers made by Apple Macintosh are often referred to as **Macs**. Introduced in 1984, the **Macintosh** or Mac is essentially a PC, although people generally don't include Macs when using the term PC. In the past, the Mac distinguished itself from other PCs by providing a user-friendly interface that utilised windows,

icons, and a mouse. The Windows interface, used on other PCs, copied many features from the Mac. There are now many different Macintosh models, with varying degrees of power.

2.5 PC parts and specifications

FAST FORWARD

The **processor** is at the heart of any computer. It consists of an arithmetic and logic unit and a control unit. Important concepts are clock speed (MHz) and RAM.

2.5.1 The processor or CPU

Key term

The **processor** or Central Processing Unit (CPU) is the collection of circuitry and registers that performs the processing in a computer. The processor is sometimes described as the 'brain' of the computer.

Two important components of the CPU are:

- The arithmetic and logic unit (ALU) which performs arithmetic and logical operations
- The control unit, which extracts instructions from memory and decodes and executes them

The set of operations that the processor performs is known as the **instruction set**.

2.5.2 Chips

On large machines, CPUs require one or more circuit boards. On personal computers and small workstations, the CPU is housed in a single **chip**. A chip is a small piece of silicon upon which is etched an integrated circuit, which consists of transistors and their interconnecting patterns on an extremely small scale. The chip is mounted on a carrier unit which in turn is 'plugged' on to a circuit board – called the **motherboard** – with other chips, each with their own functions, such as sound (a 'sound card') and video (a 'video card').

Many PCs carry a sticker saying 'Intel inside' – referring to the chips made by the Intel company. Other manufacturers include AMD and Digital.

2.5.3 MHz, cycles and clock speed

The signals are co-ordinated by a **clock** which sends out a 'pulse' – a sort of tick-tock sequence called a **cycle** – at regular intervals. Processor speed is measured in the number of these cycles produced per second.

This speed is expressed in MegaHertz (MHz) or GigaHertz (GHz).

- 1 MHz = one **million** cycles per **second**
- 1 GHz = one **billion** cycles per **second**

2.5.4 The bus

A signal travels along an electronic path that is called a **bus** in computer jargon. A 'local bus' is a particularly fast route.

2.6 Memory

The computer's **memory** is also known as main store or internal store. Memory is used to store data within the processing unit while the computer is operating. The reason for holding programs in the memory is to **speed up processing**. However, a computer's memory is limited in its size, and can only hold a certain volume of data at any time.

The memory will hold the following.

(a) **Programs**. The control unit acts on program instructions that are held in the store; these program instructions include the operating system.

(b) Some **input data**. A small area of internal store is needed to take in the data that will be processed next.

(c) A **working area**. The computer will need an area of store to hold data that is currently being processed or is used for processing other data.

(d) Some **output data**. A small area of store is needed to hold temporarily the data or information that is ready for output to an output device.

2.6.1 Bits and bytes

Each individual storage element in the computer's memory consists of a simple circuit which can be switched **on** or **off**. These two states can be conveniently expressed by the numbers **1** and **0** respectively. Any piece of data or instruction must be coded in these symbols before processing can commence.

Each 1 or 0 is a **bit**. Bits are grouped together in groups of eight to form **bytes**. Most PCs use **32 bit** or **64 bit** processors. This means that data travels around from one place to another in groups of 32 or 64 bits.

The processing capacity of a computer is in part dictated by the capacity of its memory. Capacity is calculated in **kilobytes** (1 kilobyte = 2^{10} (1,024) bytes) and **megabytes** (1 megabyte = 2^{20} bytes) and **gigabytes** (2^{30}). These are abbreviated to Kb, Mb and Gb.

| Question | Kilobytes, megabytes and gigabytes |

For convenience a kilobyte (1,024 bytes) is generally thought of as 1,000 bytes (hence the name *kilo*).

(a) Approximately how many bytes are there in a megabyte?
(b) Approximately how many megabytes are there in a gigabyte?

Answer

(a) 1 million or, more accurately, (2^{20} = 1,048,576).
(b) 1,000 or, more accurately, 1,024. ($2^{30}/2^{20}$ = 1,024)

2.7 Types of memory

A distinction can be made between two main types of memory, **RAM** and **ROM**. The term **cache** is also important.

2.7.1 RAM

Key term

> **RAM** (random access memory) is memory that is directly available to the processing unit. It holds the data and programs in current use. Data can be written on to or read from random access memory.

RAM can be defined as memory with the ability to access any location in the memory in any order with the same speed. **Random access** is an essential requirement for the main memory of a computer. RAM in microcomputers is **'volatile'** which means that the contents of the memory are **erased** when the computer's power is switched off.

The RAM on a typical modern business PC is likely to be around two gigabytes. The size of the RAM is extremely important. A computer with a two GHz clock speed but only 500 Mb of RAM will not be as efficient as a two GHz PC with 2Gb of RAM.

Question

When you start up a program on a PC you may hear a crackling noise, and see a little light flickering on the front of the base unit. What is happening?

Answer

The program is being read from the PC's hard disk into the Random Access Memory (RAM).

2.7.2 ROM

Key term

> ROM (read-only memory) is a memory chip into which fixed data is written permanently at the time of its manufacture. New data cannot be written into the memory – the data on the memory chip can't be changed.

ROM is **'non-volatile'** memory, which means that its contents do not disappear when the computer's power source is switched off. A computer's **start-up program**, known as a 'bootstrap' program, is always held in a form of a ROM. 'Booting up' means running this program.

When you turn on a PC you will usually see a reference to **BIOS** (basic input/output system). This is part of the ROM chip containing all the programs needed to control the keyboard, screen, disk drives and so on.

2.7.3 Cache

The **cache** is a small capacity but **extremely fast** memory chip which saves a second copy of the pieces of data most recently read from or written to main memory. When the cache is full, older entries are 'flushed out' to make room for new ones.

The principle is that if a piece of data is accessed once it is highly likely that it will be accessed again soon afterwards, and so keeping it readily to hand will speed up processing.

2.8 Input devices

2.8.1 The keyboard

FAST FORWARD

> Data may be input manually via a **keyboard**. Alternatively, data may be input using some **automated system**. The ideal method of data input in a given application is one which minimises input time, cost and errors.

The keyboard is the tool most often used for computer input. A computer keyboard is based on the old traditional QWERTY typewriter keyboard which includes the **alphabet**, **numbers** 0 – 9 and some basic **punctuation**, together with other keys (for example a space bar and a shift key, which allows a second set of key features to be used, including the upper case alphabet keys).

Keying data into a computer using a keyboard can be a **labour-intensive** process. In many cases the process of inputting data is speeded up through some form of automated **data capture**. We will look at automatic input devices later in this section.

2.8.2 The VDU or monitor

A VDU (visual display unit) or 'monitor' displays text and graphics. The screen's **resolution** is the number of pixels that are lit up. A **pixel** is a picture element –a 'dot' on the screen, as it were. The fewer the pixels on screen, the larger each individual pixel will be, so fewer pixels mean lower resolution or image quality. A larger number of smaller pixels will provide a higher resolution display.

Touch-sensitive screens have been developed which allow the monitor to be used as an input device. Selections are made by users touching areas of the screen. Sensors, built into the screen surround, detect which area has been touched. These devices are widely used in vending situations, such as the selling of train tickets.

2.8.3 Mouse

A **wheeled mouse** is a handheld device with a rubber ball protruding from a small hole in its base. The mouse is moved over a flat surface, and as it moves, internal sensors pick up the motion and convert it into electronic signals which instruct the cursor on screen to move.

The wheeled mouse is slowly being replaced by the **optical mouse.** The optical mouse has a small light-emitting diode (LED) that bounces light off the surface the mouse is moved across. The mouse contains sensors that convert this movement into co-ordinates the computer can understand.

A typical mouse has two or three **buttons** which can be pressed (**clicked**) to send specific signals. For example, a 'click' on the left hand button can be used to send the cursor to a new cell in a spreadsheet and a 'double click' can select a particular application from a Windows menu. Newer mice also have a **wheel** used to scroll within pages or documents that can't all be displayed on a single screen.

Similar to the mouse is the **trackball**, which is often found on laptop computers. Trackballs comprise a casing fixed to the computer, and a ball which protrudes upwards. The user moves the ball by hand. Other mobile computers use a **touch sensitive pad** for mouse functions; others have a tiny **joystick** in the centre of the keyboard.

2.9 Automatic input devices

In the following paragraphs we explain some of the most common document reading methods. Document reading methods reduce the manual work involved in data input. This **saves time and money** and also **reduces errors.**

2.9.1 Magnetic ink character recognition (MICR)

Magnetic ink character recognition (**MICR**) involves the recognition by a machine of special formatted characters printed in magnetic ink. The characters are read using a specialised reading device. The main advantage of MICR is its speed and accuracy, but MICR documents are expensive to produce. The main commercial application of MICR is in the banking industry – on cheques and deposit slips.

2.10 Optical mark reading (OMR)

Optical mark reading involves the marking of a pre-printed form with a ballpoint pen or typed line or cross in an appropriate box. The card is then read by an OMR device which senses the mark in each box using an electric current and translates it into machine code. Applications in which OMR is used include **National Lottery** entry forms, and answer sheets for multiple choice questions.

2.10.1 Scanners and Optical Character Recognition (OCR)

A scanner is device that can **read text or illustrations printed on paper** and translate the information into a **form the computer can use**. To edit text read by a scanner, you need **optical character recognition** (**OCR**) software to translate the image into text. Businesses may use a scanner and OCR to obtain 'digital' versions of documents they have only paper copies of. To enable the OCR software to recognise the characters correctly, the paper copy of the document must be good quality.

2.10.2 Bar coding and EPOS

Bar codes are groups of marks which, by their spacing and thickness, indicate specific codes or values. Electronic Point of Sale (EPOS) devices, which include bar code readers, enable supermarkets and other retailers to record and manage stock movements – and provide detailed sales information.

2.10.3 EFTPOS

Many retailers use EFTPOS systems (**Electronic Funds Transfer** at the **Point of Sale**). An EFTPOS system involves making payment electronically using a customers debit or credit card. A small terminal is used which reads the customers details and processes payment from their bank account or credit card account.

2.10.4 Magnetic stripe cards

Credit and debit cards, and some other cards, contain data held on a thin strip of magnetic recording tape stuck to the back of the card. The magnetic card reader converts this information into directly computer-sensible form. The widest application of magnetic stripe cards is as bank credit or service cards.

2.10.5 Smart cards

Because of security concerns, magnetic stripe technology is slowly being replaced in some areas by smart cards. The data on magnetic strip cards can be read, written, deleted or changed with equipment that is reasonably easy to obtain.

A smart card is a plastic card in which is embedded **a microprocessor chip**. The microprocessor replaces the 'usual' magnetic tape. The microprocessor is under a gold contact pad on one side of the card. The chip enables much **more effective security** checks to be made. The most common smart card applications include credit and debit cards, electronic cash, computer security systems and cable/satellite TV systems.

2.10.6 Voice recognition

Computer software has been developed that can convert speech into computer-sensible form via a microphone. Users are required to speak clearly and reasonably slowly.

Question	Keyboard input

In view of the above, what are the advantages and disadvantages of keyboard input?

Answer

A significant advantage of keyboard input is that the user is able to read and interpret what is being input – the user can exercise some judgement to ensure only valid data is entered.

Other advantages of keyboard input include:

(a) The person keying in the data can be in a remote location, away from the computer itself. Data can be transmitted via a communications link.

(b) The person keying in the data can check for keying errors on-screen.

(c) Keyboard input is convenient for small volumes of data when the time taken up by data input is relatively short.

Direct keyboard input has a number of disadvantages.

(a) It is unsuitable for large volumes of transaction data. Keying data manually takes time, so is not appropriate in some situations.

(b) Keyboard input is likely to be error-prone.

(c) There might be security problems. For example, keyboard input may be watched and there is the risk that unauthorised people could access a terminal or PC.

2.11 Output devices

FAST FORWARD

Output is usually sent to either the **screen**, to a **printer**, or to another **computer file** – possibly for processing by another computer.

The commonest methods of computer output are printers and screen display. Sometimes output is produced in the form of a computer file.

2.11.1 Printers

Laser printers are now widespread. They print a whole page at a time, rather than line by line. The **quality** of output with laser printers is very **high**. Laser printers are relatively expensive to purchase, but compared with inkjet printers, running costs are relatively low.

Bubblejet and **inkjet** printers are small and reasonably cheap (under £50), making them popular where a 'private' output device is required. They work by sending a jet of ink on to the paper to produce the required characters. They are fairly quiet and fast, but they may produce smudged output if the paper is not handled carefully. The price and regularity with which ink cartridges need to be replaced mean that running costs can be high.

Older style printers, that use tractor-fed rolls of paper are still used in some organisations for printing high volumes. An example is a **dot matrix printer**, which is a character printer which prints a single character at a time. Their main drawback is their **low-resolution.** They are also relatively **slow** and **noisy**, but cheap to run.

2.11.2 The VDU or monitor

Screens were described earlier in this chapter, as they are used together with computer keyboards for **input**. It should also be clear that they can be used as an **output** medium, primarily where the output **volume is low** (for example a single enquiry) and **no permanent output** is required (for example the current balance on an account).

2.11.3 The choice of output medium

Choosing a suitable output medium depends on a number of factors.

Factor	Comment
Hard copy	Is a printed version of the output needed?
Quantity	For example, a VDU screen can hold a certain amount of data, but it becomes more difficult to read when information goes 'off-screen' and can only be read a 'page' at a time.
Speed	For example if a single enquiry is required it may be quicker to make notes from a VDU display.
Suitability for further use	Output to a file would be appropriate if the data will be processed further, maybe in a different system. Large volumes of reference data might be held on microfilm or microfiche.
Cost	The 'best' output device may not be justifiable on the grounds of cost – another output medium should be chosen.

Question

Manufacturers

The next time you are in a shop that sells computer equipment, identify two manufacturers for each of the following.

(a)   PCs   (c)   Printers
(b)   Scanners

Major manufacturers include the following.

(a)   PCs – Dell, Compaq, IBM, Sony
(b)   Scanners – Canon, Epson, Hewlett Packard
(c)   Printers – Brother, Canon, Epson, Hewlett Packard, Lexmark

There are many others.

2.12 Storage devices

FAST FORWARD

The most common types of storage are magnetic tape and optical disk (eg CD and DVD).

2.12.1 Disks

Disks are the predominant form of backing storage. Disks are covered on both sides with a **magnetic** material. Data is held on a number of circular, concentric **tracks** on the surfaces of the disk, and is read or written by rotating the disk past read/write heads. The mechanism that causes the disk to rotate is called a **disk drive**.

2.12.2 Hard disks

A modern business PC invariably has an **internal hard disk**. At the time of writing the average new **PC** has a hard disk size of around 150 Gigabytes. Larger systems may use a stack of **removable disks**.

2.12.3 Memory sticks

The memory stick is a small portable storage medium which can hold around two Gb of data. It is useful for storage and for moving files between computers. The memory stick is inserted into one of the computer's USB ports.

2.12.4 Optical disks

The main types of optical disks are **CD-ROM** (Compact Disc – Read Only Memory) and **DVD** (Digital Versatile Disc). Optical disks are read and written to using lasers. Optical disks can store much more data, up to 6 gigabytes, than most portable magnetic disks.

A CD-ROM can store 700 megabytes of data. The data is permanent and can be read any number of times, but true CD-ROMs cannot be modified.

CD **recorders** are now available for use with blank CDs (CD-R) and **rewritable disks** (CD-RW). Although not strictly correct, in everyday speech these are also sometimes called CD-ROMs.

The **speed** of a CD-ROM drive is relevant to how fast data can be retrieved: for example, an **eight-speed** drive is quicker than a **four-speed** drive.

The CD format has started to be superseded by **Digital Versatile Disk (DVD)**. DVD development was encouraged by the advent of multimedia files with video graphics and sound – requiring greater disk capacity. One **DVD** can hold almost 5 gigabytes of data. Access speeds are improved as is sound and video quality.

Many people believe DVD will not only replace CD-ROMs, but also VHS cassettes, audio CDs and laser discs. DVD is backward compatible with CD-ROM, meaning a DVD drive allows users to access CD-ROMS.

2.12.5 Tape storage

Tape cartridges have a **much larger capacity** than floppy disks and they are still widely used as a **backing storage** medium. Tapes are generally measured in terms of tape width and length. For instance an 8mm tape that is 112m long can store up to 5Gb of data; a 4mm tape of 125m can store up to 12Gb. Fast tapes which can be used to create a back-up file very quickly are known as **tape streamers**.

Like an audio or video cassette, data has to be recorded **along the length** of a computer tape and so it is **more time consuming** to access a particular file than data on disk (ie direct access is not possible with tape – just like a song on a cassette tape, the tape has to be forwarded or rewound to the required location).

Exam focus point

> Computer hardware is a key topic for Paper 2 and there are likely to be two or three questions on this area.

3 Networks and communications

FAST FORWARD

> A **local area network** is a system of linked PCs and other devices such as printers. LANs can have a **server** computer holding files used by more than one computer, and providing storage capacity to the other computers in the network.
>
> A **wide area network** is a network of computers which are dispersed on a wider geographical scale than LANs. They are connected over the public **telecommunications** network. A WAN will normally use minicomputers or powerful PCs.

Computers used in organisations are usually part of a connected group of computers - known as a **network**. In this section we look at different types of computer networks. Later in the chapter we look at how computers **communicate** with each other.

A computer **network** is made up of a number of connected computers each with their own processor, for example a number of connected PCs. Networks are popular because they provide a number of users with access to **resources** (eg data files, printers, software). Therefore, a network allows computing resources to be used more efficiently between a group of users. There are two main types of network, a **local area network** (LAN) and a **wide area network** (WAN).

3.1 Local area networks (LANs)

Key term

> A **local area network** (LAN) is a network of computers located in a single building or on a single site. The parts of the network are linked by computer cable rather than via telecommunications lines.

Network topology refers to the physical arrangement of items **(nodes)** in a network. A **node** is any device connected to a network: it can be a computer, or a peripheral device such as a printer.

There are several types of LAN system configuration. For example, in a **bus structure** (diagram follows), messages are sent out from one point along a single communication channel, and the messages are received by other connected machines.

Each device can **communicate with every other device** and communication is quick and reliable. Nodes can be **added or unplugged** very easily. Locating cable faults is also relatively simple.

Bus system

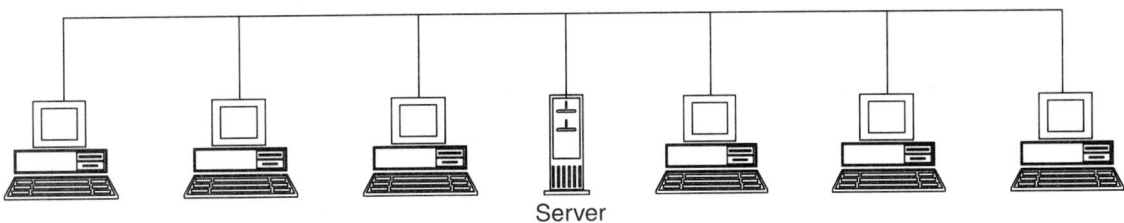

Server

Other types of LAN architectures are shown below. Which architecture is most appropriate depends upon a number of factors – such as which files are required to be accessed by many users. The number of printers to be shared and the relative power of the computers.

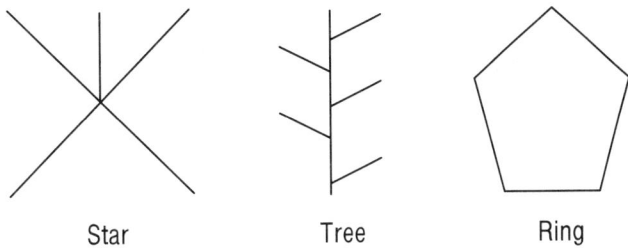

Star   Tree   Ring

Local area networks have been **successful** for a number of reasons. First of all, personal computers of sufficient power and related software were developed, so that network applications became possible. Some organisations which could not afford a mainframe or minicomputer with terminal links have been able to afford a LAN with personal computers.

3.2 Wide area networks (WANs)

Key term

Wide area networks (WANs) are networks on a number of sites, perhaps on a wide geographical scale.

WANs often use minicomputers or mainframes as the 'pumps' that keep the data messages circulating, whereas shorter-distance LANs normally use PCs for this task.

A wide area network is similar to a local area network in concept, but the key differences are:

(a)   The **geographical area** covered by the network is greater, not being limited to a single building or site.

(b)   WANs will send data over **telecommunications links.**

(c)   WANs will often use a **larger computer** as a file server.

(d)   WANs will often be larger than LANs, with **more terminals or computers** linked to the network.

(e)   A WAN can link two or more LANs.

3.3 Client-server computing

FAST FORWARD

Client-server computing is a configuration in which desktop PCs are regarded as 'clients' that request access to the services available on a more powerful server PC, such as access to a file, e-mail, or printing facilities.

Key term

The term **client-server** is a way of describing the relationship between the devices in a network. With client-server computing, tasks are distributed among the machines on the network.

A **client** is a machine which requests a service, for example a PC running a spreadsheet application which the user wishes to print out.

A **server** is a machine which is dedicated to providing a particular function or service requested by a client. Servers include file servers (see below), print servers and e-mail servers.

A client-server system allows **computer power** to be distributed to where it is most needed. The **client**, or user, will use a powerful personal workstation with local processing capability. The **server** provides services such as shared printers, communications links, special-purpose processing and database storage.

The file server may be a powerful PC or a minicomputer. As its name implies, it **serves** the rest of the network offering a generally-accessible hard disk. Clients on a network generally also have their **own hard disk** storage.

File servers must be powerful enough to handle **multiple user requests** and provide **adequate storage**. File servers are typically classified as 'low end' or 'high end'.

(a) A **low end file server** might be used in a network of around six users, running 'office' type software. A low end server is usually a highly specified standard PC.

(b) A **'mid range server'** might support 20-30 users.

(c) A **high end file server** might be used in a large department network of anywhere from 30-250 users. High end servers have now been joined by **superservers** and **'enterprise servers'** (effectively, mainframes). These are either departmental or organisation-wide, running sophisticated mission-critical systems and offering fault tolerance features.

3.3.1 The advantages of client-server computing

The advantages of a network that uses the client-server approach are as follows.

Advantage	Comment
Greater resilience	Processing is spread over several computers. If one server breaks down, other locations can carry on processing.
Scalability	They are highly scalable – hardware can be added as required.
Shared programs and data	Program and data files held on a file server can be shared by all the PCs in the network. Data duplication is avoided.
Shared work-loads	Each PC in a network can do the same work. If there were separate stand-alone PCs, A might do job 1, B might do job 2, C might do job 3 and so on. In a network, any PC, (A, B or C) could do any job (1, 2 or 3). This provides flexibility in sharing work-loads.
Shared peripherals	Peripheral equipment can be shared. For example, in a LAN, five PCs might share a single printer.
Communication	LANs can be linked up to the office communications network. Electronic mail, calendar and diary facilities can be used.
Compatibility	Client-server systems are more likely than centralised systems to have Windows interfaces, making it easier to move information between applications such as spreadsheets and accounting systems.
Ad hoc enquiries	Information may be moved to a separate server, allowing data to be manipulated without disrupting the main system.

3.3.2 The disadvantages of client-server computing

The client-server approach has two main drawbacks.

Disadvantage	Comment
Less powerful than large mainframes	Mainframes are more suited to dealing with very large volumes of transactions.
Control can be difficult	It is easier to control and maintain a system centrally. In particular it is easier to keep data secure.

3.4 Computer communications

Computers linked in a network need to be able to communicate with each other to allow the sharing of resources. Computers in one network may also require the ability to occasionally communicate with computers in a different network.

Communication may involve the transfer of data from one part of a system to another, for example transaction values may be posted from the receivables ledger module of an accounting system to the general ledger module, or could involve one-off messages, for example through the use of electronic mail.

3.4.1 Data links

When all data processing is done in the **same office**, the transmission of data between input and output devices and the central processor is usually provided for using **internal cable**.

When the input or output device is located away from the computer, so that it has to be transmitted along a **telecommunications** link (for example a telephone line) there are additional items of data transmission equipment which have to be used, and the way in which the data is to be transmitted has to be resolved.

A data link might typically connect the following.

(a)   A **computer** and a **remote terminal** (keyboard and VDU). A computer may have a number of remote terminals linked to it by data transmission equipment.

(b)   **Two computers** located some distance from each other (for example a mainframe and a PC, which would use the link to exchange data).

(c)   Several **processors** in a **network**, with each computer in the network able to transmit data to any other.

3.5 Data transmission terminology

This section explains some common terms used in the context of data communications.

3.5.1 Modems and digital transmission

New technologies require transmission systems capable of delivering substantial quantities of data at great speed. For data transmission through the existing 'analogue' telephone network to be possible, there has to be a device at each end of the telephone line that can convert (MOdulate) the data from digital form to analogue form, and (DEModulate) from analogue form to digital form, depending on whether the data is being sent out or received along the telephone line. This conversion of data is done by devices called **modems**. There must be a modem at each end of the telephone line.

Digital means 'of digits or numbers'. Digital information is information in a coded (binary) form. Information in analogue form uses continuously variable signals. It is enough for you to appreciate that there is a distinction between the two and that digital methods are more advanced.

3.5.2 Bandwidth

The amount of data that can be sent down a telecommunications line is in part determined by the bandwidth. **Bandwidth** is the range of frequencies that the channel can carry. Frequencies are measured in cycles per second, or in **Hertz**. The wider the bandwidth, the greater the amount of data the channel can carry. (See '**Broadband**' later in this section.)

3.5.3 Integrated Services Digital Networks (ISDN)

Faster telecommunications networks such as ISDN and ADSL have been developed. Digital networks for **mobile** phones also exist.

An important development of the last few years is the spread of **Integrated Services Digital Networks (ISDN)**. Data can be transmitted significantly **faster** over ISDN than over standard tele-communications lines.

3.5.4 Asymmetric Digital Subscriber Line (ADSL)

ADSL (Asymmetric Digital Subscriber Line), offers data transfer rates of up to **8 Mbps**, considerably faster than ISDN. ADSL allows information to be sent out over ordinary copper wires and simultaneous use of the normal telephone service is possible.

3.5.5 Broadband

FAST FORWARD

A fast, always-on connection to the Internet is sometimes referred to as **Broadband**.

ADSL is an example of a broadband technology. Broadband means a relatively **high capacity**, and therefore relatively **fast**, communications link. The term broadband is usually used to describe an Internet connection that is 'always on', meaning it is not necessary to dial-up to establish a connection.

3.5.6 Network cards and connections

Computers and other devices on a network are connected to each other using computer cable (known as **coaxial cable**). This cable is plugged into all devices (eg computers, printers) on the network into a slot on the device (similar to a telephone connection slot). This connection connects the cable to a **network card** that holds the circuitry required for network communication.

3.5.7 Ports

A **port** is the **socket** on a computer into which you plug a peripheral device such as a printer. Ports can be serial, parallel or Universal Serial Bus (USB) as explained below. USB ports allow faster data transfer and are expected to eventually completely replace serial and parallel ports.

3.5.8 Interfaces

The term **interface** is frequently used in computer communications contexts, but it has at least three different meanings – as shown in the following table.

Interface – possible meanings	
What links two systems	The point at which two applications software systems are linked. For example, the *interface* between a computerised payables ledger and a general ledger will normally consist of an analysis file produced by the payables ledger being read by an *interface program* in the general ledger.
How you communicate with the computer	The point of interaction between the computer and the user, principally in terms of using a display screen for input and retrieval of information. The two principal forms of interface are often described as *Graphical User Interface* (GUI) or Character-based User Interface (CUI). GUIs (eg Windows) are now more favoured than CUIs (eg MS-DOS).
Electronic connections	The circuitry which connects two devices. Interfaces may be : *Serial,* in which case data is transmitted as a stream of individual bits through a single wire, or *Parallel,* where a number of wires each carry one bit so that eight wires, for example, will enable the eight bits comprising one byte to be transferred simultaneously, or *Universal Serial Bus (USB)* – a more recent type of port that supports data transfer at very fast rates. Most computer peripherals are now connected using USB.

3.5.9 Mobile communications

Networks for mobile telephone communications have grown since the development of mobile phones, also known as **'cellular phones'**, in the late 1980s.

Digital networks have been developed, which are better able to support data transmission than the older analogue networks. Digital networks offer **higher transmission speeds** and less likelihood of data corruption. Internet access through mobile phones is available, and combined handheld computer/cellular phones have been developed.

4 Software

FAST FORWARD

Operating system software manages computer resources and supervises the running of other programs. It provides a 'bridge' between software programs and the hardware.

Key term

Software is the name given to programs or sets of programs that tell the computer what to do.

We now turn our attention to the sets of instructions (programs) used with computers. These are referred to as software.

There are two main types of software. The **operating system** provides the link between hardware and software, and it controls the interaction between the user and the computer, via the human-computer interface, or HCI. **Applications software** is any computer program designed to help the user perform a task - rather than to control the operation of the computer.

Question   Software packages

Name three software packages and state the role or type of the package.

Answer

There are many examples to choose from. Here are four.

(a)   Microsoft Windows 95/98/ME/XP/2000/NT/Vista – variations of the Microsoft Windows operating system
(b)   Microsoft Word – word processing software
(c)   Microsoft Excel - spreadsheet
(d)   Sage Line 50 – an accounting package

4.1 The operating system

Key term

The **operating system** is concerned with the operation of the computer. It provides the link between the computer hardware, the user and other software.

An **operating system** is a program that provides the 'bridge' between **applications** software (such as word processing packages, spreadsheets or accounting packages) and the **hardware**. For example, access to data files held on disk during the processing of a business application would be managed by the operating system.

An operating system will typically perform the following tasks.

(a)   Initial **set-up** of the computer once it has 'booted up' via the BIOS.
(b)   Checking that **hardware** (including peripherals) is functioning properly.
(c)   Calling up of program files and data files into **memory**.
(d)   **Opening and closing** of files

(e)   Maintenance of **directories** (folders) in disk storage.

(f)   Controlling **input and output** devices.

(g)   Controlling system **security** (for example monitoring the use of passwords).

(h)   Handling of **interruptions** (for example program abnormalities or machine failure).

(i)   Managing **multitasking** (ie using more than one application at one time, for example printing out a Word document while you work on an Excel spreadsheet).

4.1.1 Microsoft Windows

FAST FORWARD

The most widely used operating system is **Microsoft Windows**, which is available in a range of versions for both PCs and networks. Other operating systems include Novell Netware, the Mac OS system, Unix and Linux.

The most popular computer operating system, particularly for PCs and small networks, is Microsoft Windows.

Microsoft Windows includes the following features.

(a)   A **'Desktop'**, which is a general area from which programs etc may be accessed. Shortcuts to disk drives, folders (directories), applications and files can all be placed on the Desktop.

(b)   A **'Taskbar'** which includes the **Start** button (from which applications may be launched) and buttons providing quick access to currently open applications.

(c)   A **Recycle Bin** for easy deletion and recovery of files.

(d)   Easy integration with **networking** software.

(e)   **Multitasking** is available, allowing more than one program to be active at one time.

(f)   The **Microsoft Internet Explorer** browser is included.

Although (as with almost all software) it does contain bugs and irritations, Microsoft Windows provides a **comprehensive working environment**, managing programs specifically written for it. This makes it **easier for beginners** to learn, as applications tend to look and 'feel' the same.

Other features of Windows are explained in the table below.

Feature/area	Comment
User-friendly	User interface enhancements include easier navigation, such as **single-click launching** of applications, icon highlighting, forward/backward buttons, and an easy to customise Start Menu. Application packages written for Windows are generally **similar in design** providing a familiar look and feel. This **reduces training time** and costs and makes **skills transferable**.
Reliability	(a) Windows can be set up to regularly **test** the user's hard disk, system files, and configuration information to increase the system reliability, and in many cases fix problems automatically. (b) Enhanced **backup** and **restore** functions.
Web integration	**There are a variety of features designed to enhance** Internet access **and use of Internet facilities and technologies, and integrate them with the users system.**
Multimedia	Windows has **graphics** and **video capabilities** and support for **games** hardware such as joysticks. It supports **digital video disks** (DVD).
Graphical user interface (GUI)	Windows has a **user-friendly** GUI (some say this was copied from the Macintosh Operating System). Most dialogue between the user and software is conducted through the mouse and on-screen images rather than typed text. The GUI has certain features, explained below, which can be remembered by the abbreviation **WIMP** (which stands for 'Windows, Icons, Mouse and Pull-down menu').

4.1.2 Windows (as in a section of the screen rather than the operating system)

The screen can be divided into sections ('windows') of flexible size, which can be opened and closed. This enables two or more programs to be open and viewed at the same time, for example an Excel spreadsheet and a Word document.

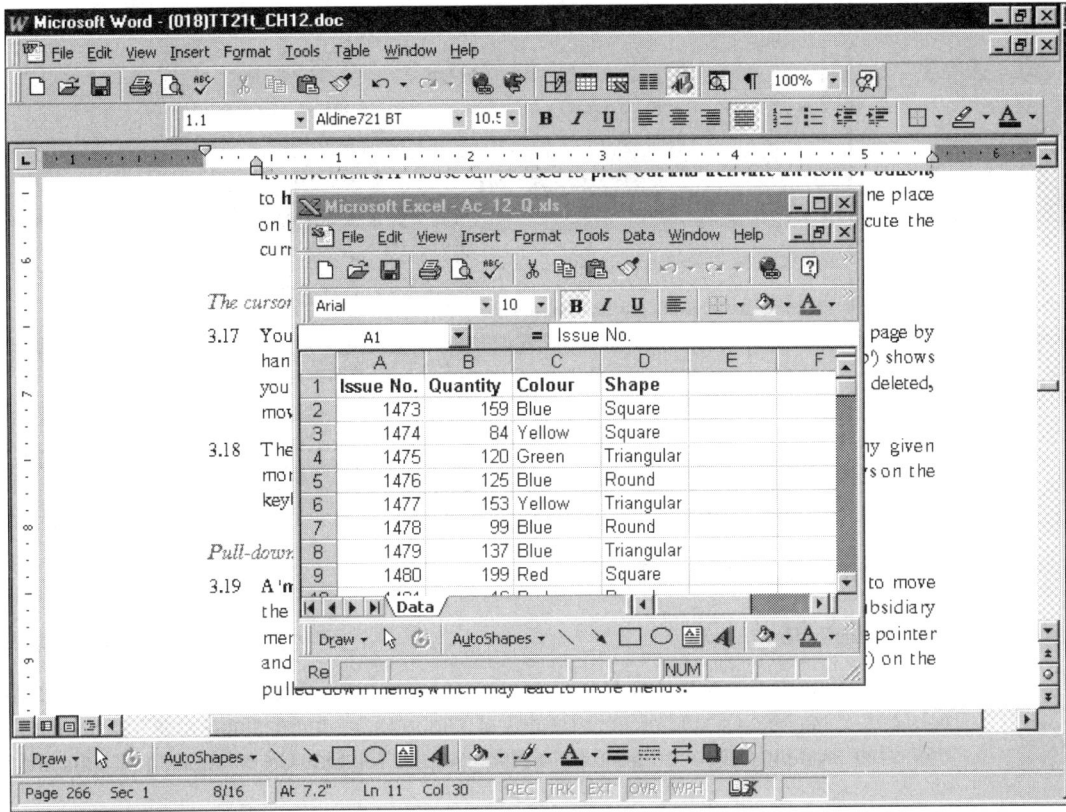

4.1.3 Icons

An icon is an image of an object used to represent a function or a file in an obvious way. For instance Windows based packages use a **picture of a printer** which is simply clicked to start the printing process.

4.1.4 Mouse

As the mouse moves around on the desktop a *pointer* (cursor) on the screen mimics its movements. The mouse has buttons which are **clicked** to execute the current command. Common actions performed using a mouse include activating an icon or button, selecting text and **dragging** data from one place then **dropping** in another.

4.1.5 Pull-down menu

A **'menu-bar'** will be shown across the top of the screen. Using the mouse to move the pointer to the required item in the menu, the pointer **'pulls down'** a subsidiary menu – somewhat similar to pulling down a roller blind at a window. The pointer and mouse can then be used to **select** (input) the required item (output) on the pulled-down menu, which may lead to more menus.

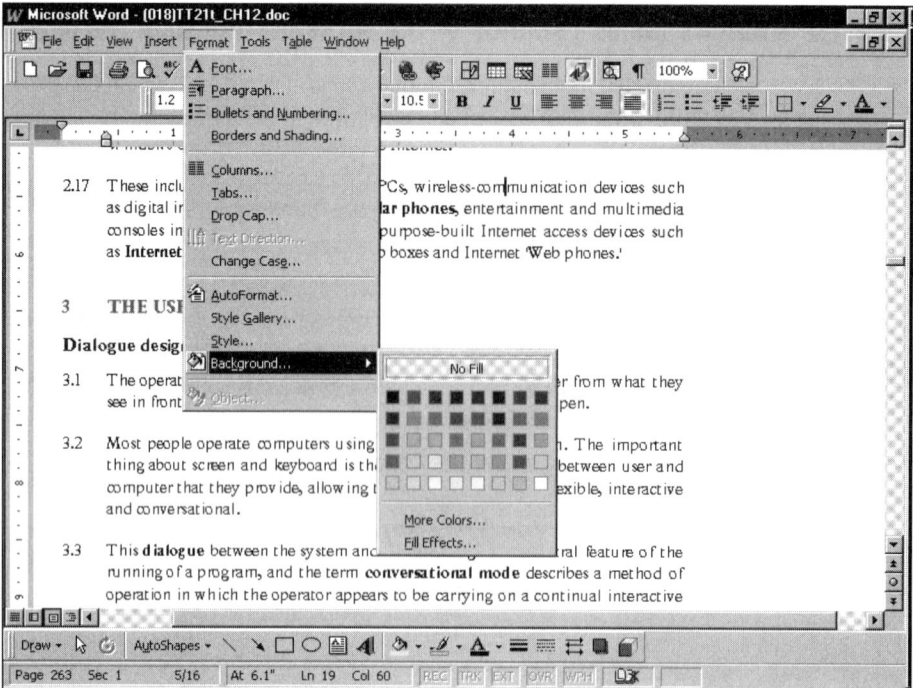

4.2 Other operating systems

4.2.1 Mac OS

Apple Macintosh computers or **Macs** use a completely different operating system called **Mac OS**. Recent versions of the Mac OS and recent versions of Windows are increasingly able to use data files created on the 'other' system. Other competitors to Windows and the Mac OS exist, such as **Unix** and **Linux**.

4.2.2 Unix

The **UNIX operating system** was developed as a **non-proprietary** (ie not specific to one manufacturer) operating system. UNIX works equally well in a PC network environment or in a mainframe system. Particular areas where UNIX has demonstrated its capabilities are **communications**, where the ability to accommodate PC operating systems in the UNIX environment supports the use of electronic mail, and **engineering**, where UNIX's capabilities are suited to driving high-resolution graphics systems.

4.2.3 Linux

Linux is a freely-distributable operating system that runs on many hardware platforms, including networks, PCs and Macintoshes. Linux has become a popular alternative to more traditional operating systems.

4.2.4 Novell Netware

NetWare is a popular local area network (LAN) operating system developed by Novell Corporation. NetWare runs on a variety of different types of LANs.

Question   Operating systems

List five tasks typically performed by an operating system.

The operating system performs the following tasks.

(a) Initial set-up of the computer once it has 'booted up'.
(b) Checking that the hardware (including peripheral devices such as printers) is functioning properly.
(c) Calling up of program files and data files into memory.
(d) Opening and closing of files and folders.
(e) Controlling input and output devices, including the interaction with the user.
(f) Controlling system security (for example monitoring the use of passwords).
(g) Handling of interruptions (for example program abnormalities or machine failure).
(h) Managing multitasking.

4.3 Applications software

FAST FORWARD

Software which processes data for a particular purpose, or which is written for a particular data processing function, is known as **applications software**. An example is a payroll package.

General purpose software allows data to be handled in a particular way, for example in a spreadsheet, but its specific use in a particular situation is determined by the user.

The term **integrated software** is generally used in two different situations. Accounts packages often consist of individual program **modules** that link together while some packages include programs that provide a **range of tools**, such as word processing, spreadsheets and a database.

Key term

Applications software consists of programs which carry out a task for the user as opposed to programs which control the workings of a computer.

Whenever a computer is being used, it will be under the control of an **application program**, for example controlling inventory, designing a car, dispensing cash, preparing accounts, running a computer game, word processing, economic forecasting, statistical analysis or recording sales at a cash desk.

Within applications software, a distribution can be made between **application packages** and **general purpose packages**.

4.3.1 Application packages

An **application package** is a program or set of programs that will carry out a specific processing application or job – for example, a payroll package is used for payroll processing. Application packages may be either written from scratch or purchased off-the-shelf. **Off-the-shelf** application packages are available for a wide range of business applications and provide a tested and cheaper means of obtaining a program than would be the case writing the programs from scratch.

4.3.2 General purpose packages

A **general purpose package** is an off-the-shelf program that can be used for processing of a general type, but the computer user can apply the package to a variety of uses. Spreadsheet packages and word processing packages are examples of general purpose packages.

4.3.3 Integrated software

The trend in applications software is towards integrated software packages. Integrated software refers to programs, or packages of programs, that perform a variety of different processing operations, using **data which is compatible** with whatever operation is being carried out. The term is generally used in two different situations.

(a) **Accounts packages** often consist of individual program **modules** that link together into a complete accounting system. For example, there will be a receivables ledger module, a payables ledger module a general ledger module and so on. Output from one 'module' in an integrated system can be used as input to another, without the need for re-entry of data.

(b) Some software packages include programs that provide a range of tools, such as word processing, spreadsheets and a database. Examples of integrated software packages include Lotus Smartsuite, Microsoft Works (a low specification package) and Microsoft Office (a collection of high specification programs).

Exam focus point

Any questions on computer software will be general questions and will not require detailed knowledge of any particular package.

Chapter Roundup

- A computer may be defined as a device which will accept **input** data, **process** it according to certain rules and stores or **outputs** data.

- Computers have traditionally been classified as supercomputers, mainframes, minicomputers and microcomputers (or **PCs**), but the distinctions are less distinct with modern systems.

- The **processor** is at the heart of any computer. It consists of an arithmetic and logic unit and a control unit. Important concepts are clock speed (MHz) and RAM.

- Data may be input manually via a **keyboard**. Alternatively, data may be input using some **automated system**. The ideal method of data input in a given application is one which minimises input time, cost and errors.

- **Output** is usually sent to either the **screen**, to a **printer**, or to another **computer file** – possibly for processing by another computer.

- The most common types of storage are magnetic **tape** and **optical disk** (eg CD and DVD).

- A **local area network** is a system of linked PCs and other devices such as printers. LANs can have a **server** computer holding files used by more than one computer, and providing storage capacity to the other computers in the network.

- A **wide area network** is a network of computers which are dispersed on a wider geographical scale than LANs. They are connected over the public **telecommunications** network. A WAN will normally use minicomputers or powerful PCs.

- **Client-server** computing is a configuration in which desktop PCs are regarded as 'clients' that request access to the services available on a more powerful server PC, such as access to a file, e-mail, or printing facilities.

- **Faster telecommunications** networks such as ISDN and ADSL have been developed. Digital networks for **mobile** phones also exist.

- A fast, always-on connection to the Internet is sometimes referred to as **Broadband**.

- **Operating system software** manages computer resources and supervises the running of other programs. It provides a 'bridge' between software programs and the hardware.

- The most widely used operating system is **Microsoft Windows**, which is available in a range of versions for both PCs and networks. Other operating systems include Novell Netware, the Mac OS system, Unix and Linux.

- Software which processes data for a particular purpose, or which is written for a particular data processing function, is known as **applications software**. An example is a payroll package.

- **General purpose software** allows data to be handled in a particular way, for example in a spreadsheet, but its specific use in a particular situation is determined by the user.

- The term **integrated software** is generally used in two different situations. Accounts packages often consist of individual program **modules** that link together while some packages include programs that provide a **range of tools**, such as word processing, spreadsheets and a database.

Quick Quiz

1   Which one of the following options describes the term 'hardware'?

    A   A set of programs that tell the computer what to do
    B   A system of linked PCs
    C   The various physical components which comprise a computer system
    D   A storage device

2   The most powerful computers are known as

    A   Special computers
    B   Super computers
    C   Mainframe computers
    D   Personal computers

3   Which one of the following options is sometimes described as the brain of the computer?

    A   The ROM
    B   The file server
    C   The central processing unit
    D   The RAM

4   Memory that is directly available to the processing unit is called?

    A   RAM
    B   ROM
    C   REM
    D   RUM

5   Which one of the following is an output device?

    A   A keyboard
    B   A scanner
    C   A smart card
    D   A printer

6   Which of the following options refers to a network of computers which are connected over the public telecommunications network?

    A   LAN
    B   WAN
    C   TAN
    D   PAN

7   What is the name usually used to describe an Internet connection that is 'always on'?

    A   Broadbean
    B   Bandwidth
    C   Broadband
    D   Bandaid

8   Two statements follow about the operating system:

1   An operating system is a program that provides the 'bridge' between applications software and the hardware.

2   An operating system controls input and output devices.

Are the above statements true or false?

A   Both are false
B   Both are true
C   Statement 1 is false but statement 2 is rue
D   Statement 1 is true but statement 2 is false

9   Which one of following options is not an operating system?

A   Unix
B   Linux
C   Word
D   MacOS

Answers to Quick Quiz

1	C	Option A refers to software. Option B refers to a local area network.
2	B	Option A is fictitious. Mainframe and PCs are not as powerful as supercomputers.
3	C	The CPU is the collection of circuitry and registers that performs the processing in a computer.
4	A	Random access memory is memory that is directly available to the processing unit.
5	A	A printer. The other options are input devices.
6	B	Wide area network. These are dispersed on a wider geographical scale than LANs.
7	C	Broadband. (This is an easy question but highlights the need to read the options carefully!)
8	B	Both statements are true.
9	C	Word. The others are operating systems.

Using computers: the basics

2

29

Study guide

			Syllabus reference
1	(c)	Describe the hardware and software components of a computer system.	1(b), 3(b) (iii)
	(d)	Describe simple visual checks on computer hardware and ancillaries (plugs and cables) and explain their importance.	1(a)
	(e)	Describe the correct process for powering up and for shutting down computer systems	1(a), 1(b)

1 Introduction

The chapter aims to teach you the basics of using a PC and dealing with problems that may occur while using a PC and printer. It covers only very basic functions and operations. You will learn more about software, particularly spreadsheets and word processing, in Chapter 3.

2 Basic PC operation and troubleshooting

FAST FORWARD

A small part of the **operating system** controls the initial start-up or **boot** process when a computer is switched on.

If a computer or a peripheral fails to respond correctly, one simple check is to check all **cables** are connected correctly.

2.1 Before you turn your PC on

When you plan to use a computer, you should perform a few quick **visual safety checks** before switching the machine on.

(a)   Are all hardware components in place? Check the main unit and peripherals such as printers have not been moved.

(b)   Ensure there are no liquids on or around the computer and your working area.

(c)   Check all cables are connected and haven't become lose.

(d)   Ensure the computer has sufficient space around it for heat to dissipate.

(e)   Make sure power sockets aren't overloaded with excessive numbers of plugs.

2.2 What happens when you turn on your PC?

In this section we run through the process that occurs when you turn on your PC.

Step 1   **Turn on the power**
Most PCs are turned on using a single switch, usually found on the cover of the main unit. Other machines require the monitor to be turned on separately. The Power button is usually marked by an open circle with a straight line coming through the top or the side. Ensure you are aware of how to turn your PC on correctly.

Step 2   **The boot program**
Your computer hardware requires instructions to tell it what to do. The program the Central Processing Unit (CPU) looks for first is a very small part of the operating system known as the boot program. This program 'boots' the computer into action.

Step 3   **The power-on self test**
The CPU performs what is known as a Power-On Self Test (POST). This tests that various parts of the system are functioning correctly, including memory and peripherals. During this test the little lights on your keyboard and printer may turn on and off, and then a beep may indicate that everything is fine.

Step 4   **Searching for the operating system**
The CPU then goes hunting for the rest of the operating system.

Step 5   **Microsoft Windows starts**
As soon as the CPU locates the operating system, it loads it into memory. You should see the Microsoft Windows logo. The screen you are presented with will depend on the version of Windows being used, whether the PC is connected to a network and how the system has been set up.

Step 6   **Logging on to a network**
If you are on a network, or if you share your computer with other people, each of whom has a different user profile, you'll need to enter your name and password before you arrive at the desktop. (A user profile is a collection of information about a user's preferences regarding the appearance of the screen, the items on menus, and so on.) This process is known as logging on or logging in.

2.3 Turning your PC off

2.3.1 Should I turn it off?

In general, you should turn off your computer only when you don't plan on using it again for several hours. Leaving the computer on causes less wear and tear than turning it off and then on again. However, if you leave the PC you should ensure that a password protected screensaver is activated to prevent unauthorised access.

2.3.2 What steps should I follow?

Step 1   **Shut down active applications**
One by one, close down each application using their Exit options. (Remember to Save any work you don't wish to discard.)

Step 2   **Exit from Microsoft Windows**
Go to Start, and then select Shut Down. If Windows displays a box with the title Shut Down Windows, select the Shut Down option (this is the default) and click on OK. (Later versions of Windows have different options – for example under Windows XP you should first choose to 'Log off', and then choose the 'Turn off' option.)

Step 3   **Be patient**
Most PCs running Windows now switch themselves off without further user intervention. If you are using earlier versions of Windows, you should wait for the 'It is Now Safe to Turn Off Your Computer' message before switching the PC off using the On/Off switch.

Step 4   **Turning the computer back on**
If you turn your computer off and then decide to turn it on again, you should wait for approximately thirty seconds before doing so. This will ensure all shutting down processes are complete and will allow all electrical charges to dissipate from the machine.

2.4 What should I do if the PC doesn't 'boot' correctly?

2.4.1 Booting: Nothing happens

Step 1   **Press the power button again**
Wait a moment, and then try your power button again. Press firmly on the button. Some models require the On/Off button to be held in for about five seconds.

Step 2 **Check connections**

Check the power cable coming into the back of the PC from the power outlet. Make certain the cable is firmly attached. Retry the power button.

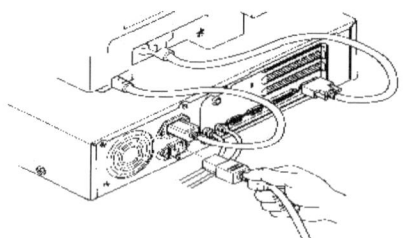

Step 3 **Check the power supply**

Check other devices that may be plugged into the power supply outlet to see if they have power. If so, try swapping the power cable plug for the PC into another outlet you know is working. Try the power button again. Make sure the unit is turned off then push the plugs into the sockets and turn the unit back on.

Step 4 **Call for assistance**

If, following these basic checks the PC is not operating as intended, call for assistance (for example from your organisation's IT support).

2.4.2 I heard the PC 'boot', but the screen is blank

Step 1 **Make sure the monitor power switch is turned on**

Some PCs have an On/Off switch on the monitor as well as on the main unit. Ensure this switch is turned on.

Step 2 **Make sure the monitor power cord is attached**

Make sure the unit is turned off then push the plug into the socket and turn the unit back on.

Step 3 **Make sure the monitor video cable is attached**

Turn the PC and monitor off, then ensure the cable running from the monitor to the PC is firmly attached. Turn the unit back on.

Step 4 **Call for assistance**

If, following these basic checks the PC is not operating as intended, call for assistance (for example from IT support staff).

2.5 Other common PC problems and error messages

2.5.1 The keyboard isn't responding

If your keyboard does not respond to keystrokes you should check that the **cable** connector for the keyboard is firmly connected to the keyboard port on the back of the PC. Also check to see if the cable has been pulled loose at the keyboard end.

2.5.2 Mouse problems

If moving your mouse has no effect at all, check that the **cable** connector for the mouse is firmly plugged into the mouse port. If possible, try using another mouse. If moving the mouse results in erratic cursor movement, and you aren't using an optical mouse, you should open the bottom of the mouse, remove the ball, and **clean** the runners that the wheel rubs against. Reassemble the mouse and try again.

2.5.3 General Protection Faults

A common error message is the message that states there has been a General Protection Fault (GPF). This means that the computer has had a problem accessing a part of a program, a network, or a file. The message will instruct you to save your files and restart Windows. One of the main causes of a GPF is

having too many programs open at one time. To avoid this problem, open only the program or programs needed to complete your task. If this doesn't solve your problem try closing all of your programs, exit Windows and **reboot** your computer.

2.5.4 Damaged or corrupt files

If you attempt to open a file with an application, but receive an error message along the lines of 'Unable to open file' it is possible that there is physical **damage** to the area of the **disk** the file is held on. Alternatively, the **contents** of the file itself could be damaged (corrupted). In both of these cases, the damaged file is unlikely to be of any further use. Restoring a copy of the file, taken before the damage occurred, is the most common solution to this problem.

2.5.5 What software should I open this file with?

Another reason you may not be able to open a file is that you don't know **what software** to use to open the file. The file extension part of the file name (eg doc, xls, jpg etc) provides a clue as to the software required to access the file. For example a file with a '.doc' extension is a Microsoft Word document; an '.xls' file is an Excel spreadsheet. Files with a 'jpg' or 'gif' extension are image files that could be opened in Paint or an image manipulation package.

Some users 'Zip' the contents of multiple file attachments into one Zip file to send via e-mail (some e-mail programmes do this automatically). To open the Zipped files, you must first unzip (extract) the zip file using software such as WinZip or PKZip. The extracted files will then show their file extensions, and may be opened using the appropriate software.

2.5.6 I need a file that's been deleted

On a PC, deleted files are held in the **Recycle Bin** (until the bin is emptied). If you have deleted a file that you shouldn't have, open the recycle bin, and if the file is there, restore it. Failing this, an older version of the file should be available from the regular system back-ups.

2.6 Computer lock-ups

FAST FORWARD

When a computer stops responding it is said to have '**locked-up**'. Causes of lock-ups include; too many programs running, not enough memory to support the running programs, corrupt files, hardware failure and viruses.

If your computer system stops responding you may lose control of the program running and the keyboard and mouse may not respond correctly. When a computer stops responding it is said to have 'locked-up'. A computer may stop responding due to a wide variety of reasons. **Common causes** of computer lock-ups include:

- Too many programs running at the same time
- Not enough memory to support the running programs
- Corrupt (damaged) or incorrectly installed software
- Power management or screensaver problems
- Improper operating temperatures and humidity levels
- Hardware failure
- Corrupt device driver (drivers are software files that tell your computer how to communicate with hardware (the modem, the printer etc)
- A virus has infected the computer

The following paragraphs contain general advice relating to how you could deal with a computer lock-up. However, many organisations prefer staff (or students) to seek assistance whenever a computer lock-up occurs. Ensure you **follow the procedures that apply to your organisation or college**. Unfortunately, it is likely you will lose any unsaved information in the program you were working on.

2.6.1 Soft lock-ups

If the computer stops responding while working in a particular program, try to close the offending program. To do this, hold down the Ctrl and Alt keys, and then press Delete (Ctrl+Alt+Delete). If Ctrl+Alt+Delete brings up the close program dialog but, the computer is said to be in a soft lock-up. Sometimes it takes several seconds for the Close Program dialog box to appear.

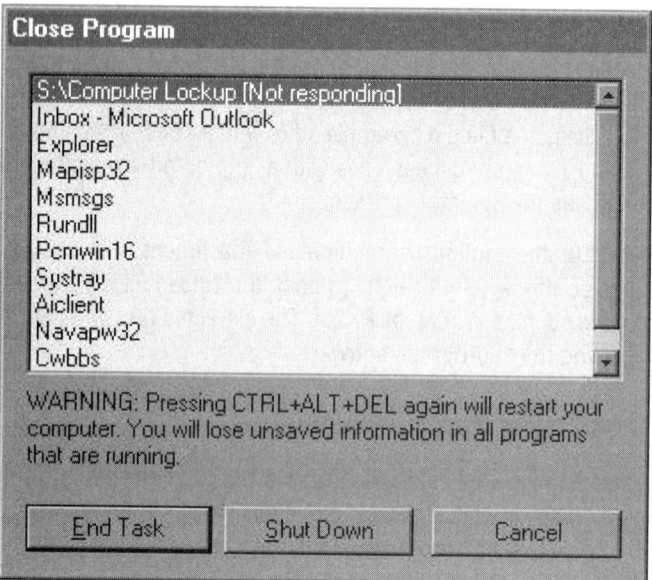

Look through the list of Programs and find an item that says 'Not responding' after it. If there is not an item that states 'Not responding' after it, click **Cancel** and then try the Ctrl+Alt+Delete again. Sometimes items do not immediately report that they are not responding. Select the 'Not responding' item, and then click **End Task**. After several seconds, an **End Task** dialog box may appear. Click **End Task** to finish closing the offending application. This process may need to be repeated.

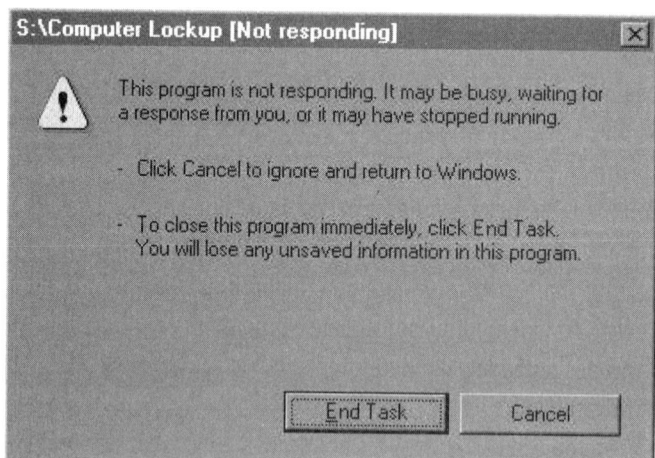

2.6.2 Hard lock-ups

If Ctrl+Alt+Delete has no affect, the computer is said to be in a **hard lock-up**. The only option in this situation is to turn **the PC off** using the power button. Then restart the PC.

2.6.3 Investigating recurring lock-ups

If your PC locks-up frequently, you should **gather** as much **information** as you can to enable suitably qualified staff to investigate the problem. Answers to the following questions should help identify the cause of the problem:

- When did the problem start?
- Does it happen only in one application or in any application?
- What application does it occur in?
- Does it only occur when performing a certain function within the application?
- How often does it occur?
- Are there any error messages that are displayed before the computer locks up?

2.6.4 Error report

In Windows XP, when an application program crashes you may see the following dialogue box.

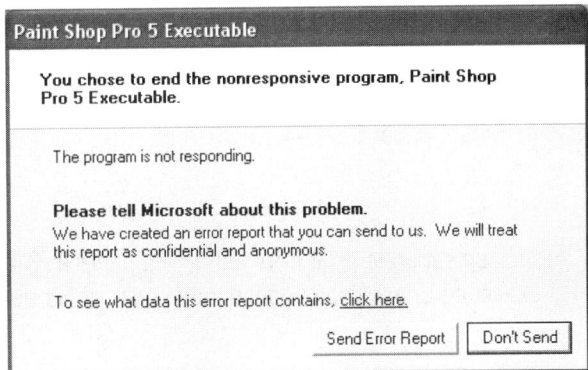

This box gives users with an Internet connection the opportunity to ensure Microsoft is kept informed about possible conflicts or bugs – with the intention of improving future versions of Windows. To send an error report to Microsoft, simply click Send Error Report. Relevant information, such as active programs and tasks at the time of the crash, are then forwarded to Microsoft.

2.6.5 Printing problems

Most printers used in business today are laser printers – this section refers to laser printers only. There are a vast number of laser printers in common use. The following paragraphs may not apply to your particular printer, but they may be adaptable to your situation.

2.6.6 The printer doesn't respond

If after you send a job to a printer 'nothing happens', check the following: None of the lights are on.

- Check the printer display and lights – is the printer power switch turned on?
- Ensure both ends of the power cord are plugged in.
- When possible check the power outlet is working using another electrical item.
- Make sure the Printer Cable is plugged into the PC.

If these obvious checks don't reveal the problem, it could be that your job has been routed to a different printer, or there may be another problem. You should request further assistance.

2.6.7 Printer error 'Toner low'

As pages are printed the ink in the toner cartridge is used. When the ink level drops to a low level, the message 'toner low' is displayed. Often however it is only the centre of the toner which is used, there may still be a reasonable amount of ink in the cartridge, towards the sides. If you remove the cartridge from the printer, (open the 'lid' and slide the cartridge upwards and out) shake it and tap it on both ends, the ink congealed in the sides will level out. Put the cartridge back and you should enjoy some further use of that cartridge.

2.6.8 Printer error 'Paper jam'

Paper jams may occur as a result of using incorrect paper (wrong weight), or paper which is 'dog eared' or damp. Before loading paper, flick it to ensure that the pages are not stuck together.

In the event of paper jams, **turn off** the printer and disconnect it from the mains. Then remove the paper tray, the upper and rear covers and the toner and extricate any paper you can see. If you can see jammed paper but cannot pull it out, seek further assistance from IT support staff.

2.6.9 'Load letter' or 'Load legal'

This error crops up frequently when printer or software settings are set to **Letter size paper** rather than A4 size. A simple but time consuming 'work around' is to press the continue button on the printer for every page you print!

To resolve the load letter error, ensure that all settings for the printer are set to A4 and not Letter. Printer settings can be accessed through Start, Settings, Printers, and then highlighting the relevant printer and choosing File Properties. The Printing Preferences button will bring up a range of options including Paper size – this should be A4.

Paper size should also be set to A4 within the individual software application. For example, in Microsoft Word under the File menu select Page Setup, Paper Size, A4.

2.6.10 'Load A4'

The printer may be out of paper, or may be set up to print from a different paper tray (eg the message **'Manual feed'** means the printer is expecting to use paper loaded in the manual fee tray).

2.6.11 Help!

Windows includes a Help function - which is like a user manual accessible on-screen. The Help function is accessed through the Help menu. For general Windows help, select **Help** from the **Start** menu. (The appearance of the menu will differ depending on the version of Windows you are using.)

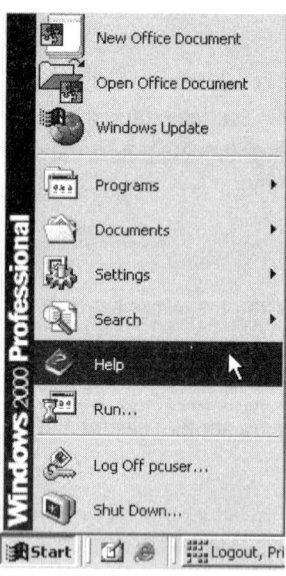 

Exam focus point

Questions could be set on any of these problem areas testing whether candidates know how to deal with the problem.

3 Using Microsoft Windows: The basics

FAST FORWARD

The **Desktop** is the 'starting' point in Microsoft Windows. Applications may be started from the desktop using either an icon (or 'shortcut') or by navigating through the menus that branch out from the **Start** button.

3.1 Why Microsoft Windows?

The syllabus and study sessions for this paper do not specify any particular software packages. However, you are required to be able to describe the hardware and software components of a computer system, to describe the correct process for powering-up and shutting down computer systems and to be able to save, transfer and print documents. These skills require practical computer skills. Using a computer requires some knowledge of the operating system. The most popular operating system in use today is Microsoft Windows.

This section aims to teach you some basic Microsoft Windows skills. Microsoft Windows is available in a number of different variations (eg Windows 2000, Windows NT, Windows XP). The functions we describe in this section are not significantly different across the different versions.

Question

Windows version

Find out which version of Windows is loaded on the PC you will be using. Ensure you are aware of the correct starting-up and shutting down procedures for your PC and know who to contact should you run into difficulties.

Answer

The version of Windows you are using should display sometime during the 'boot-up' process.

3.2 The Desktop

In Microsoft Windows, the initial screen is called the **Desktop**. The **Desktop** is the 'starting' point. Application programs may be started from the desktop using either an icon (or 'shortcut') or by navigating through the menus that branch out from the **Start** button. An example of a Desktop is shown below.

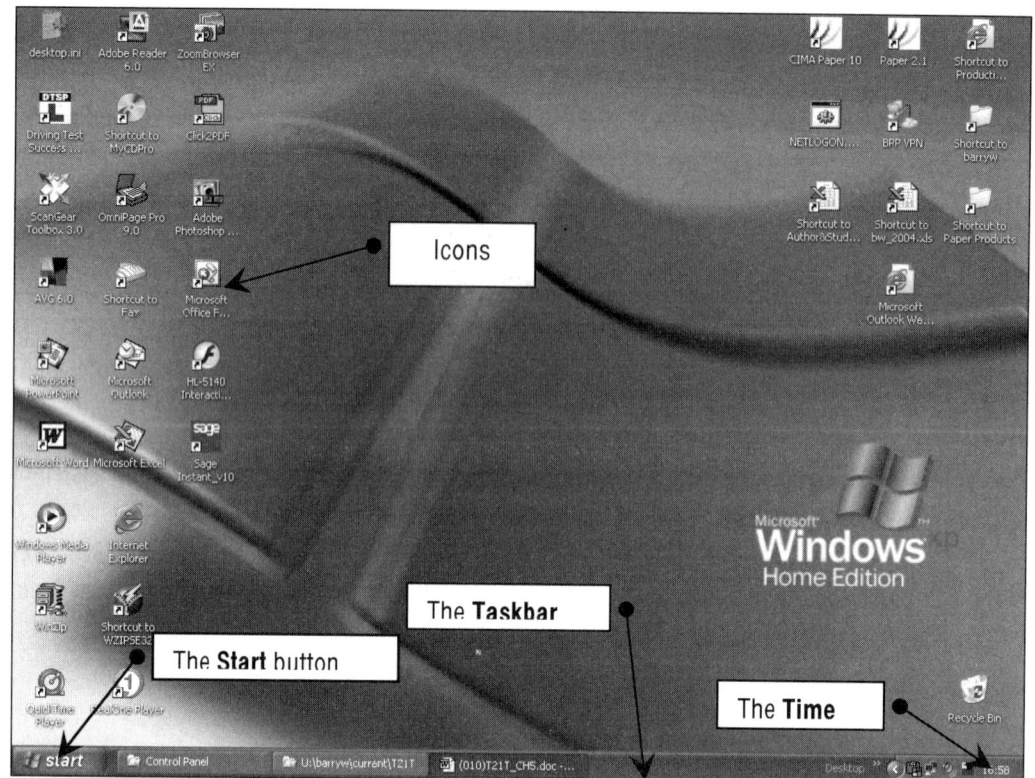

3.3 Title bar

When an application is started (eg Microsoft Word) each program or activity is launched in a separate window. Each window has a **Title bar** - a strip at the top of the window - for example when Microsoft Word is launched it opens a new document in a window with a Title bar like that shown below.

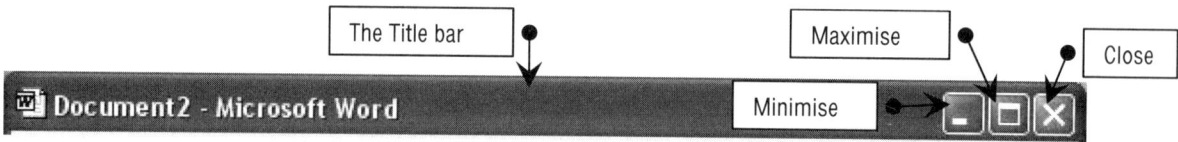

The Title bar may be used to **maximise**, **minimise** or **move** a window. Clicking on the symbol in the **top-left hand corner** (in our example above the Word symbol) reveals options used to close the window or to hide (minimise it). (The symbol is different depending upon which program you are using.)

In the **top right-hand corner** of each window are three symbols.

(a)   There is a line, which minimises the window, reducing it to a button on the 'task bar' at the bottom of the screen.

(b)   There are either two squares, one on top of the other or a single square. If there are two squares clicking on this button will make the window smaller, so you can see what other windows are open. If your window is already in its 'smaller' state only one square is shown (as in our example above). Clicking on this button makes the window bigger again.

(c)   There is an **X.** This closes the window altogether.

3.3.1 Moving windows

You may reposition a window on the desktop by using the Title bar to **drag** it to a new position. To do this, position the pointer in the Title bar then hold down the mouse button and drag the window to move it. When you release the mouse button, the window will remain where you have **dropped** it. Moving windows is sometimes useful if you wish to view more than one window at once.

3.3.2 Resizing windows

To change the **size** of a window, move the pointer to one of the edges of the window. Just as it passes over the edge it changes shape and becomes a two-headed arrow. If you click and hold down the mouse button which this arrow is in view, you will be able to pull out the side of the window. You can resize a window in two dimensions at once if you point at one of the corners until the pointer turns into the two-headed arrow and then hold down the mouse button and drag.

3.4 Scrolling within windows

A window will often be too big to display all contents on screen at one time. A scroll bar appears down the right hand side of large windows to allow you to scroll the on-screen display. There are many ways to scroll:

(a)   Using the **Scroll bar**. This may be used in a number of ways for example by clicking on the up or down arrows either end of the bar, by clicking within the bar above or below the Slider or by dragging the slider up or down within the bar.

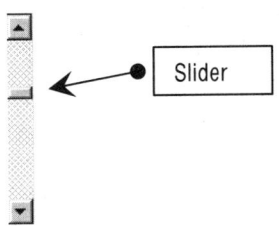

(b)   Using the **direction arrow keys** (the arrow keys to the left of the numeric keypad).

(c)   Using the **Page Up** and **Page Down** keys.

(d)   If your mouse is relatively new, you may have a '**wheel**' between the two mouse buttons. If you turn this wheel when a window with a scroll bar is 'active', the contents of the window will scroll.

(e)   You may move to the last line again of a window by holding down the **Ctrl** key and pressing the **End** key. The **Ctrl** and press **Home** keys may be used in the same way to go to the first line.

3.5 Switching between applications using the Taskbar

As we explained earlier, windows allows multi-tasking which means you are able to have a number of applications open at any one time (eg Word and Excel).

As with many Microsoft Windows operations, there is **more than one way** to switch between open applications. One popular method of switching between applications is to simply click on the icon of the relevant open application displayed on the Windows **Taskbar**. The Taskbar (shown below) usually shows at the bottom of the screen, although some systems are set-up to 'hide' the Taskbar.

3.5.1 Switching between applications using Alt + Tab

Another way to switch between applications is to use Alt and Tab keys. If you press and hold down the Alt key, then press the Tab key, a box will appear in the centre of the screen showing all open applications. You can Tab through the applications showing in this box – when you release the Alt key you will transfer to the application currently 'framed' within the grey box.

Hands-on practice

You may well be familiar with the skills explained above. If not, ensure you practice these skills hands-on at a PC – using applications such as Word and Excel.

Hands-on, practical experience is vital if you are to gain a good understanding of the material covered in this chapter.

FAST FORWARD

Windows Explorer allows you to see how the files and applications on your hard drive are organised – it enables you to become familiar with the file structure on your PC.

You may also **move**, **copy**, **rename** or **delete** files from within Windows Explorer.

3.6 Windows Explorer

One of the most important applications in Windows is **Windows Explorer**. Amongst other things, this allows you to see what folders and files are on a disk, make copies of files and disks, move files around from one directory to another, look at the files in a directory in date order, or name order, or file type order, and to search for files.

It is quite possible, however, that your college system prevents you from using Explorer. This will be to stop people accessing files and folders (also known as directories) that the college wishes to keep secure. (Don't confuse Windows Explorer with the Internet browser software Microsoft Internet Explorer.)

Windows Explorer enables you to see the files held on the computer hard disk and other removable disks. To open Windows Explorer:

*   Click Start

*   Point to Programs to display the Programs menu

*   Click Windows Explorer

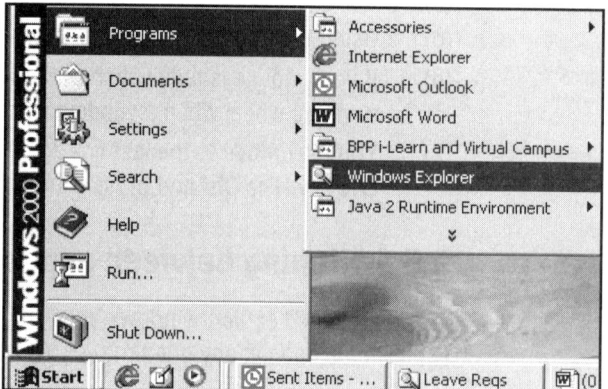

3.6.1 The folder or directory structure

Windows Explorer allows you to see how the files and applications on your hard drive are organised – it enables you to become familiar with the file structure on your PC. When you open Windows Explorer, you are able to see how files and folders (or directories) 'are stored. A 'file' in a computer system is a single document (or other collection of data) of a particular type. A word-processed letter would be one document file. In a computer system a file is saved in a location called a folder, or a directory.

On the hard disk, the 'first level' is the hard disk itself, which is usually named **C drive** (C:). If you make a folder or save a file directly to **C:**, you are placing it in the **root directory**. A file saved inside a folder that branches off the root directory is in the **second level**. The **third level** branches off the second level and so on.

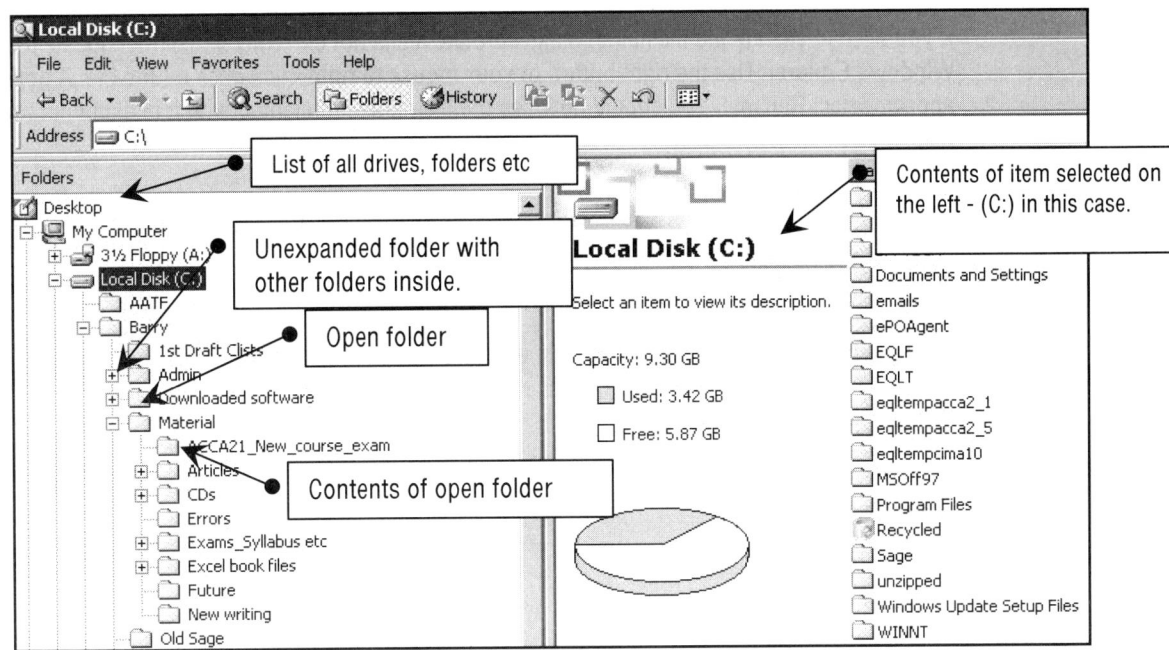

3.7 Moving, copying, renaming and deleting files

Note: You should never move, rename or delete files unless you are 100% clear what you are doing – and you have explicit permission to do so.

3.7.1 Moving files

As you can see above, the main Explorer window has two panes. To view the contents of a 'collapsed' folder, click on the plus sign (+) to the left of a folder; the folder will expand and the sign will become a minus (-) sign. You could have also just double clicked on the folder itself. To close or re-collapse the folder, click this minus sign.

You can move files around by 'dragging and dropping' them in Windows Explorer. To move file(s) or folder(s), firstly locate the file(s)/folder(s) you wish to move by double-clicking on the appropriate drive and folders until you reach their location. Highlight (by single-clicking on) the file(s) or folder(s), and, holding the left button of the mouse down, drag and drop the highlighted items in the desired location in the other pane of the window.

3.7.2 Copying files

You can copy files from within Explorer using Copy and Paste. To do this using the keyboard, locate the files using Windows Explorer and highlight the file(s)/folder(s) you wish to copy. Then hit the key combination **Ctrl-C** to copy your file onto the computer's '**clipboard**'. Then move to the location you wish to Copy the files to and select **Ctrl-V** to Paste the contents of the clipboard to the new location.

Another way of achieving the same thing is to use the **Copy** and **Paste** commands from the **Edit** menu within Explorer. As with the keyboard commands, you first must highlight the file(s)/folder(s) you want to duplicate (use a single-click), then select Copy from the Edit menu of that window. Next, put your cursor in the window where you wish the copy to be located, and then from the Edit menu, select Paste.

The copy and paste commands are also available in the 'context sensitive' menus that appear when you right-click on a given file or selected item.

The copy and paste commands may also be used within a single application, or to copy data between applications (eg Excel and Word). This is explained in Chapter 3.

3.7.3 Renaming files

If you wish to change the file name, make sure the file is not currently in use then locate the file within Windows Explorer. Use the right button of your mouse to right-click once on the file. A pop-up menu will appear; select Rename. You should now see the file name highlighted with a blinking cursor as shown below.

Type the new file name, including the file extension (.doc in this case).

3.7.4 Deleting files

To delete the file 'paper one', right-click once on it and select Delete from the pop-up menu. (Files must be closed to be deleted.)

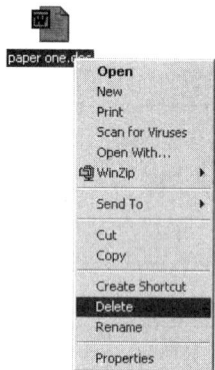

The system will ask for confirmation that you really want to send the file to the Recycle Bin as shown below.

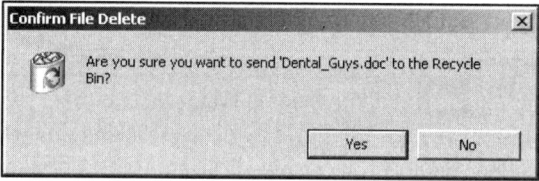

Click 'Yes' to delete. The same thing could have been achieved by clicking on the file pressing the 'Delete' key, or by highlighting and dragging the item to the Recycle Bin.

Files sent to the Recycle Bin are not really deleted. The files may be restored (undeleted) by accessing the Recycle Bin, either through Explorer or through an icon on your desktop, then selecting the file(s) to Restore and choosing File, Restore from the menu.

Note also that there may be some files that you are unable to send to the Recycle bin. For example, if you are on a network your **network rights** may only allow you to modify or delete certain files. Or, it may be that someone has set-up a Word or Excel file with **password protection** allowing read-only access to other users. This is covered in Chapter 5.

3.8 Saving files from within an application

In the following paragraphs we demonstrate some basic skills relating to saving files in certain locations. We explain these functions through the use of a **practical example**. You should follow this example hands-on, at a PC.

Start the application known as Notepad (by clicking on Start, Programs, Accessories then Notepad). Type your name and address into the Notepad document. Then either click on the ⊠ symbol in the top left corner of the window, or select **File** from the menu, and then **Exit**. You should then see the following message.

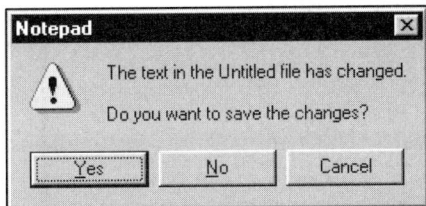

This message provides the opportunity to **save** the Notepad file you have created. If you click **Yes**, a new window will appear – the Save As window (see the name 'Save as' in the Title bar).

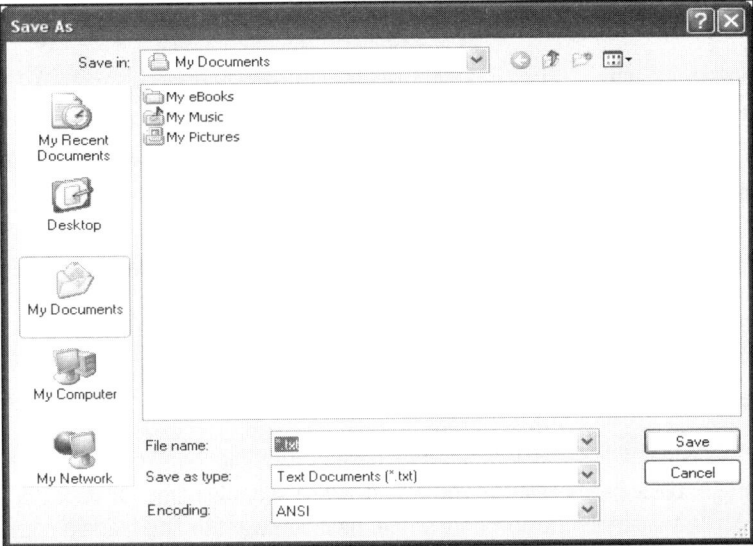

3.8.1 Save as

We now have the Save As window on screen. The Save As window is common to all Windows-based applications that have a facility for storing data in a file. We could have activated this window from within Notepad by selecting File, Save or File, Save As from the main menu. File Save is usually used to update an existing file, Save As is used to Save another copy of an existing file leaving the original file in place.

As we are creating a new file, both File Save and File Save As will activate the Save As window. When the window first appears the File Name box is highlighted. You can move from section to section of this window by pressing the **Tab** key. This is the key above the Caps Lock key on your keyboard. Pressing the Tab key will move the cursor around the different items in the window. Try this out.

You can move back and forward between consecutive items if you wish. To move back you hold down the **shift** key – the one you would use for capital letters – and press **Tab**. Try this out too. We will now explain the options available from within the Save As window.

3.8.2 Save in

Near the top of the Save As window is the **Save in** box. This is where you specify where you want to save your file. This is like deciding what folder you would file a paper document in. As we explained earlier, the hard drive is usually called drive C and the CD-ROM/DVD drive is assigned another letter.

Click on the down arrow at the right of the **Save in** box. A list of the drives available will appear and you can select the appropriate drive by clicking on its name. To select the C drive, click on it as shown in the following illustration.

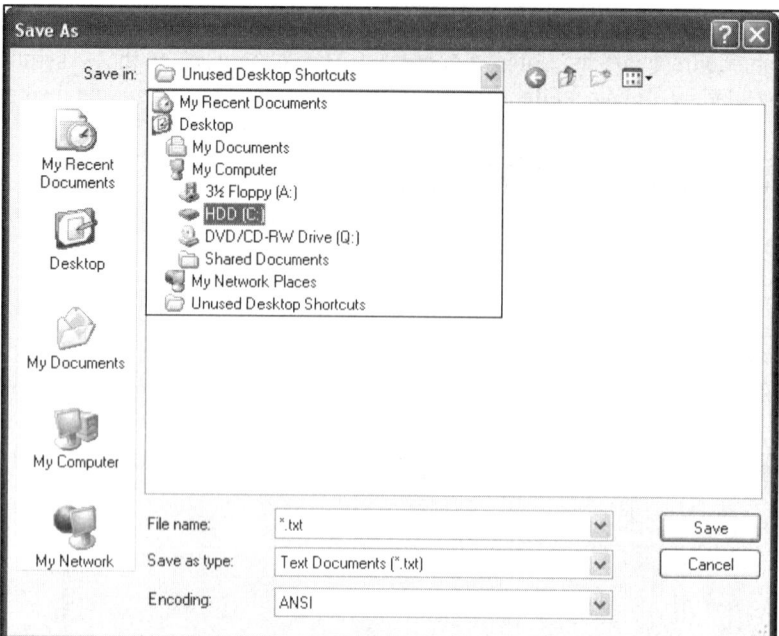

If you were going to save your file you would now search for an appropriate folder. For example, if you wanted to save this file in an existing folder called 'Notes', which was located on a CD currently inserted into the 'Q' drive, you would click on the down arrow next to the 'Save in' box, select Q drive, then double-click on the Notes folder.

3.8.3 File name

When the Save As window first appears, the **File name** box is highlighted. It shows an asterisk, a full stop and three letters. In place of the asterisk you would type a suitable name for your file. You should use file names that will help to identify the contents of the file if you want to find it again at a later date.

The format of the file is reflected in the file name by the three characters after the full stop. This is known as the file *extension.* Usually, there is no need to change the file extension suggested. ────────

3.9 Save as type

Below the File name box in the Save As window is the **Save as type** box. As a rule you won't need to do anything with this box. It specifies the format in which the file will be saved. The default suggestion will be the usual format for files created in the program you are using. For the Notepad application the usual format is a Text (.TXT) file. For Microsoft Word, the default is a document (.doc) file. For a spreadsheet created in Microsoft Excel it is an (.xls) file, and so on.

The file type shown in the File Type box also determines what files are listed in the box above it. In our example, there are no TXT files in the windows sub-directory, so there is nothing listed in this box.

3.9.1 Existing from Notepad

We have now explained the options contained in the Save As window. Click on the **Cancel** button, then choose File, Exit and answer No when asked if you wish to save your changes.

3.10 Closing down Microsoft Windows

We explained the procedures for shutting down Microsoft Windows in the previous chapter. If you do not feel confident shutting Windows down and turning off your PC, you should revisit the previous chapter now. You must be familiar with the 'Shut down' procedures you are expected to follow at your college or place of work.

4 Electronic mail (e-mail)

FAST FORWARD

E-mail is used for communication within organisations and between organisations. The term 'electronic mail', or e-mail, is used to describe various systems of sending data or messages electronically using a computer.

4.1 Introduction

4.1.1 What is e-mail?

Key term

> The term **electronic mail**, or **e-mail**, is used to describe various systems of sending data or messages electronically using a computer.

In a typical e-mail system, information is 'posted' by the sender to a central computer which allocates disk storage as a **mailbox** for each user. The information is subsequently collected by the receiver from the mailbox.

(a) Senders of information thus have **documentary evidence** that they have given a piece of information to the recipient and that the recipient has picked up the message.

(b) Receivers are **not disturbed** by the information when it is sent (as they would be by face-to-face meetings or phone calls), but collect it later at their convenience.

Each user will typically have **password protected access** to their individual inbox, outbox and filing system. Users may prepare and edit text and other documents using a **word processing** function, and send mail using **standard headers** and **signatures** to an individual or a group of people on a prepared **distribution list**.

E-mail use is now widespread both **within organisations** and **between** them – via the Internet.

4.1.2 Advantages of e-mail

E-mail has the following **advantages**.

(a) **Speed** (transmission, being electronic, is almost instantaneous). E-mail is far faster than post. It is a particular time-saver when communicating with people overseas.

(b) **Economy** (no need for stamps etc). E-mail is reckoned to be 20 times cheaper than fax.

(c) **Efficiency** (a message is prepared once but can be sent to thousands of employees at the touch of a button).

(d) **Security** (access can be restricted by the use of passwords).

(e) Documents can be attached from **word-processing** and other packages.

(f) Electronic **delivery and read receipts** can be requested.

4.1.3 Dangers of e-mail

E-mail has the following dangers:

- **Confidentiality** – passwords must be safeguarded
- Used to **replace** other communications that may be more appropriate (eg conversation)
- Too much going to **people who don't need it** as it is so easy to send to many recipients

 Question   Sending an email

There are many types of e-mail software. Perhaps the most common is Microsoft Outlook. Ensure you can send a message using the e-mail system at your work or college. Find out how to attach a file (such as a spreadsheet) to your message.

Another practical activity. Learning to send file attachments is a very useful skill.

5 The Internet

FAST FORWARD

The **Internet** is accessed via an Internet Service Provider (such as Virgin Media or AOL) and a browser (such as Microsoft Internet Explorer). Searches are done using a search engine (such as Google).

5.1 What is the Internet?

Key term

The **Internet** is a global network connecting millions of computers. The Internet allows any computer with a telecommunications link to send and receive information to and from any other suitably equipped computer.

5.2 Websites

Key term

A **website** is a collection of images and text which may be viewed on the World Wide Web.

Most organisations and many individuals now have a website. Some sites are able to process transactions (known as electronic commerce or e-commerce).

5.3 Internet Service Providers (ISPs)

Connection to the Internet is made via an **Internet Service Provider** (ISP). ISPs, such as AOL and Virgin, provide their own information services in addition to Internet access and e-mail capability.

5.4 Browsers and search engines

Users access the Internet through interface programs called **browsers**. The most popular and best known is **Microsoft Internet Explorer**, another is **Netscape Navigator**.

Browser software packages provide a facility to **store Internet addresses** so that users can access frequently-visited sites without having to go through a long search process. Thus in business use, workers who **regularly need up-to-date information**, say, on stock market movements, or new government legislation, or the activities of a competitor, can simply click on the appropriate entry in a personal 'favourites' directory and be taken straight to the relevant site.

Searching the Net is done using a **search engine**. Popular search engines include **Google**, Lycos, Yahoo! and AllTheWeb. These guide users to destinations throughout the web: the user simply types in a word or phrase to find related sites and documents.

Question

Hardware for the internet

Do you have access to the Internet? If not, seek out a friend or colleague with a suitably equipped PC who will let you get hands-on experience of using the Internet.

What **hardware** do you think you need to get onto the Internet?

The minimum **hardware** requirements are a PC, a modem and a conventional telephone line.

Ideally you would have a powerful PC with a broadband link such as ADSL.

5.5 Getting on to the Internet

If the hardware and software required to access the Internet has been set up correctly, accessing the Internet is simple. All you have to do to get started is **double-click** on the correct program icon. The 'correct' icon depends on how your PC has been set up. It may be a **browser** icon such as Netscape Navigator or Microsoft Interest Explorer, or an icon for an Internet Service Provider such as AOL or Virgin.

Depending how your system is set up, you may need to supply a **password**. Check with your tutor or system administrator which icon you should use, and if you require a password.

Once you have got past the password stage, the information on-screen will depend on **which ISP** and **browser** you are using.

5.6 Searching the internet

5.6.1 Search engines

The first thing you have to do is choose which **search engine** to use to find the information you are looking for. Your have a choice from a number of engines such as:

- Google
- AltaVista
- WebCrawler
- Lycos
- Yahoo!
- AskJeeves

There is **no limitation** on which search engine you can use: they are all freely available. (Most will display advertising material – this is how they make a large part of their income.) If you do not like the results given by, say, Alta Vista, you can simply **perform another search**, using, say, Google or Yahoo!.

5.6.2 Specifying what to search for

All search engines work in a similar way. The illustrations that follow show the opening ('home') page of Google.co.uk. To perform a search, you simply click in an empty box (if the cursor isn't flashing there already), type in a word or words and click on **Search** or, for Google, on Google Search.

In the following example, the user is using the Google.co.uk search engine to find web pages from the UK containing information regarding share prices.

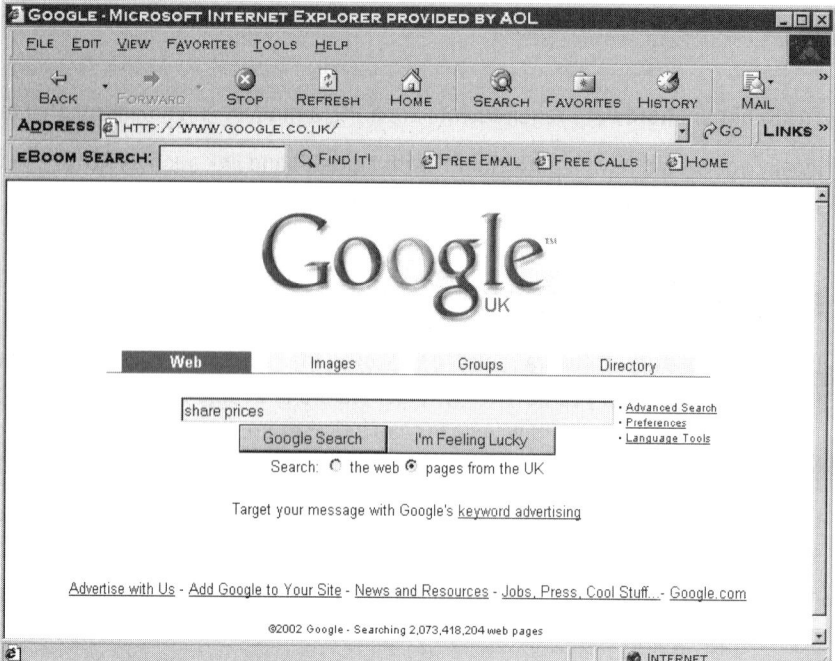

The results of the search are shown below.

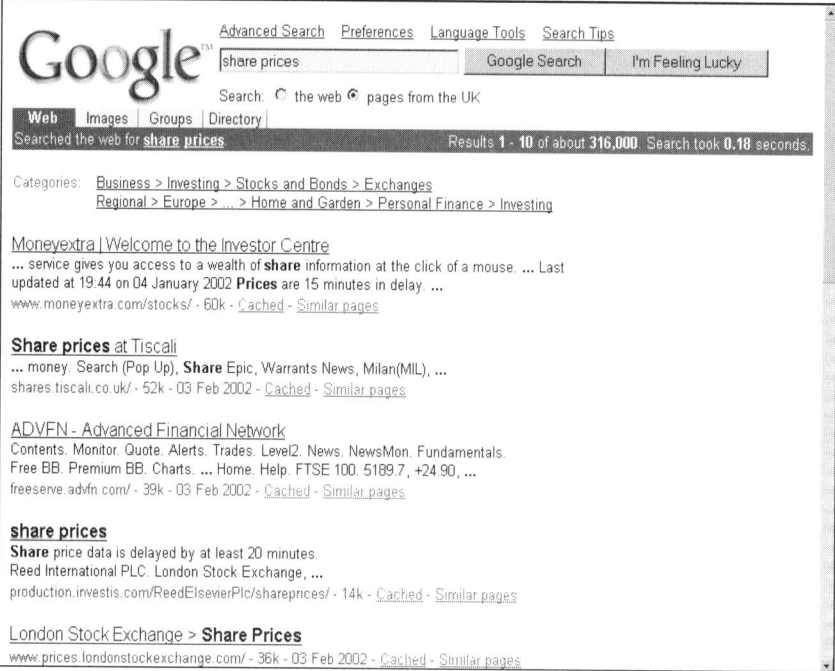

Google found hundreds of websites or documents relating to share information. To view a document, you simply click on the highlighted document title.

5.6.3 The quality of information

Remember, when you are looking at information on the Internet it is **not necessarily good information**, just because it is 'published'. **Anybody** can put information on the Internet.

The **known reliability** of the source is the key matter. The BBC for instance is a respected worldwide news organisation. If the next page you consult is called 'Fred's Financial Advice page', you should not necessarily trust the information that it provides.

5.6.4 Refining your search

Google came up with thousands of pages that were relevant to a search for **share prices.** One reason why it found so many pages is because it searched for and found **all** pages that contain the word **share** and all pages that contain the word **prices,** not just pages with the specific phrase 'share prices'.

Pages are listed in **batches** of ten or twenty, which makes the results more manageable, and the results are sorted by **relevance**, so the first few results will have 100% matches for both 'share' and 'prices', and are likely to contain a lot of material relevant to your enquiry.

Try to **be as specific as you possibly can** about what it is you are looking for. In the search we have just illustrated, if you were interested in technology share prices it would have been more sensible to include the word 'technology' in your search.

Question	Google

Using Google, search the web for a site that would enable you to order a laptop computer on-line (don't actually place the order!).

Answer

PC's may be ordered on-line from specialist PC suppliers such as Dell - or from the websites of computer retailers (such as PC World) or department stores (such as John Lewis). It sometimes saves time to look at what is available on a number of websites - even if then you then travel to a traditional shop to make the purchase.

Search engines generally have options to restrict the number of sites searched, for instance to **UK sites** only, or to **English language** sites only. We used the 'pages from the UK' option on Google.

5.6.5 Links within websites

Many organisations provide **links** to other people's websites within their own web pages. A link is a word, phrase or image that may be clicked to navigate for a new address. Links within text are often identified through the use of underlining or a different colour.

5.6.6 'Advanced' search techniques

In many (though **not all**) search engines you can use **symbols** and/or what are known as **Boolean operators** to help the search engine to understand what it should and should not look for. These so-called 'advanced' searching techniques aren't actually particularly advanced, and they are **extremely useful**.

(a) **Plus signs (+)**

 If you put a plus sign (+) directly in front of a word (with no space) this tells the search engine that the word **must** be present in all the pages that are found. So if you type **+financial+information**, you will only get pages that contain both words (though not necessarily together or in this order). You can use as many pluses and words as you like.

 Instead of + you can use the word AND (in capitals, with spaces) if you prefer: **financial AND information**

(b) **Minus signs (-)**

 As you might expect, the – sign works in the opposite way to +. If you put a minus sign directly in front of a word the search engine will **ignore** any documents that contain that word. So, if you type **+financial+information-bank** you will avoid all the pages that have references to banking issues.

 However clever you are at using the minus sign you are still likely to get some information that you are not interested in. You simply would not think of typing, say, **+financial+information-cat,** for

example, because it would not occur to you that there happened to be a page of advice for penniless cat-owners.

Instead of – you can use the words AND NOT (in capitals, with spaces) if you prefer: **financial AND information AND NOT banks**

(c)   **Quotation marks (")**

To find **only** pages that contain the words **financial information** together in that order, you enclose them in quotation marks: **"financial information"**.

(d)   **OR**

If there is a chance that pages relevant to you will use alternative words, you can use OR to make the search engine look for pages that contain at least one of the alternatives: for instance **financial OR economic**

(e)   **Brackets**

Brackets can be used to devise more complicated searches. For instance **financial AND (information OR advice)** will find pages containing the word 'financial' and either the word 'information' or the word 'advice'

 Case Study

How to search the web

It helps to understand the basics of how search engines get their listings. There are two main ways: human beings or automated 'crawlers'. Yahoo is a great example of a search engine that uses human beings. Its editors classify websites into different categories. So a search for 'travel' reveals categories such as Travel Booksellers, Travel Companies and Hawaiian travel. Clink on a topic and you'll be shown a list of sites that an editor has selected for that particular category.

In contrast, a search engine like Google sends robot crawlers out across the web to read automatically a large number of pages. The text is stored in what you can think of as a big book.

It is also helpful to understand the basic search engine 'maths'. This means that by using symbols such as + or –, you can get better search results. For instance, say you were looking for 'football' and kept getting answers about the NFL, the National Football League in the United States. Try searching again like this: football-nfl. The minus symbol tells the search engine to look for pages that say football then to subtract any pages that contain the word NFL. That makes it more likely that you'll get pages about Liverpool FC rather than the Miami Dolphins!

In fact, you can use the + symbol to get even closer to Liverpool. Try a search like this: football+liverpool. That tells the search engine to find all the pages with football on them, then to show you only pages that also say "liverpool". By searching in lower case, you'll find both lower and upper-case versions.

Another way to get better results can be to use multiple search engines. No two search engines are exactly the same and if you use only one, you might miss good results that another might have. Since they are all free, don't be afraid to try a couple when searching the web.

The best places to start looking

Yahoo: www.yahoo.com
The oldest major human powered search engine on the web.

AltaVista: www.altavista.com
Crawler based service that's an excellent choice for finding unusual of very specific information. Offers the ability to search within the UK or across the entire web.

Google: www.google.co.uk

Crawler based service with a unique ranking system that finds great answers, even when seeking general information.

Ask: www.ask.co.uk
Many like its unusual style of asking you questions to get you to the right website.

www.alltheweb.com
Crawler based service with a large number of listings. Good for unusual information.

www.go2net.com
Site that lets you query many popular search engines at once.

5.6.7 Going directly to an Internet address (URLs)

If the address of a website is known, users may access the site directly without the need for a Search engine.

Typically, a website address will be given in the format **'http://www.bbc.co.uk'** (although increasingly organisations are leaving out the http:// prefix as this is not required). The address is called a **URL** or **Uniform Resource Locator** (sometimes referred to as Uniform Resource Location).

URL element	Explanation
http://	**Hypertext Transfer Protocol**, the protocol or accepted format used on the World-Wide Web for the exchange of documents produced in what is known as 'hypertext mark-up language' (HTML). The two forward slashes after the colon introduce a 'host name' such as **www**. Browsers such as Microsoft Internet Explorer no longer require users to type the http:// part of the address. This has led to many website addresses now being quoted as starting with www.
www	This stands for **World Wide Web**. This is the part of the Internet that contains websites.
bbc	This is the **domain name** of the organisation or individual whose site is located at this URL
co	This indicates the type of organisation concerned, in this case a company. Other designations include: .com — Commercial .ac or .edu — Educational and research .org — Usually non-commercial institutions .net and .biz — Inconsistent, an 'overflow' from .com and .org .tv — Inconsistent, often used to imply a high multimedia content .mil — Military .gov — Government agencies
uk	This indicates that the organisation is located in the UK. For a full list of country codes used on the web visit; www.dundee.ac.uk/english/url-jav.htm

Question   URLs

Here are some other useful URLs. Visit and explore as many of these as you can.

www.microsoft.com

www.bbc.co.uk

www.amazon.co.uk

www.streetmap.co.uk

www.dictionary.com

www.ft.com

www.the trainline.com

www.open.gov.uk

www.accaglobal.com

Answer

These sites show just how versatile the World Wide Web is. Organisations of all types and sizes offer information and/or trading facilities on the web.

5.6.8 Favourites

If you locate a site that is particularly useful to you, you do not have to do a fresh search for it every time you want to consult it again. ISPs and browsers usually have an option for users to compile and save their list of **'favourites'** for future use.

5.6.9 Downloading files

We have talked about downloading **pages** from the Internet in the preceding pages. This simply means that the page can be viewed via your ISP and browser while you are connected to the Internet. The page is not stored on your computer unless you **actively choose** to save a copy (by selecting **File** and then **Save**, just like in any other Windows program).

Downloading a **file** is a different procedure that involves saving a copy of the file to your hard drive. You might want to download files, for instance, if they contain **trial versions** of a new software product, or to obtain your **own copy of a document** available on the Internet.

5.6.10 After you've downloaded a file

When you download a file, be sure to make a note of the folder in which you have chosen to save the file. If the file is large, it may be designed to download in a compressed form – a Zip file. Depending on your ISP, and on your browser settings, the Zip file may **extract automatically** to a **temporary directory** on your hard drive when you log-off the Internet.

If you download software, among the files downloaded will usually be one called **Read.Me**, which contains further instructions for installing the program, and one called **setup.exe**, which performs the installation process.

5.6.11 Viewers

Documents available for download are often in Portable Document Format (**PDF**) format. To open pdf files a viewer such as **Adobe Acrobat Reader** is required. This allows documents to be read as they were intended to be read, including all formatting such as bold headings, paragraph spacing and so on, and all diagrams.

Question

Adobe Acrobat

If you don't have Adobe Acrobat Reader already, find the Adobe site on the Internet and download Adobe Acrobat reader onto your computer.

The Adobe site can be found at www.adobe.com.

5.6.12 Warning!

Never download files from the Internet unless you are sure that they are from a reliable source.

5.7 A practical exercise

The following activity is an **information finding exercise** that you should try out the next time you are sitting at a computer with access to the Internet. There are **no definitive solutions** to some of these activities: it depends when you do them and what links you choose to follow up. However, we give some further hints in the answer in case you get stuck.

Question   Surfing the internet

These activities are likely to take at least an hour to complete satisfactorily, and probably a lot longer if it is your first real go at the Internet. You may prefer to do them, say, two at a time over a series of sessions.

On this occasion feel free to look at any other information that interests once you have reached the site suggested, since you are learning how to use the Internet as well as finding specific information. You will quickly realise that on other occasions you need to be more disciplined, otherwise you will waste a lot of time.

(a)   Find and visit the site of a firm of certified accountants in the UK. Note down the information provided there and any other features of interest.

(b)   Visit the site of the UK HM Revenue and Customs and find out why the tax year starts on April 6. (Enter the Individuals, Frequently Asked Questions, General section to find this out.)

(c)   Visit the site of a newspaper, eg www.guardian.co.uk. What is the top news story of the day?

(d)   Visit the UK site of Sage – www.sage.co.uk What other Accounting and Finance products do Sage produce besides the Sage 'Line 50' accounting package?

(e)   You want to buy some blank CDs and a new printer cartridge. Can you find a supplier on the Internet?

(f)   You have come across the phrase 'data warehousing' in a newspaper article. What does it mean?

(g)   When was the UK Prime Minister Gordon Brown born?

(h)   Via its 'Information Society Initiative', the Department of Trade and Industry have a number of useful documents available on the Internet. Find, and if possible save and print out, its guide to the Internet and the World Wide Web.

Answer

(a)   The site we found had a sections on: Mergers and Acquisitions (with links to other mergers and acquisitions related sites), Audit & Accounting Services, Corporate Finance, Raising Venture Capital or Development Capital, Employee Rewards, Taxation, Trusts and Estates, Financial Services including pensions and investments, Forensic Accounting & Litigation Support, Information Technology (including a job vacancy), Industry Specific Services & Information (Agriculture, Care Homes, Construction, Dentists, Entertainment & Sport, GP's, Medical, Motor Industry, Legal, Vets), Career Opportunities, Recruitment & Training and Training & Standards.

(b)   You can find the HM Revenue and Customs site at hmrc.gov.uk. The reason dates back to the change from the Julian calendar to the Gregorian calendar back in 1752 (you don't need to know this!).

(c)   Most newspapers provide 'free' access to their web-based editions.

(d)   Other Accounting and Finance products available from Sage include: Instant Accounts, Line 100, Line 200 and Line 500.

(e)   Try searching for related words such as 'computer consumables'. If you don't want to shop on-line, you could use the electronic yellow pages (www.yell.co.uk in the UK) to find a 'traditional' supplier.

(f)   There are many pages of information relevant to data warehousing. The term is used to describe a database that brings together a number of other databases. This activity shows that you may need to look through a number of different sources of information before finding one that is suitable.

(g)   He was born in 1951 and went to school at Kirkcaldy High School. You can find this quite quickly by entering +Gordon+Brown+biography. Alternatively you could go to the Labour Party's site (www.labour.org.uk).

(h)   Try www.open.gov.uk as a starting point.

Chapter Roundup

- A small part of the **operating system** controls the initial start-up or **boot** process when a computer is switched on.

- If a computer or a peripheral fails to respond correctly, one simple check is to check all **cables** are connected correctly.

- When a computer stops responding it is said to have '**locked-up**'. Causes of lock-ups include; too many programs running, not enough memory to support the running programs, corrupt files, hardware failure and viruses.

- The **Desktop** is the 'starting' point in Microsoft Windows. Applications may be started from the desktop using either an icon (or 'shortcut') or by navigating through the menus that branch out from the **Start** button.

- **Windows Explorer** allows you to see how the files and applications on your hard drive are organised – it enables you to become familiar with the file structure on your PC.

- You may also **move**, **copy**, **rename** or **delete** files from within Windows Explorer.

- **E-mail** is used for communication within organisations and between organisations. The term 'electronic mail', or e-mail, is used to describe various systems of sending data or messages electronically using a computer.

- The **Internet** is accessed via an Internet Service Provider (such as NTL or AOL) and a browser (such as Microsoft Internet Explorer). Searches are done using a search engine (such as Google).

1   Two statements follow about turning a PC off:

    1   Applications should be closed down one by one.

    2   To close down Microsoft Widnows, you first click on the start button.

Are the above statements true or false?

A   Both statements are false
B   Both statements are true
C   Statement 1 is false but statement 2 is true
D   Statement 1 is true but statement 2 is false

2   In the context of computuing, what does POST stand for?

A   Power-on safety test
B   Processor-on self test
C   Processor-on safety test
D   Power-on self test

3   A General Protection Fault means which one of the following?

A   The computer has had a problem accessing a part of a program, a network or a file
B   A file is corrupt
C   The computer has a virus
D   There is a paper jam in the printer

4   What can Windows Explorer NOT be used for?

A   Viewing how files and applications on the hard drive are organised
B   Moving files
C   Re-naming files
D   Browsing the Internet

5   Which one of the following is a possible disadvantage/danger of e-mail?

A   Economy
B   Speed
C   Delivery and read receipts
D   Large volumes of information

6   Two statements follow about the Internet:

    1   Information published on the Internet is reliable information.
    2   Connection to the internet is made via an Internet search processor.

Are the above statements true or false?

A   Both statements are false
B   Both statements are true
C   Statement 1 is false but statement 2 is true
D   Statement 1 is true but statement 2 is false

7   What is a Uniform Resource Locator?

A   A search engine
B   A website address
C   An Internet service provider
D   A global network

1	B	Both statements are true.
2	D	Power-on self test.
3	A	One of the main causes of a GPF is having too many programs open at one time.
4	D	Do not confuse Windows Explorer with Microsoft Explorer.
5	D	The danger with e-mail is that too much information will go to people who don't need it because it is so easy to send to many recipients
6	A	Anybody can put information on the internet so it is not necessarily reliable. Connection is made via an Internet service provider (not search processor).
7	B	A website address is called a URL.

Using word processing software and spreadsheets

3

Study guide

			Syllabus reference
1	(f)	Describe how to save, transfer, and print documents	3(b)(iii)
4	(b)	Describe the nature of general purpose application software packages, including word processing and spreadsheets	3(b)(iii)

1 Introduction

Much of the information used for management control today is analysed or presented using spreadsheet or word processing software.

2 Using word processing software

FAST FORWARD

Word processing software, such as **Microsoft Word**, is used to produce text-based documents such as letters, memos and reports.

It includes a wide range of tools that allow the **professional presentation** of information.

Key term

Word processing software enables you to use a computer to create a document, store it electronically, display it on-screen, modify it by entering commands and characters from the keyboard, and print it using a printer.

In this section, we cover some basic functions of Microsoft Word, the most popular word processing software package. You should work through this section hands-on, at a computer that has Microsoft Word available. We have used Word 2003 as this is still the most widely used version of Word. There is a new version called Word 2007 and this looks slightly different.

After working through this section, you may wish to experiment with other functions of word processing software – explore the Microsoft Word on-line Help facility (**Help** from the Word main menu) for detailed guidance.

2.1 Starting Microsoft Word

Microsoft Word is launched by double-clicking on the Word **icon** or button, or by choosing Microsoft Word from the **Start** menu (maybe from within the **Microsoft Office** option). When Word starts, you are presented with a blank document. To open an existing document, you select File, Open from the main menu.

The document itself displays in the centre part of the screen. Above the document is a bank of toolbar buttons. These buttons serve a variety of functions. In recent versions of Word, if you let the mouse pointer linger over a particular button (without clicking on it) a little label soon pops up telling you what it does. The menu choices just below the title bar offer a range of further functions and options. We are going to look at several of the most commonly used.

2.2 File: Open

Click on the word **File** and a menu will drop down which includes the item **Open.** If you click on this, a window like the following will appear.

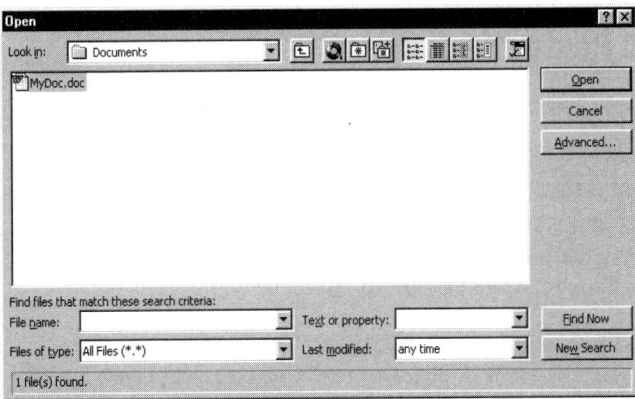

To open an existing file, click on the **Look in** box arrow and then locate the file by navigating through the folder structure (these skills were covered in Chapter 2). When you locate the document, click on the file name and then click on OK to open the file. *Double-clicking* on a file name has the effect of both selecting it and clicking on OK to open it.

2.3 File: Save As

If you open an existing file (that will obviously already have an existing file name), then make some changes to it which you want to save, but you also wish to leave the original document intact, you should use the File, Save As option, and give the amended file a new name.

The file you originally opened will remain in its original form, and the file with the new name will include all of your changes. For example, you could open a file containing a letter to Mrs Smith called Smith.Doc, change the name and address details, and save it as Jones.Doc. You would end up with *two* files – one called Smith.Doc and the other called Jones.Doc.

2.4 File: Close

To close a Word file simply select **File** and then **Close**. If you haven't already done so you will be asked if you want to save any changes you made.

2.5 File: Print

If you have a document open and you wish to print it, click on the **Print** option in the **File** menu. The following box will appear.

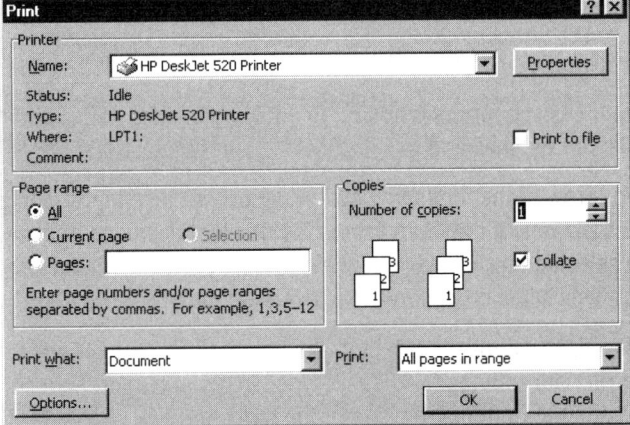

There are options to select a different printer (if you are on a network and have other printers available), to print more than one copy, to print only the current page or only text you have already selected or to print specific pages only. Experiment with these options yourself – hands on practice is essential.

2.6 Edit: Cut, Copy and Paste

The cut, copy and paste facilities are available via toolbar buttons or as menu items. They are used as follows.

(a) The first step is to highlight (select) the text you wish to format. To select text using your mouse, position the mouse pointer at the beginning of the first word, then hold down the left mouse button and move the pointer across the text you wish to select. Then release the mouse button. The portion of text will now be highlighted as shown below.

> This·text·is·selected· ·This·text·isn't·selected

To select using the keyboard, move the cursor to the beginning of the area to be selected. Hold down the Shift key, and while holding it down, use the navigation (arrow) keys to highlight the required area. (To unselect text, click anywhere in your document except inside the selected region.)

(b) With the required text highlighted, click on **Edit** from the main menu.

    (i) To retain the highlighted text in its current place and also to make a copy of it which is retained temporarily on the computer's 'clipboard', click on **Copy**.

    (ii) To remove the highlighted text from its current place, but also place it temporarily on the computer's clipboard, click on **Cut**. The highlighted text will disappear.

(c) Move the cursor to the point in your document where you want to place the text.

(d) Click on Edit again and choose **Paste**. The text you highlighted will reappear here.

Note also that there are keyboard shortcuts for cutting, copying and pasting. These are listed on the **Edit** menu –for example pressing the Ctrl and V keys at the same time is the same as selecting Paste from the Edit menu. Another option, that achieves the same as cutting and pasting, is to *drag* the selected text and *drop* it in the new place. Try doing this yourself.

2.7 Format: Font

Microsoft Word allows you to apply a range of fonts (character styles) to text. Word also allows you to format text with features such as bold, underline, italics and colour.

Formatting options are accessed either via the Format menu or through the Formatting tool bar (shown below). If you can't see these options available on-screen, select View, Toolbars, Formatting from the main menu.

The formatting toolbar allows you to select a font, a font size, to apply bold, italic and underline options, to justify text, apply numbers or bullets or outlines and to select font colour options.

To change the font, click the down arrow of the font name box. A list of the currently available fonts appears in the box. You may select any one of the fonts listed. The name of the newly selected font will appear in the font name box. Any selected text will have the new format, any text entered after the font selection will have the new format. This same procedure works for the font size as well.

The bold (**B**), italic (*I*) and underline (U) buttons do exactly that, they bold, italicise, or underline the current selection, or make the appropriate settings for the text typed in at the cursor. Font colour can be modified by using the underlined capital A button at the end of the tool bar. Click on the down arrow next to the A, the colour you then select is the colour that will be applied to selected text.

Explore these same options using the items available under the Format menu rather than using the toolbar buttons.

2.8 Format: Paragraph

This item on the **Format** menu offers you (amongst other things) a consistent and professional way of spacing out paragraphs. You should use this option rather than pressing return several times to leave blank lines.

Clicking on the **Paragraph** option in the **Format** menu brings up the Indents and Spacing tab. The Spacing option allows you to specify the number of 'points' (small units of vertical space) before paragraphs and after them. For example there are '6 pts' between this paragraph and the previous one.

2.8.1 Paragraph justification

'Justification' refers to how the text is laid out on the screen.

(a)   Left justification has the left side of the text even and aligned, while the right side remains jagged.

(b)   Right justification is just the opposite, where the right margin is smooth and the left margin is left jagged.

(c)   Centre justification has each line is positioned in the centre of the page.

(d)   Full justification forces both right and left margins to be even and aligned by putting very small spaces between the words to make up for the extra space you would normally find at the end of a line.

All of these options are also available through menu selections. The formatting options we have described are available through the Format menu.

2.9 Ruler bars

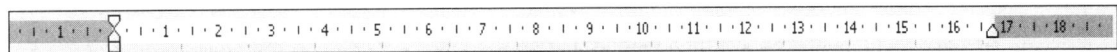

The Ruler bars are located above and to the left of your document. They display the arrangement of your margins, your paragraph indents, tab settings, and page layout information. If the ruler bars do not appear, they have simply been turned off. If you cannot see your rulers, select Ruler from the View menu.

The horizontal ruler bar (shown above) allows you to set tabs, indents and margins. The white areas of the ruler bar determine where text can be placed. The margin is shown where white meets grey. No text will be displayed beyond the white area. You can adjust the margin simply by moving the mouse over the separator line between white and grey, then when the pointer becomes a two-pointed arrow, click and drag the margin to the required position.

The triangle like shapes on the horizontal ruler bar are used for paragraph indents. These may be dragged to indent paragraphs as required.

The top-left triangle (pointing down) is the First Line Indent – the position where the first line will start.

The left edge of all other lines in the paragraph are aligned with the bottom triangle on the left side of the ruler bar. This is the Hanging Indent.

Below the Hanging Indent triangle is a small rectangle. This is the Left Indent control – if you drag this rectangle it will move the First Line Indent and the Hanging Indent in unison. The triangle on the right side of the ruler bar is for right indentation.

The vertical ruler bar is similar to the horizontal ruler bar. You adjust the vertical margins by using the same procedure you used with the horizontal ruler bar. Note that changes to margins affect the entire page, while indent settings apply only to the current paragraph.

2.10 Tabs ⌶

Tabs are used to space text across the page. The Tab tool is shown on-screen in the top left corner of the page. There are four types of Tab, each representing a different type of alignment. Clicking on the Tab tool changes the type of Tab to be inserted.

To place a tab in your document, click on the ruler bar where you want the tab stop to go. A symbol, identical to the one in the tab box, will appear on the ruler bar. To move the tab, drag the tab marker to the left or right. To remove a tab, drag the marker down and drop it anywhere below the ruler.

There are four main types of Tabs (later versions of Word include more but these four are the most commonly used).

⌐ **Left** Tab Stop – Text jumps to the tab stop and then shows to the right of the tab stop.

⊥ **Centre** Tab Stop – Text centred on this tab stop.

⌐ **Right** Tab Stop – Text jumps to the tab stop and then will show to the left of the tab stop.

⊥ **Decimal** Tab Stop – Text jumps to the tab stop and then will show to the left of the tab stop. Decimal places are aligned consistently on each line.

As with all of the features we have covered, you should experiment using Tabs yourself hands-on.

2.11 Tools: Spelling

Finally we come to one of the most popular features of word processing software. Click on **Tools** and then on **Spelling** in the drop down menu. Word will work right through your document seeing if the spelling matches the spelling of words in the computer's dictionary. If not it suggests alternatives from which you choose the correct one. For example, if you type 'drp', the choices you are offered include 'drip', 'drop', 'dry' and 'dip'.

The spell-checker will identify all words that don't appear in the word processing package's dictionary. Remember that not all of the words highlighted will actually be mistakes, for example the word 'spreadsheeting' (eg 'this job requires good spreadsheeting skills') is suggested as a mistake.

Also, some mistakes won't be highlighted as the incorrect spelling matches another word. For example, you may type 'form' when you meant 'from' – this won't be highlighted as a spelling mistake.

So, when using the spell checker always take your time before deciding whether to accept or ignore the suggested change. Also, ensure the correct dictionary is being used, for example English UK rather than English US.

Ensure the dictionary selected is correct (eg English UK)

2.12 Tables

Some information to be included in a report, letter, memo or other document may best be presented in a table. We will briefly explain how to create and format a table using menu items. As with many Microsoft Word functions, the same process could be performed using toolbar buttons (if you wish to experiment using toolbar buttons, activate the Tables and Borders toolbar by selecting View, Toolbars, Tables and Borders from the main menu).

To create a simple table follow the following steps.

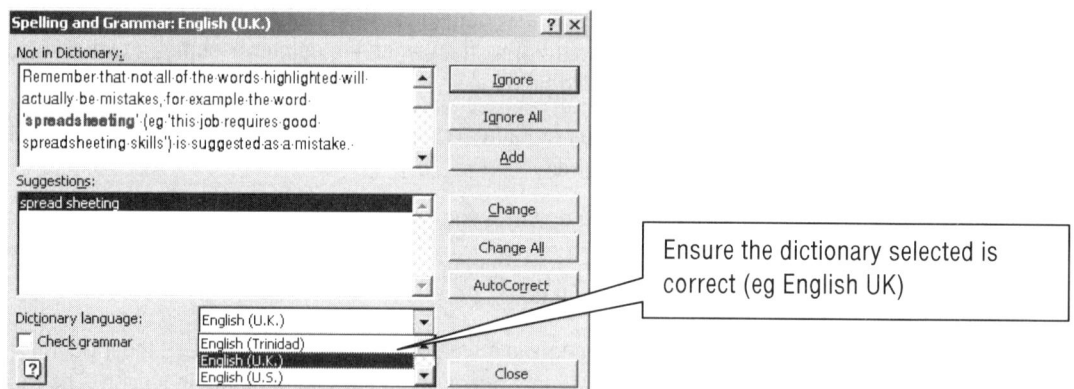

Step 1   Click where you want to create a table within your document.

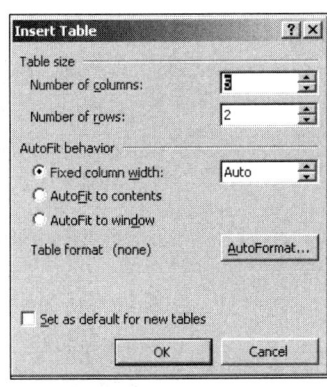

Step 2   From the main menu select, Table, Insert, Table.

Step 3   The Insert Table dialogue box will appear as shown (if you are using an earlier version of Word the box will appear slightly different). Enter the required number of vertical columns and the number of horizontal rows (don't worry if you are not 100% sure as these options may be changed later). Accept the column width default setting of Auto. Click OK.

Step 4   You should now have a Table in your document. For example, if you had chosen 4 Columns and 10 rows, you would have the table shown.

Step 5   The table you have created is a starting point only. As you add data to your table you may decide to format the contents of particular cells in a certain way, or to insert or delete columns or rows.

Instructions for some useful actions associated with tables are shown in the table below.

Table action	Explanation
Entering text and moving around the table	Click into the appropriate cell (individual area of the table) and start typing. When you reach the end of the cell the text will continue on the next line, and the cell height will adjust automatically. Move to a different cell by using your mouse to click the cursor in the new cell. If you prefer, you can move around the table using the following keys. Tab – takes you to the next cell. Shift + Tab – takes you 'back' a cell. (The Shift key is above the Ctrl key) Up or Down direction arrow key – takes you up or down a row. Return or Enter – takes you to a new line within the same cell.
Aligning text	The default is to align text in tables to the left. To align text in the centre or to the right, use the alignment buttons on the standard toolbar. 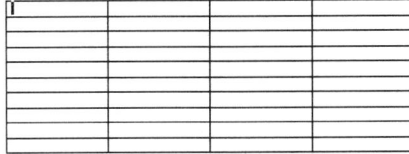
Formatting text	You format text in a table just as you would format normal text – by selecting it then using toolbar buttons or the Format menu.
Selecting rows	Position the cursor to the left of the row you wish to select. The cursor will become an arrow pointing towards the top of the row. Click to select the row. If you prefer, click into the row you wish to select, then choose Table, Select, Row from the menu.
Selecting columns	Position the cursor just above the column you wish to select. The cursor will become a black, downward pointing arrow. Click to select the column. If you prefer, click into the column you wish to select, then choose Table, Select, Column from the menu.

Table action	Explanation
Selecting a single cell	Position the cursor just inside the left border of the cell you wish to select. The cursor will become a black arrow pointing towards the top of the cell. Click to select the cell. If you prefer, click into the row you wish to select, then choose Table, Select, Cell from the menu.
Selecting the entire table	Click in any cell in the table. Choose Table, Select, Table from the menu.
Changing row height and column width	Move the cursor over the border you wish to move until it becomes two lines with arrows pointing up and down (rows) or left and right (columns). Hold down the mouse button and drag the boundary to the required height or width.
Deleting rows and columns	Select the row or column as above. Then chose Table, Delete, Rows or Table, Delete, Columns from the menu.
Deleting the contents of rows and columns	To clear the contents of a row or column select the area to be cleared then press the Delete key.
Adding rows and columns	To add an extra row, select the row below where you wish the new row to be then chose Table, Insert, Rows from the menu. To add an extra column, select the column to the right of where you wish the new column to be then chose Table, Insert, Columns from the menu.
Merging cells	Joining two cells together to contain text that spans two or more columns is called merging cells. This is useful, for example, to provide a cell at the top of a table suitable for a heading that spans across all columns. To merge cells, you must first select the cells you wish to merge – then choose Table, Merge Cells from the menu.
Borders and shading	Word inserts a simple line border around all cells in a new table. You may change some or all borders, or add shading, or remove all border lines, by using the options available under Format, Borders and Shading. You should experiment with these options.

2.13 House style

With such a wide range of fonts, formats and other options available, it is possible to produce documents with a vast range of appearances. To present a consistent, professional image, some organisations specify the same font and formatting options for all documents. This ensures consistency and presents a professional image.

For example, the headings and areas of text within this book use the same fonts each time they appear – and each chapter uses the same styles, headers and footers.

If your organisation has a house style, ensure you know how to apply it to your documents.

Question

Using Word

Type the following paragraph into a new Microsoft Word document. Use Times New Roman font, size 12pt.

This Activity covers formatting and fonts. You will use this paragraph to practice different functions. When you have completed this activity, you should be able to change font sizes, font typefaces and apply other formats. Now work through the Tasks that follow.

(a)   Highlight the phrase font sizes. Click on the font size drop-down box and change the font size to 18.

(b)   Highlight the phrase 'font typefaces'. Click on the drop box which currently displays Times New Roman and change it to Tahoma.

(c)   Highlight the phrase 'other formats'. Use the appropriate button from the formatting toolbar to underline the text.

(d)   Highlight the first sentence. Click on Format, Font and click on the checkbox next to Outline.

(e)   Highlight the last sentence. Select Format, Font from the main menu and experiment with the different options available including colour.

Answer

Your answer should look like the paragraph below.

This Activity covers formatting and fonts. You will use this paragraph to practise different functions. When you have completed this activity, you should be able to change font sizes, font typefaces and apply other formats. Now work through the Tasks that follow.

3 Spreadsheets

FAST FORWARD

A **spreadsheet** is basically an electronic piece of paper divided into **rows** and **columns**. The intersection of a row and a column is known as a **cell**.

Numbers can be **formatted** in several ways, for instance with commas, as percentages, as currency or with a certain number of decimal places.

Much of the information presented to management in the modern office is produced and/or presented using spreadsheet software. You should be able to produce clear, well-presented spreadsheets that utilise basic spreadsheet functions such as simple formulae.

3.1 What is a spreadsheet?

Key term

A **spreadsheet** is essentially an electronic piece of paper divided into rows (horizontal) and columns (vertical). The rows are numbered 1, 2, 3 . . . etc and the columns lettered A, B C . . . etc. Each individual area representing the intersection of a row and a column is called a 'cell'.

A cell address consists of its row and column reference. For example, in the spreadsheet below the word Jan is in cell B2.

The main examples of spreadsheet packages are Lotus 1 2 3 and Microsoft Excel. We will be referring to Microsoft Excel 2003, as this is the most widely-used spreadsheet. (Microsoft Excel 2007 is now available but it is not yet used by the majority of businesses. The 2007 version looks slightly different.) A simple Microsoft Excel spreadsheet, containing budgeted sales figures for three geographical areas for the first quarter of the year, is shown below.

	A	B	C	D	E	F
1	BUDGETED SALES FIGURES					
2		*Jan*	*Feb*	*Mar*	*Total*	
3		£'000	£'000	£'000	£'000	
4	North	2,431	3,001	2,189	7,621	
5	South	6,532	5,826	6,124	18,482	
6	West	895	432	596	1,923	
7	Total	9,858	9,259	8,909	28,026	
8						

3.2 Why use spreadsheets?

Spreadsheets provide a tool for calculating, analysing and manipulating numerical data. Spreadsheets make the calculation and manipulation of data easier and quicker. For example, the spreadsheet above has been set up to calculate the totals **automatically.** If you changed your estimate of sales in February for the North region to £3,296, when you input this figure in cell C4 the totals (in E4, C7 and E7) would change accordingly.

3.2.1 Cell contents

The contents of any cell can be one of the following.

(a) **Text**. A text cell usually contains **words**. Numbers that do not represent numeric values for calculation purposes (eg a Part Number) may be entered in a way that tells Excel to treat the cell contents as text. To do this, enter an apostrophe before the number eg '451.

(b) **Values**. A value is a **number** that can be used in a calculation.

(c) **Formulae**. A formula **refers to other cells** in the spreadsheet, and performs some sort of computation with them. For example, if cell C1 contains the formula =A1-B1, cell C1 will display the result of the calculation subtracting the contents of cell B1 from the contents of cell A1. In Excel, a formula always begins with an equals sign: = . There are a wide range of formulae and functions available.

4 Spreadsheet formulae

FAST FORWARD

Relative cell references (B3) change when you copy formulae to other locations or move data from one place to another. **Absolute** cell references ($B$3) stay the same.

The following illustration shows the formula bar in an Excel spreadsheet. The formula bar allows you to see and edit the contents of the active cell. The bar also shows the cell address of the 'active cell' (C3 in this example), which is the cell that the cursor is currently in.

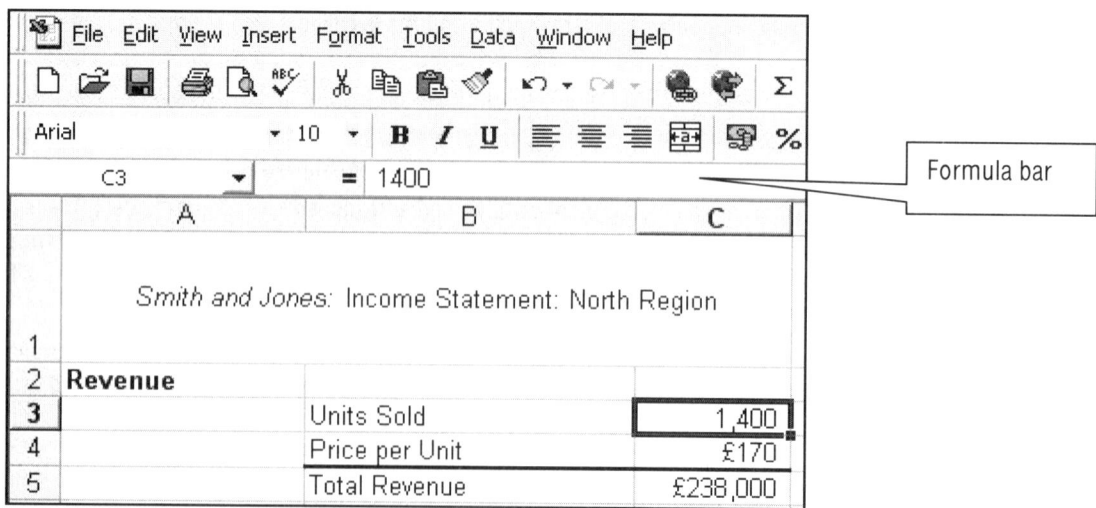

LEARNING MEDIA

4.1 Examples of spreadsheet formulae

Formulas in Microsoft Excel follow a specific syntax that includes an equal sign (=) followed by the elements to be calculated (the operands) and the calculation operators. Each operand can be a value that does not change (a constant value), a cell or range reference, a label, a name, or a worksheet function.

Formulae can be used to perform a variety of calculations. Here are some examples.

(a)   =C4*5. This formula **multiplies** the value in C4 by 5. The result will appear in the cell holding the formula.

(b)   =C4*B10. This **multiplies** the value in C4 by the value in B10.

(c)   =C4/E5. This **divides** the value in C4 by the value in E5. (* means multiply and / means divide by.)

(d)   =C4*B10-D1. This **multiplies** the value in C4 by that in B10 and then subtracts the value in D1 from the result. Note that generally Excel will perform multiplication and division before addition or subtraction. If in any doubt, use brackets (parentheses): =(C4*B10)−D1.

(e)   =C4*117.5%. This **adds** 17.5% to the value in C4. It could be used to calculate a price including 17.5% sales tax.

(f)   =(C4+C5+C6)/3. Note that the **brackets** mean Excel would perform the addition first. Without the brackets, Excel would first divide the value in C6 by 3 and then add the result to the total of the values in C4 and C5.

(g)   = 2^2 gives you 2 **to the power** of 2, in other words 2^2. Likewise = 2^3 gives you 2 cubed and so on.

(h)   = 4^ (1/2) gives you the **square root** of 4. Likewise 27^(1/3) gives you the cube root of 27 and so on.

Excel calculates a formula from left to right, starting with the equals. You can control how calculation is performed by changing the syntax of the formula. For example, the formula =5+2*3 gives a result of 11 because Excel calculates multiplication before addition. Excel would multiply 2 by 3 (resulting in 6) and would then add 5.

You may use parentheses to change the order of operations. For example =(5+2)*3 would result in Excel firstly adding the 5 and 2 together, then multiplying that result by 3 to give 21.

Question   Spreadsheets

	A	B	C	D	E	F
1	BUDGETED SALES FIGURES					
2		Jan	Feb	Mar	Total	
3		£'000	£'000	£'000	£'000	
4	North	2,431	3,001	2,189	7,621	
5	South	6,532	5,826	6,124	18,482	
6	West	895	432	596	1,923	
7	Total	9,858	9,259	8,909	28,026	
8						

(a)   In the spreadsheet shown above, which of the cells have had a number typed in, and which cells display the result of calculations (ie which cells contain a formula)?

(b)   What formula would you put in each of the following cells?

   (i)   Cell B7
   (ii)   Cell E6
   (iii)   Cell E7

(c)   If the February sales figure for the South changed from £5,826 to £5,731, what other figures would change as a result? Give cell references.

(a)   Cells into which you would need to enter a value are: B4, B5, B6, C4, C5, C6, D4, D5 and D6. Cells which would perform calculations are B7, C7, D7, E4, E5, E6 and E7.

(b)   (i)   =B4+B5+B6 or better =SUM(B4:B6)

(ii)   =B6+C6+D6 or better =SUM(B6:D6)

(iii)   =E4+E5+E6 or better =SUM(E4:E6) Alternatively, the three monthly totals could be added across the spreadsheet: = SUM (B7: D7)

(c)   The figures which would change, besides the amount in cell C5, would be those in cells C7, E5 and E7. (The contents of E7 would change if any of the sales figures changed.)

4.2 Relative and Absolute Cell references

We will explain this concept by using an example. Formulae in 'standard' form, for example the formula =SUM(B7:B9) located in cell B10, are said to be relative. This formula does not really mean 'add up the numbers in cells B7 to B9'; it actually means 'add up the numbers in the three cells above this one'. So, if this **relative** formula was copied to cell C15 it would become =SUM(C12:C14). Sometimes this automatic amendment to copied formulae may not be required. In this situation you should use **absolute** referencing.

If we insert a dollar sign $ before the column letter, this makes the column reference absolute. So, copying =(SUM$B7:$B9) from B10 to C15 would give =SUM($B12:$B14).

A dollar sign before the row number makes the row number absolute. So, copying =(SUMB$7:B$9) from B10 to C15 would give =SUM(C$7:C$9).

A dollar sign before the column letter and row number makes the complete cell reference absolute. So, copying =(SUM$B$7:$B$9) from B10 to C15 would give =(SUM$B$7:$B$9).

You do not need to type the dollar signs, you can highlight the cell references you wish to make absolute and then press F4. This adds dollar signs to cell references in the formula, for example C31 would become $C$31. If you pressed F4 again, the reference becomes C$31. Press it again: the reference becomes $C31. Press it once more, and the simple relative reference is restored: C31.

Exam focus point

You could be asked a question in the exam about the users of spreadsheets or even to determine a formula for a cell in a spreadsheet.

5 Basic spreadsheet skills

FAST FORWARD

Essential basic **skills** include how to **move around** within a spreadsheet, how to **enter** and **edit** data, how to **fill** cells, how to **insert** and **delete** columns and rows and how to improve the basic **layout** and **appearance** of a spreadsheet.

In this section we explain some **basic spreadsheeting skills**. We give instructions for Microsoft Excel, the most widely used package. Our examples should be valid with all versions of Excel released since 1997. You should read this section while sitting at a computer and trying out the skills we describe, **'hands-on'**. Come back to this section later if you cannot do this right now.

5.1 Examples of useful spreadsheet skills

Start Microsoft Excel by double-clicking on the Excel **icon** or button (it will look like an X), or by choosing Excel from the **Start** menu (maybe from within the **Microsoft Office** option).

5.1.1 Moving about

The F5 key is useful for moving about large spreadsheets. If you press the function key **F5**, a **Go To** dialogue box will allow you to specify the cell address you would like to move to. Try this out.

Also experiment by holding down Ctrl and pressing each of the direction arrow keys in turn to see where you end up. Try using the **Page Up** and **Page Down** keys and also try **Home** and **End** and Ctrl + these keys. Try **Tab** and **Shift + Tab**, too. These are all useful shortcuts for moving quickly from one place to another in a large spreadsheet.

5.1.2 Editing cell contents

Suppose cell A2 currently contains the value 456. If you wish to **change the entry** in cell A2 from 456 to 123456 there are four options – as shown below.

(a)   Activate cell A2, **type** 123456 and press **Enter**. (To undo this and try the next option press **Ctrl + Z**: this will always undo what you have just done.)

(b)   **Double-click** in cell A2. The cell will keep its thick outline but you will now be able to see a vertical line flashing in the cell. You can move this line by using the direction arrow keys or the Home and the End keys. Move it to before the 4 and type 123. Then press Enter.

After you have tried this, press Ctrl + Z to undo it.

(c)   **Click once** on the number 456 in the line that shows the active cell reference and cell contents at the top of the screen. Again you will get the vertical line and you can type in 123 before the 4. Then press Enter, then Ctrl + Z.

(d)   Press the **function key F2**. The vertical line cursor will be flashing in cell A2 at the *end* of the figures entered there (after the 6). Press Home to get to a position before the 4 and then type in 123 and press Enter, as before.

5.1.3 Deleting cell contents

You may delete the contents of a cell simply by making the cell the active cell and then pressing **Delete**. The contents of the cell will disappear. You may also highlight a range of cells to delete and then delete the contents of all cells within the range.

For example, enter any value in cell A1 and any value in cell A2. Move the cursor to cell A2. Now hold down the **Shift** key (the one above the Ctrl key) and keeping it held down press the ↑ arrow. Cell A2 will stay white but cell A1 will go black. What you have done here is **selected** the range A1 and A2. Now press Delete. The contents of cells A1 and A2 will disappear.

5.1.4 Filling a range of cells

Start with a blank spreadsheet. Type the number 1 in cell A1 and the number 2 in cell A2. Now *select* cells A1: A2, this time by positioning the mouse pointer over cell A1, holding down the left mouse button and moving the pointer down to cell A2. When cell A2 goes black you can release the mouse button.

Now position the mouse pointer at the **bottom right hand corner** of cell A2. (You should be able to see a little black lump in this corner: this is called the **'fill handle'**.) When you have the mouse pointer in the right place it will turn into a black cross.

Hold down the left mouse button again and move the pointer down to cell A10. You will see an outline surrounding the cells you are trying to 'fill'.

Release the mouse button when you have the pointer over cell A10. You will find that the software **automatically** fills in the numbers 3 to 10 below 1 and 2.

Try the following variations of this technique.

(a)   Delete what you have just done and type in **Jan** in cell A1. See what happens if you select cell A1 and fill down to cell A12: you get the months **Feb, Mar, Apr** and so on.

(b)   Type the number 2 in cell A1. Select A1 and fill down to cell A10. What happens? The cells should fill up with 2's.

(c)   Type the number 2 in cell A1 and 4 in cell A2. Then select A1: A2 and fill down to cell A10. What happens? You should get 2, 4, 6, 8, and so on.

(d)   Try **filling across** as well as down. In Excel you can fill in any direction.

(e)   What happens if you click on the bottom right hand corner using the **right mouse button**, drag down to another cell and then release the button? You should get a menu giving you a variety of different options for how you want the cells to be filled in.

5.1.5 The Sum button Σ

Start with a blank spreadsheet, and then enter the following figures in cells A1:B5.

	A	B
1	400	582
2	250	478
3	359	264
4	476	16
5	97	125

Make cell B6 the active cell and click *once* on the sum button (the button with a Σ symbol on the toolbar – the Σ symbol is the mathematical sign for 'the sum of'). A formula will appear in the cell saying =SUM(B1:B5). Above cell B6 you will see a flashing dotted line encircling cells B1:B5. Accept the suggested formula by hitting the Enter key. The formula =SUM(B1:B5) will be entered, and the number 1465 will be appear in cell B6.

Next, make cell A6 the active cell and **double-click** on the sum button. The number 1582 should show in cell A6.

5.1.6 Multiplication

Continuing on with our example, next select cell C1. Type in an = sign then click on cell A1. Now type in an **asterisk *** (which serves as a **multiplication sign**) and click on cell B1. Watch how the formula in cell C1 changes as you do this. (Alternatively you can enter the cell references by moving the direction arrow keys.) Finally press Enter. Cell C1 will show the result (232,800) of multiplying the figure in Cell A1 by the one in cell B1.

Your next task is to select cell C1 and **fill in** cells C2 to C5 automatically using the filling technique described earlier. If you then click on each cell in column C and look above at the line showing what the cell contains you will find that the software has automatically filled in the correct cell references for you: A2*B2 in cell C2, A3*B3 in cell C3 and so on.

(**Note**: The forward slash / is used to represent division in spreadsheet formulae).

5.1.7 Inserting columns and rows

Suppose we also want to add each row, for example cells A1 and B1. The logical place to do this would be cell C1, but column C already contains data. We have three options that would enable us to place this total in column C.

(a)   Highlight cells C1 to C5 and position the mouse pointer on one of the **edges**. (It will change to an arrow shape.) Hold down the **left** mouse button and drag cells C1 to C5 into column D. There is now space in column C for our next set of sums. Any **formulae** that need to be changed as a result of moving cells using this method should be changed **automatically** – but always check them.

(b)   The second option is to highlight cells C1 to C5 as before, position the mouse pointer anywhere **within** column C and click on the **right** mouse button. A menu will appear offering you an option

Insert... . If you click on this you will be asked where you want to shift the cells that are being moved. In this case you want to move them to the *right* so choose this option and click on OK.

(c)   The third option is to **insert a whole new column**. You do this by clicking on the letter at the top of the column (here C) to highlight the whole of it then proceeding as in (b). The new column will be inserted to the left of the one you highlight.

You can now display the sum of each of the rows in column C.

You can also insert a **new row** in a similar way (or stretch rows).

(a)   To insert **one** row – for headings say – click on the row number to highlight it, click with the right mouse button and choose insert. One row will be inserted **above** the one you highlighted. Try putting some headings above the figures in columns A to C.

(b)   To insert **several** rows click on the row number **immediately below** the point where you want the new rows to appear and, holding down the left mouse button select the number of extra rows you want – rows 1, 2 and 3, say, to insert three rows above the current row 1. Click on the highlighted area with the right mouse button and choose insert.

5.1.8 Changing column width

You may occasionally find that a cell is not wide enough to display its contents. When this occurs, the cell displays a series of hashes ######. There are two options available to solve this problem.

(a)   One is to **decide for yourself** how wide you want the columns to be. Position the mouse pointer at the head of column A directly over the little line dividing the letter A from the letter B. The mouse **pointer** will change to a sort of **cross**. Hold down the left mouse button and, by moving your mouse, stretch Column A to the right, to about the middle of column D, until the words you typed fit. You can do the same for column B. Then make your columns too narrow again so you can try option (b).

(b)   Often it is easier to **let the software decide for you**. Position the mouse pointer over the little dividing line as before and get the cross symbol. Then double-click with the left mouse button. The column automatically adjusts to an appropriate width to fit the widest cell in that column.

You can either adjust the width of each column individually or you can do them all in one go. To do the latter click on the button in the top left hand corner to **select the whole sheet** and then **double-click** on just one of the dividing lines: all the columns will adjust to the **'best fit'** width.

5.1.9 Keyboard shortcuts and toolbar buttons

Finally a few tips to improve the **appearance** of your spreadsheets and speed up your work. To do any of the following to a cell or range of cells, first **select** the cell or cells and then:

(a)   Press Ctrl + B to make the cell contents **bold.**

(b)   Press Ctrl + I to make the cell contents *italic.*

(c)   Press **Ctrl + C** to **copy** the contents of the cells.

(d)   Move the cursor and press **Ctrl + V** to **paste** the cell you just copied into the new active cell or cells.

There are also **buttons** in the Excel toolbar (shown below) that may be used to carry out these and other functions. The best way to learn about these features is to use them – enter some numbers and text into a spreadsheet and experiment with keyboard shortcuts and toolbar buttons.

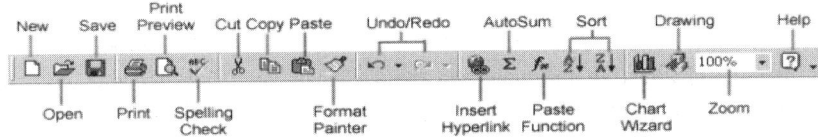

6 Spreadsheet format and appearance

FAST FORWARD

A spreadsheet should be given a **title** which clearly defines its purpose. The contents of rows and columns should also be clearly **labelled**. **Formatting** should be used to make the data held in the spreadsheet easy to read and interpret.

It is important that the information provided in a spreadsheet is easy to understand. Good presentation can help people understand the contents of a spreadsheet.

6.1 Titles and labels

A spreadsheet should be headed up with a title which **clearly defines its purpose**. Examples of titles are follows.

(a) Income statement for the year ended 30 June 200X

(b) (i) Area A: Sales forecast for the three months to 31 March 200X
    (ii) Area B: Sales forecast for the three months to 31 March 200X
    (iii) Combined sales forecast for the three months to 31 March 200X

(c) Salesmen: Analysis of earnings and commission for the six months ended 30 June 200X

Row and **column** headings (or labels) should clearly identify the contents of the row/column. Any assumptions made that have influenced the spreadsheet contents should be clearly stated.

6.2 Formatting

There are a wide range of options available under the **Format** menu. Some of these functions may also be accessed through toolbar **buttons**. Formatting options include the ability to:

(a) Add **shading** or **borders** to cells.

(b) Use **different sizes of text** and different **fonts**.

(c) Choose from a range of options for presenting values, for example to present a number as a **percentage** (eg 0.05 as 5%), or with commas every third digit, or to a specified number of **decimal places** etc.

Experiment with the various formatting options yourself.

6.3 Formatting numbers

Most spreadsheet programs contain facilities for presenting numbers in a particular way. In Excel you simply select **Format** and then **Cells ...**to reach these options.

(a) **Fixed format** displays the number in the cell rounded off to the number of decimal places you select.

(b) **Currency format** displays the number with a '$' in front, with commas and not more than two decimal places, eg $10,540.23.

(c) **Comma format** is the same as currency format except that the numbers are displayed without the '$'.

(d) **General format** is the format assumed unless another format is specified. In general format the number is displayed with no commas and with as many decimal places as entered or calculated that fit in the cell.

(e) **Percent format** multiplies the number in the display by 100 and follows it with a percentage sign. For example the number 0.548 in a cell would be displayed as 54.8%.

(f) **Hidden format** is a facility by which values can be entered into cells and used in calculations but are not actually displayed on the spreadsheet. The format is useful for hiding sensitive information.

6.4 Gridlines

One of the options available under the **Tools**, **Options** menu, on the **View** tab, is an option to remove the gridlines from your spreadsheet.

Compare the following two versions of the same spreadsheet. Note how the formatting applied to the second version has improved the spreadsheet presentation.

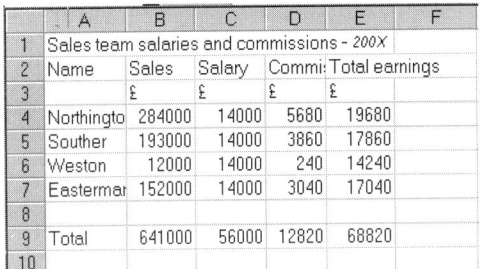

7 Using spreadsheets with word processing software

Spreadsheets can be **linked** to and exchange data with **word processing documents** – and vice versa.

There may be a situation where you wish to incorporate the contents of all or part of a spreadsheet into a **word processed report**. There are a number of options available to achieve this.

(a) The simplest, but least professional option, is to **print out** the spreadsheet and interleave the page or pages at the appropriate point in your word processed document.

(b) A neater option if you are just including a small table is to select and **copy** the relevant cells from the spreadsheet to the computer's clipboard by selecting the cells and choosing Edit, Copy. Then switch to the word processing document, and **paste** them in at the appropriate point.

(c) Office packages, such as Microsoft Office, allow you to **link** spreadsheets and word processing files.

For example, a new, blank spreadsheet can be '**embedded**' in a document by selecting Insert, Object then, from within the Create New tab, selecting Microsoft Excel worksheet. The spreadsheet is then available to be worked upon, allowing the easy manipulation of numbers using all the facilities of the spreadsheet package. Clicking outside the spreadsheet will result in the spreadsheet being inserted in the document.

The contents of an existing spreadsheet may be inserted into a Word document by choosing Insert, Object and then activating the Create from File tab. Then click the Browse button and locate the spreadsheet file. Highlight the file, then click Insert, and then OK. You may then need to move and resize the object, by dragging its borders, to fit your document.

Chapter Roundup

- Word processing software, such as **Microsoft Word**, is used to produce text-based documents such as letters, memos and reports.

- It includes a wide range of tools that allow the **professional presentation** of information.

- A **spreadsheet** is basically an electronic piece of paper divided into **rows** and **columns**. The intersection of a row and a column is known as a **cell**.

- **Numbers** can be **formatted** in several ways, for instance with commas, as percentages, as currency or with a certain number of decimal places.

- **Relative** cell references (B3) change when you copy formulae to other locations or move data from one place to another. **Absolute** cell references ($B$3) stay the same.

- Essential basic **skills** include how to **move around** within a spreadsheet, how to **enter** and **edit** data, how to **fill** cells, how to **insert** and **delete** columns and rows and how to improve the basic **layout** and **appearance** of a spreadsheet.

- A spreadsheet should be given a **title** which clearly defines its purpose. The contents of rows and columns should also be clearly **labelled**. **Formatting** should be used to make the data held in the spreadsheet easy to read and interpret.

- Spreadsheets can be **linked** to and exchange data with **word processing documents** – and vice versa.

Quick Quiz

1   What does the term 'justification' refer to?

   A   The character style
   B   The way that the text is laid out
   C   The way that the file is saved
   D   The contents of a cell

2   Which one of the following statements about spreadsheets is incorrect?

   A   Spreadsheets make calculations easier and quicker
   B   Data can be manipulated more easily
   C   'Totals' figures can be calculated automatically
   D   The information will always be accurate

3   Cell C4 contains a sales price net of sales tax. Which one of the following formulae would NOT give the gross sales price?

   A   C4 * 117.5%
   B   C4 * 1.175
   C   C4 * (1 + 0.175)
   D   C4 + 17.5%

4   In order to move quickly from one place to another in a large spreadsheet, which one of the following key controls would be unhelpful.

   A   F2
   B   Page up
   C   F5
   D   Ctrl and an arrow key

5   If a spreadsheet column is not wide enough to display its contents, which of the following would appear?

   A   #REF!
   B   #NUM!
   C   #####
   D   #DIV/O!

6   Which of the following options would perform the 'paste' function?

   A   Ctrl + P
   B   Ctrl + R
   C   Ctrl + T
   D   Ctrl + V

Answers to Quick Quiz

1   B   Justification refers to how the text is laid out on the screen. Text can be subject to left justification, right justification, centre justification or full justification.

2   D   The spreadsheet itself won't make errors but it is still subject to human error. If, for example, the data which is input is incorrect then the output information will be incorrect.

3   D   Try this using a figure of 100 in cell C4.

        The first three options will return a figure of 117.50. Option D will return a figure of 100.175 because Excel has added 0.175 to the 100.

4   A   F2 will not be helpful as this is an edit key.

5   C   When this occurs, the cell displays a series of hashes.

6   D   Ctrl + V will paste. (Note that Ctrl + P will tell the computer to print.)

Computer security and legal issues

4

Study guide

			Syllabus reference
1	(g)	Outline the requirements of health and safety legislation related to the use of computer hardware.	2c(iii)
2	(d)	Discuss security issues related to the location of hardware and software.	2b(i),(iii)
	(c)	Discuss the prevention of computer fraud and data corruption, and of hardware/software problems and failure.	2b(i)-(v)
	(e)	Outline the requirements of data protection legislation relating to computer software/information.	2c(i),(ii)

1 Introduction

Information technology has brought many changes to working practices and procedures. Much information processing is now **faster**, more **accurate** and more **reliable** than was ever possible using manual processing methods. Computers can tackle **complex** tasks and can handle **huge volumes** of data.

Computers are used widely in many organisations, and those organisations often depend entirely on their IT resources to support the smooth and continuing day-to-day operation of the business.

A high degree of reliance on computers can mean a high level of exposure to computer failure. If users do not put adequate security measures and procedures into place, computer failure can result in the loss of much valuable data. Security measures to protect against damage and disruption to computer data and services are therefore essential.

Key term

> **Security** involves the prevention of unauthorised modification, disclosure or destruction of data and the maintenance of uninterrupted computing services.

2 Risks

FAST FORWARD

> There are many different **risks** to computer systems. Sources of risk include authorised users and staff, unauthorised users and intruders, faulty hardware, software or storage media, fire, terrorism and other major incidents and natural disasters.

Risks to computer systems come from a variety of **sources**, including:

* Authorised users and staff
* Unauthorised users and intruders
* Faulty hardware, software or storage media
* Fire, terrorism and other major incidents
* Natural disasters

Specific risks are identified and explained in the following table.

Risk to computer systems	
Risk	**Explanation**
Human error	The mistakes staff and other people make are a threat. For example a person may input a transaction to the wrong account, key an incorrect value, or forget to check a back-up has completed properly. Incorrect data prevents the system operating as it should.

Risk to computer systems	
Risk	**Explanation**
Hardware, software and storage media	Computer systems involve the interaction of various hardware, software and storage media. Hardware failure is relatively uncommon but has the potential to prevent the system from operating. A software fault is referred to as a bug. Minor bugs may be 'worked around' for a time but major bugs must be corrected. A faulty disk is likely to prevent the system retrieving data held on it.
Fire, terrorism and other major incidents	Fire is a serious hazard to computer systems – it can destroy hardware, software and data. Water damage from fire fighting can also cause problems. Terrorist acts such as bombs could cause devastation of buildings and contents including computer systems – as could a major incident such as a vehicle hitting a building.
Theft	Computer equipment theft may be carried out by staff or intruders. A laptop computer will fit easily into a briefcase or bag. One person can carry a laser printer or a desktop PC unit reasonably easily. Other theft risks include: • Chip theft – computers being opened up and the microchips and memory removed • Theft of storage media such as CD-Rs • Theft or unauthorised copying of company software • Theft of commercially valuable data (either by hackers or authorised users)
Malicious damage or harm	Outsiders (whether gaining physical entry or through 'hacking' - explained later) or staff with a grudge may damage systems deliberately. A fairly new threat, relating to Internet websites is the 'denial of service attack'. This involves an organised campaign to bombard an Internet site with excessive volumes of traffic at a given time, with the aim of overloading the site.
Fraud	Fraud may be committed regardless of the type of information system used (manual or computerised). Computer fraud may be committed by disgruntled employees, by interested outsiders (who may bribe an employee to breach the organisation's defences) and by hackers. Examples of common methods of fraud are given below. • Creation of false supplier accounts and submission of false invoices • Loading unauthorised discounts on customer accounts • Falsifying inventory records to cover up the theft of inventory • Creating fictitious staff on the payroll
Weather and other natural disasters	In some areas flooding is a natural risk, for example in towns and cities near rivers or coasts. Wind and rain can also cause substantial damage to buildings. Flooding, lightning and electrical storms pose a threat to power supplies. Power surges may occur when services are restored which may affect computer operations. Other natural disasters such as earthquakes are a risk in some countries.
Hackers and eavesdroppers	Hackers attempt to gain unauthorised access to computer systems. They may attempt to damage a system or steal information. Hackers use tools like electronic number generators and software which enables rapid password attempts. Data that is transmitted across telecommunications links is exposed to the risk of being intercepted or examined during transmission (eavesdropping).

Risk to computer systems	
Risk	**Explanation**
Viruses	A virus is a small piece of software which performs unauthorised actions and which replicates itself. Viruses may cause damage to files or attempt to destroy files and damage hard disks. When transmitted over a network, such as the Internet, into a 'clean' system, the virus reproduces, thus infecting that system. Types of virus include: • E-mail viruses spread using e-mail messages and replicate by mailing themselves to addresses held in the users contacts book • Worms copy themselves from machine to machine on a network • Trojans or Trojan horses are hidden inside a 'valid' program but perform an unexpected act. Trojans therefore act like a virus, but they aren't classified as viruses as they don't replicate themselves. • Trap doors are undocumented access points to a system allowing controls to be bypassed. • Logic bombs are triggered by the occurrence of a certain event. • Time bombs are triggered by a certain date.

3 Controls

FAST FORWARD

Risks should be **controlled** - as much as is practically possible.

Physical access controls attempt to stop **intruders** or other unauthorised persons getting near to computer equipment or storage media. Controls include **door locks** and **card entry systems**.

Logical access controls are concerned with preventing those persons who have gained physical access from gaining unauthorised access to data or software. Passwords are one example of a logical access system.

Organisations should take steps to minimise or control the possible impact of risks to computer systems. In this section we explain the main types of control.

Computer system controls		
Control type	**Relevant risk(s)**	**Control explanation**
Physical access controls	**Theft, malicious damage**	The first line of protection against individuals seeking unauthorised access to equipment or systems is to control physical access to the building. Physical access controls include: • Personnel (security guards). • Personal identification numbers (PINs) required to be keyed into keypads to gain entry to the building and/or areas. PINs differ from combination keypad locks, as a system that uses PINs involves an individual PIN being used by each person – rather than having one combination used by all. PIN systems may be used in conjunction with a magnetic stripe card – or a smart card. • Door locks (key operated or combination). Key control or combination control if security is to be maintained. (The combination lock approach differs from a PIN system, as the same combination is used by all.) • Magnetic strip cards or smart card systems may be used to allow access to a building or to parts of a building.

Computer system controls		
Control type	**Relevant risk(s)**	**Control explanation**
		• Closed circuit television (CCTV) allows movements to be monitored. • Burglar alarms may deter intruders outside office hours. • Systems able to identify people through the use of fingerprints or retina scans are available. However these are too expensive for most organisations.
Logical access controls	**Fraud, unauthorised access, unauthorised copying**	Logical access controls prevent actual entry to computer system software and data. Examples include: • Passwords required to log on or to gain access to certain files or functions (covered in detail in the next chapter). • Users should be required to log off when they leave their PC. PC's should have password protected screensavers that automatically activate on idle machines. • Computer terminals/PCs should be sited where the risk of unauthorised use is minimised. • Printouts that contain confidential or sensitive data should be stored securely - and shredded when no longer needed. • Disks and CDs containing data should not be left lying around - they could get lost, stolen or damaged.
Hardware, software and storage media controls	**Hardware, software and storage media faults, theft, data loss**	The risk of hardware and software failure can be minimised by ensuring the system installed is **capable** of performing the tasks required – and is thoroughly **tested**. Smaller items of equipment, such as laptop computers (left on the premises) should be **locked** securely away. Desktop PCs may be **bolted** to desks. Equipment should be **marked** with the organisation's name and asset number – to prevent thieves passing off the equipment as their own and to enable the return of any equipment that is stolen and later recovered. A **log** of all equipment should be maintained. Staff allocated portable equipment such as laptops should sign acknowledging responsibility for the equipment. The log and **booking procedures** aim to reduce the likelihood of theft by people who have official access to equipment. External storage media such as memory sticks, CDs and tapes should be **stored securely** and handled with care. • CDs should be protected from dust, scratches and fingerprints. They should be held along the outer edge or by the centre hole. If written on, this should be on the 'label' side and only with a felt-tip pen. • Tapes can be snipped with scissors, or get knotted up, and they can also be damaged by magnets, heat and liquid.

Computer system controls		
Control type	**Relevant risk(s)**	**Control explanation**
Hardware, software and storage media controls (continued)	Hardware, software and storage media faults, theft, data loss (continued)	Data loss from hard disks can be protected against by taking **back-ups** (covered in detail in the next chapter). Storage media holding back-up files and copies of software CDs should be stored in a fireproof locked cabinet or safe. Some back-ups of data should be stored off-site.
Input controls	Human error	Many applications include input checks that prevent obviously incorrect data being entered (eg accounting software would not accept text in the 'amount' field or a transaction date outside the accounting year).

However, it is not possible to prevent all errors - such as selecting an incorrect account or keying an incorrect amount. Procedures requiring input to be checked before being posted should be implemented to minimise these errors. |
| Building location and layout, protected power supply | Weather and other natural disasters | The risk posed by weather (eg flooding) and natural disasters should be considered when considering the location and layout of the building.

The loss of the mains power supply may be protected against by the use of a separate generator and a device known as a UPS (uninterrupted (protected) power supply). The UPS also protects equipment from fluctuations in the supply. |
| Fire safety plan | Fire, terrorism and other major incidents | A fire safety plan is an essential feature of security procedures, in order to prevent fire, detect fire and put out the fire. Fire safety includes:

Site preparation (for example, appropriate building materials, fire doors)

Detection (for example, smoke detectors)

Extinguishing (for example, sprinklers)

Training for staff in observing fire safety procedures

Water damage from fire fighting may be minimised through the use of waterproof ceilings and floors together with the provision of adequate drainage. |
| Controls over staff | Theft, fraud, human error, malicious damage | Controls relating to staff include the following.

Careful selection of personnel. Staff should be recruited with care. They should be honest and should have the qualities and experience required. Reference checks should be carried out.

Segregation of duties (division of responsibilities). Dishonest behaviour is most likely to occur when an individual is able to act alone. To reduce the opportunity for an individual to be dishonest (or to commit fraud), no one person should be responsible for performing and checking or approving a particular task.

Job rotation, so that employees change jobs at random intervals, thus making it uncertain that an individual will be able to set up a breach of security in the time available.

Enforced holidays (employees who have committed fraud or another offence may be reluctant to take holidays for fear that the person taking over their duties will detect their actions).

Access to sensitive information granted on a need-to-know basis. |

Computer system controls		
Control type	**Relevant risk(s)**	**Control explanation**
Virus protection, network and telecommunications security	**Viruses, hackers, eavesdroppers**	The main protection against viruses is anti-virus software. Anti-virus software, such as McAfee or Norton's searches systems for viruses and removes them. Anti-virus programs include an auto-update feature that downloads profiles of new viruses, enabling the software to check for all known or existing viruses. Very new viruses may go undetected by anti-virus software (until the anti-virus software vendor updates their package - and the organisation installs the update).
		Organisations should ensure all files received via e-mail are virus checked.
		External e-mail links can be protected by way of a firewall that may be configured to virus check all messages, and may also prevent files of a certain type being sent via e-mail (eg .exe files, as these are the most common means of transporting a virus).
		Firewalls can be implemented in both hardware and software, or a combination of both. A firewall disables part of the telecoms technology to prevent unauthorised intrusions. However, a determined hacker may well be able to bypass this.
		Data that is transmitted across telecommunications links is exposed to the risk of being intercepted or read during transmission. Encryption is used to reduce this risk. Encryption involves scrambling the data at one end of the line, transmitting the scrambled data, and unscrambling it at the receiver's end of the line. A person intercepting the scrambled data is unable to make sense of it.
		Authentication is a technique of making sure that a message has come from an authorised sender. Authentication involves adding extra data in a form previously agreed between sender and recipient.
		Dial-back security operates by requiring the person wanting access to dial into the network and identify themselves first. The system then dials the person back on their authorised number before allowing access.

Many of the controls covered in this section will be included in a formal organisation security plan, including the steps to be followed in case of a major disaster. We look at the contents of a formal security policy in Chapter 5.

Within the risks and controls covered above are several key terms. These are shown below.

Key terms

Fraud refers to any activity deliberately practiced with the aim of gaining an unlawful advantage or gain.

A **hacker** is a person who attempts to access a system they are not authorised to enter.

A **virus** is a piece of software which infects programs and data and possibly damages them, and which replicates itself.

3.1 Advantages and disadvantages of controls

Almost all controls involve a **trade-off** between providing **protection** against unauthorised or unwanted access and damage – and allowing people enough **flexibility** and freedom to perform their duties efficiently.

A balance is required that provides sufficient protection without hindering the performance of employees.

The **cost** of the control measures also needs to be considered and balanced against the potential damage the measure is designed to prevent.

Controls that involve people – such as security guards controlling access – have the advantage of allowing judgement to be exercised. For example, a security guard can recognise a long-serving employee who may have lost their ID card and arrange temporary access.

Mechanical or automated access controls, such as a PIN system, do not exercise judgement – if the correct PIN is entered by an unauthorised person they will gain access. On the other hand, if a bona-fide employee forgets their PIN the system won't allow access.

The 'best' controls depend upon the circumstances involved eg cost, size of the organisation, nature of the business etc.

4 Hoaxes

FAST FORWARD

Hoaxes often take the form of a warning about viruses contained in e-mail. Hoaxes waste the time of all concerned.

There are a vast number of common hoaxes, most of which circulate via **e-mail**. Many are a variation of one of the most 'popular' early hoaxes - the **Good Times** hoax. This hoax takes the form of a warning about viruses contained in e-mail. People pass along the warning because they are trying to be helpful, but they are in fact wasting the time of all concerned.

A number of websites provide information on hoaxes and 'real' viruses - for example www.sophos.com. If you receive a warning of a virus or the promise of rewards for forwarding an e-mail to a number of others, this is a good place to look to establish if the warning is a hoax or not.

Question   Hardware security

Your department is located in an open-plan office. The office contains five networked desktop PCs and two laser printers.

You have just read an article suggesting that the best form of security is to lock hardware away in fireproof cabinets, but you feel that this is impracticable. Make a note of any alternative security measures which you could adopt to protect the hardware and data held on the system.

Answer

(a)   'Postcode' (ie mark with your postcode or company name) all pieces of hardware. Invisible ink post coding is popular, but visible marking may be a better deterrent.

(b)   Mark the equipment in other ways. Some organisations spray their hardware with permanent paint using stencilled shapes.

(c)   Hardware can be bolted to desks. If bolts are passed through the desk and through the bottom of the hardware casing, the equipment can be rendered immobile.

(d)   Ensure that the organisation's standard security procedures (magnetic passes, keypad access to offices, signing-in of visitors etc) are followed.

(e)   Ensure all data held on the PCs is backed up regularly

Question   Fire and flooding risks

Your company is reviewing all areas of computer operations and the associated risks. You realise that no-one has considered the risks of fire or flooding. Make a note of the issues you consider relevant to these areas.

(a) Fire. Fire security should include preventative, detective and corrective measures. Preventative measures include sitting of the computer in a building constructed of suitable materials and the use of a site which is not affected by the storage of inflammable materials (stationery, chemicals). Detective measures involve the use of smoke detectors. Corrective measures may include installation of a sprinkler system (water-based or possibly gas-based to avoid electrical problems), training of fire officers and good sitting of exit signs and fire extinguishers.

(b) Flooding. Water damage may result from flooding or from fire recovery procedures. It may not be sensible to site large mainframe computers in a basement.

Question — Security guards and identification devices

What are the relative advantages and disadvantages of security guards and electronic identification devices?

Answer

Security guards can get to know the staff and can act on their own initiative if intruders are spotted. On the other hand, they are expensive and they may become lax about security procedures.

Electronic identification devices are cheap to run and always apply controls to the same standard. On the other hand, they cannot show initiative, and a device which reads a card cannot tell if a card has been stolen and is being used by an intruder.

Question — Data Security

(a) Identify the main threats that an organisation holding sensitive data on computer storage must guard against?

(b) To protect such data, a logical access system is essential. What is a logical access system, and how might it work?

(c) Explain the significance of the following terms in the context of data security:
- Encryption
- Hacking
- Computer viruses

Answer

(a) **Threats to data**

Threats which a company holding sensitive data on a magnetic storage medium must guard against include the following.

(i) Contravention of Data Protection legislation. If the data falls within the scope of the legislation care must be taken that control to ensure compliance is exercised at all times.

(ii) Losing the data through physical threats. The data can be lost as a result of a number of factors, which include both external and internal influences: fire, theft, floods, physical damage to the storage media, or erasure of the storage media by magnetic or electrical means. 'Man-made' physical threats also exist, for example from hackers and disgruntled employees or ex-employees.

(iii) Corruption of the data. Many of the factors which might result in a total loss of data can also play a similar part in partially corrupting the data held on the medium. This corruption, if it goes undetected, is potentially more damaging than a total loss of the data would be, since there is a chance that the corrupted data is treated as correct. In addition, rogue software

such as poorly written programs, viruses and misused utility programs can both corrupt and erase data.

(iv)   Releasing the data to unauthorised persons. If the data is released to outsiders, then the value of the data can be negated as well as providing opportunities for the unauthorised person either to misuse the data, to sell it or just to pass it over to other parties. Data could be transmitted over communications links, or copied to floppy disk, Zip disk or CD, all of which are easily concealed and very portable.

(b)   **Logical access**

A logical access system is an entry system based on logical (program) controls rather than physical (keys, etc) controls. The logical access system will allocate passwords in a variety of forms at different levels of access to the system. A password may need to be given when first accessing the overall computer facility, when asking to use specific systems on the computer, and when accessing particular files, or specific fields within files. Whether passwords are allocated at a particular level would depend on the importance of the data at that level as well as the degree of sensitivity of the data.

When a user attempts to access a protected part of the system he or she would have to enter a password using the keyboard, or some form of input device and/or some form of physical scanning device to establish their credentials. Incorrect passwords would result in the attempted access being logged and perhaps shut down the terminal being used for the attempt.

When passwords are established they should be set by the person subsequently using them, and re-set at regular intervals.

(c)   (i)   **Encryption**

Encryption is the deliberate coding or altering of data, before transmission, so that any unauthorised party intercepting or eavesdropping on the transformation is unable to make sense of it. Encryption ranges from the simple substitution of one character for another to more secure methods, such as using a data encryption standard to change data to what is, effectively an unreadable state. Decryption of the data, which has to take place to allow it to be read, happens by reversing the substitution. Authorised recipients have the required decryption key (the process usually occurs without user intervention).

More secure methods of encryption make unauthorised reading of data difficult, and, therefore, discourage theft of the information. In addition encryption can make it more difficult to corrupt the data without the corruption being detected.

Encryption techniques are particularly valuable where data is transmitted electronically, for example via networks or over public telecommunications links.

(ii)   **Hacking**

Hacking is the attempted or actual access to a computer system which the hacker is not entitled to access. Examples have included people looking at private mail on public network systems. Hackers can both steal data, with the attendant problems, and corrupt data without removing it. Both of these events are better prevented if possible.

Many hackers are children who see hacking as a game or a challenge. There are numerous examples of hackers accessing private systems, including those belonging to educational establishments, public utilities and defence ministries. Hackers access systems through the telephone network; they then try out passwords either by guesswork or by using simple programs. Once inside a system, a hacker's opportunity to cause damage is high.

(iii)   **Computer viruses**

Computer viruses are small programs which, when executed, damage data and/or programs. Viruses have the ability to spread, replicating themselves like a biological virus. The damage or corruption can take the form of changes (such as an increase in the size of the corrupted program) to more complex ones (where the corrupted program might erase all the data on a disk when a specific event occurs). Both data loss and corruption are better prevented. Prevention on PCs involves using only software from recognised sources, running virus protection and detection software and not accepting e-mail attachments from unknown sources.

Two types of virus are logic bombs and time bombs.

(1)   A logic bomb is a piece of code triggered by certain events. A program will behave normally until a certain event occurs, for example when disk utilisation reaches a certain percentage. A logic bomb, by responding to set conditions, maximises damage. For example, it will be triggered when a disk is nearly full, or when a large number of users are using the system.

(2)   A time bomb is similar to a logic bomb, except that it is triggered at a certain date. Companies have experienced virus attacks on April Fool's Day and on Friday 13th. These were released by time bombs.

An activated virus can show itself in a number of ways. The Jerusalem virus slows down the operation of the infected machine so much that it becomes virtually unusable, then deletes files. Cascade causes letters on the screen to 'fall' to the bottom of the screen and may reformat the hard disk. The Melissa virus corrupts Microsoft Office documents.

Question

Looking after a CD

The diagram shows an illustration found on a CD. What does it mean?

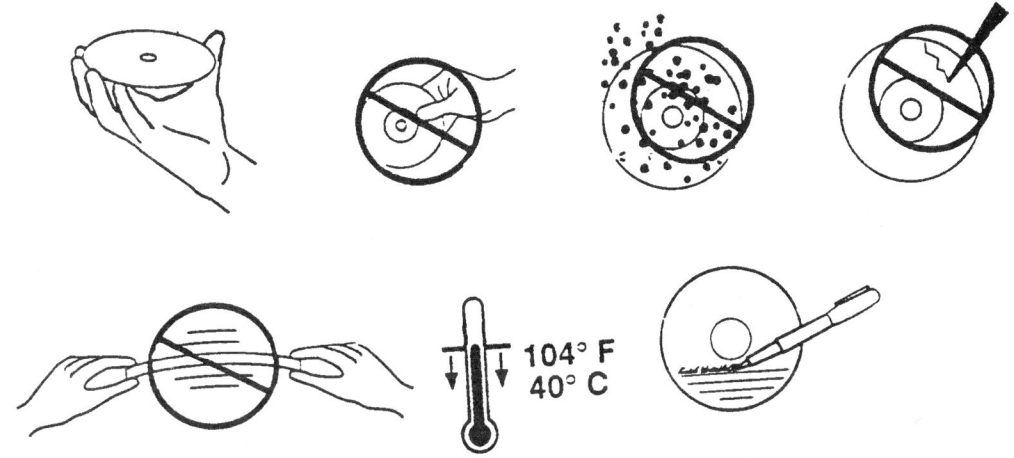

Answer

(a)   Hold the CD by its edges.
(b)   Do not touch the surface of the CD with your fingers.
(c)   Do not allow the CD to get dirty or dusty.
(d)   Do not scratch the surface of the CD.
(e)   Do not bend the CD.
(f)   Store below 40ºC (104ºF).
(g)   Only write on the label side and only use a felt-tip pen.

Question

Hoaxes

In the context of computer viruses, what is a hoax and what is the point of a hoax? How could you check if a hoax is 'real'?

Hoaxes do not do any physical harm, and there is *no* point. They are a serious problem however as they waste people's time.

A number of websites provide information on hoaxes and 'real' viruses - for example http://www.sophos.com/virusinfo/hoaxes/

5 Legal regulations

FAST FORWARD

In many countries, government agencies have introduced **health and safety regulations** relating to the use of computer equipment. These aim to **protect users** from risks associated with computer use.

In recent years, there has been concern about the dangers to computer users of working with computers for significant parts of their working day. There has also been concern about how the increasing amount of information held about individuals on computers could be misused.

In many countries, government agencies have introduced to regulate computer use at work. Many governments have also introduced Data Protection legislation providing rules about how information held on computer may be used. In this chapter we look at health and safety regulations relating to the used of computers and at issues related to data protection.

Most concern relating to possible health risks of extensive computer use has centred around constant exposure to Visual Display Units (VDU) or computer monitors. In many countries, government agencies have introduced health and safety regulations relating to the use of VDUs. In the United Kingdom, the relevant regulations are **The Health and Safety (Display Screen Equipment) Regulations 1992**.

Under these regulations, any organisation that employs staff who spend a significant amount of time using computers has a range of **responsibilities** to all staff that use display screen equipment as a significant part of their normal work.

Employer responsibility	Comment
To **assess** and **reduce** the **risks** associated with the use of computers.	Risks include aches and pains in the arms, wrists or hands associated with the use of keyboards (sometimes known as Repetitive Strain Injury or **RSI**), as well as **headaches** and **eye strain**. To reduce these risks, employees should be made aware of correct **posture** for computer use and take **regular breaks** from computer work. Breaks should allow employees to stop using a computer for a while, which might involve performing another task. The regulations state that frequent, short breaks are better than longer, less frequent ones.
Ensure that workstations and the working environment **meet** the **minimum requirements**.	The requirements include the provision of adjustable **chairs** and non-glaring **lighting**. **Screens** should be adjustable, for brightness and contrast, and should be able to be tilted and turned. They should be free of reflective glare. **Keyboards** should be tiltable, durable, and easy to use. **Desks** should be large enough to allow equipment used on them a choice of positions. Chairs should be stable and adjustable. Lower back support is important. The **office environment** should provide sufficient room for individual workers, should be suitably lit, free from glare and noise, and of an appropriate temperature.

Employer responsibility	Comment
Employers should provide **health and safety** information and **training**.	Employees should be **trained** to use their workstations correctly. This includes, for example, guidance relating to seating and posture. Important factors to consider are **lower back support**, having forearms parallel to the desk, limiting wrist movement, and having a space in front of the keyboard to rest hands on.
To pay for a full **eye test**.	Under the regulations, a VDU user is entitled to a full eye and eyesight test by an optician or other qualified person at their company's expense. A company may offer its own quick eye test, but this is not a substitute for an employee's right to a full test.
Software regulations and monitoring employee work.	Computer software must be **appropriate** for individual users, and not used to measure a user's work without their knowledge.

6 Minimising risks to computer users

 FAST FORWARD

Risks to the **computer user** include the usual office hazards, and some particularly associated with computers such as eye strain, back strain and RSI.

The specific legal regulations described above aim to minimise many of the risks faced by computer users. There are other more general risks in environments that contain computers, or indeed any other **electrical equipment**. For example, the risks of **injury** from **electric shock**, attraction of **static electricity** and the hazard of loose or badly-routed computer **cabling**.

A summary of the main steps recommended in the legal regulations, plus steps to minimise other risks, is provided below:

(a) Ensure that your place of work is **comfortable** and conducive to maintaining a **good posture**. For example ensure that the **layout** of the workstation does not require **awkward posture** or movements.

(b) Take **occasional breaks** and change your posture from time to time to prevent muscle strain.

(c) Try out different ways of **positioning** the keyboard, VDU and input documents to find one that suits you.

(d) Reduce the **glare** from your screen through tilting the monitor and perhaps the use of a glare guard. Focus should be **sharp**, characters should **not flicker** and there should be **no reflections**.

(e) Ensure all **cables are secured** in such a way that they can not be tripped over.

(f) Don't **overload power points** with clusters of double-adapters and plugs - use approved power point boards that provide sockets for a number of plugs.

(g) Ensure users are **appropriately trained** in the use of the equipment and software they need to use.

Question   Workstation health and safety

You have been asked to enter a batch of invoices into the payables ledger. Unfortunately a colleague has spilt a cup of coffee over your keyboard and some of the keys are sticking. There is a spare terminal in the office and so you decide to use this. List the adjustments you should consider making to ensure the workstation is suited to your requirements.

You should consider whether any of the following are necessary.

(a) Adjustment of chair (height of seat and angle of back support).

(b) Layout of desk. There should be space for input documents (both those processed and those to be processed) and the keyboard should be positioned to allow you to adopt a natural typing posture.

(c) Position of screen. The screen should be angled so that you can see it without having to move or stretch.

(d) 'Look' of screen. There should be no reflections visible on the screen and you should minimise glare by adjusting the brightness/contrast and by fitting an anti-glare filter if necessary.

(e) Other. Check that there are no electric cables which you might trip over.

Question

Computer health risks

Many call centre staff could potentially work in front of a computer screen and keyboard most of the day, entering information into the system. What health risks are these employees exposed to and how might these be addressed?

Answer

The health risks faced by these employees could include:

- Repetitive Strain Injury (RSI) caused by the over-use of certain parts of the body
- Back ache possibly caused by poor posture
- Injuries caused by tripping over computer cables or equipment
- Eye strain from excessive screen use

These risks may be addressed by:

- The use of adjustable chairs and appropriate desks
- Requiring employees to take regular breaks from screen-based tasks
- Ensuring lighting is appropriate and screen glare guards are available
- Offering to facilitate regular eye check-ups

7 The Data Protection Act

FAST FORWARD

The **Data Protection Act 1998** aims to protect the rights of **individuals** in relation to information organisations hold about them.

7.1 Why is privacy an important issue?

In recent years, there has been a growing popular fear that **information** about individuals which was stored on computer files and processed by computer could be **misused**. In the UK the current legislation is the **Data Protection Act 1998**. This Act replaced the earlier Data Protection Act 1984.

Key term

Privacy is the right of a person to be free of unwanted intrusion by others into their lives or activities.

7.2 The Data Protection Act 1998

The Data Protection Act 1998 is an attempt to protect the **individual**. The Act covers manual and computer systems.

7.2.1 Definitions of terms used in the Act

In order to understand the Act it is necessary to know some of the technical terms used in it.

(a) **Personal data** is information about a living individual, including expressions of opinion about him or her. The 'living individual' could come from within the organisation or from outside eg job applicant, person who works for a supplier, person who works for a customer etc.

(b) **Data users** are organisations or individuals who control personal data and the use of personal data.

(c) A **data subject** is an individual who is the subject of personal data.

7.2.2 The data protection principles

There are certain Data Protection Principles which data users must comply with.

DATA PROTECTION PRINCIPLES

1   Personal data shall be processed fairly and lawfully and, in particular, shall not be processed unless:

   (a)   At least one of the conditions in Schedule 2 of the Act is met. The Schedule 2 conditions are shown below (only one of these need be met):

      (i)   With the consent of the subject. Consent cannot be implied: it must be by freely given, specific and informed agreement.

      (ii)   As a result of a contractual arrangement.

      (iii) Because of a legal obligation.

      (iv)   To protect the vital interests of the subject.

      (v)   Where processing is in the public interest.

   (b)   In the case of sensitive personal data, the processing of 'sensitive data' is not allowed, unless express consent has been obtained or there are conflicting obligations under employment law. Sensitive data includes data relating to race, political opinions, religious beliefs, physical and mental health, sexual orientation and trade union membership.

2   Personal data shall be obtained only for one or more specified and lawful purposes, and shall not be further processed in any manner incompatible with that purpose or those purposes.

3   Personal data shall be adequate, relevant and not excessive in relation to the purpose or purposes for which they are processed.

4   Personal data shall be accurate and, where necessary, kept up to date.

5   Personal data processed for any purpose or purposes shall not be kept for longer than is necessary for that purpose or those purposes.

6   Personal data shall be processed in accordance with the rights of data subjects under this Act.

7   Appropriate technical and organisational measures shall be taken against unauthorised or unlawful processing of personal data and against accidental loss or destruction of, or damage to, personal data.

8   Personal data shall not be transferred to a country or territory outside the European Economic Area unless that country or territory ensures an adequate level of protection for the rights and freedoms of data subjects in relation to the processing of personal data.

7.2.3 Registration under the Act

The Data Protection Registrar keeps a Register of all data users. Unless a data user has an entry in the Register they may not hold personal data. Even if the data user is registered, they must only hold data and use data for the **purposes** which are registered.

7.2.4 The rights of data subjects

The Act includes the following rights for data subjects.

(a) A data subject may seek **compensation** through the courts for damage and any associated distress caused by the **loss**, **destruction** or **unauthorised disclosure** of data about himself or herself or by **inaccurate data** about himself or herself.

(b) A data subject may apply to the courts for **inaccurate data** to be **put right** or even **wiped off** the data user's files altogether. Such applications may also be made to the Registrar.

(c) A data subject may obtain **access** to personal data of which he is the subject. (This is known as the 'subject access' provision.) In other words, a data subject can ask to see his or her personal data that the data user is holding.

(d) A data subject can **sue** a data user for any **damage or distress** caused to him by personal data about him which is **incorrect** or **misleading** as to matter of **fact** (rather than opinion).

Exam focus point

> The Data Protection Act is important and a question on its principles or application is entirely possible.

8 Other relevant acts

FAST FORWARD

> The **Computer Misuse Act 1990** makes it a criminal offence to attempt to access, use or change any computer system to which you do not have authorised access rights.
>
> In the UK most law relating to copyright is contained within the **Copyright Designs and Patents Act 1988**. Computer software is covered by copyright legislation.   A breach of **software licence** conditions usually means the owners' copyright has been infringed.

In this section we take a brief look at two other Acts relevant to computer systems. We look at Acts from the UK - many other countries have similar legislation. The two acts we will look at are The Computer Misuse Act 1990 (relating to hacking) and The Copyright Designs and Patents Act 1998 (covering copying of software).

8.1 The Computer Misuse Act 1990

The Computer Misuse Act 1990 makes it a criminal offence to attempt to access, use or change any computer system to which you do not have authorised access rights. Therefore, it is a criminal offence to attempt to by-pass security controls such as passwords. Hacking falls under the terms of the Act, which also makes it an offence to deliberately introduce a virus to a system.

8.2 The Copyright Designs and Patents Act 1998

In the UK most law relating to copyright is contained within the Copyright Designs and Patents Act 1988. The Copyright (Computer Software) Amendment Act 1985 had already granted computer programs the status of a literary work - and therefore entitled to copyright protection granted under copyright legislation.

When a user purchases software they are merely buying the rights to use the software in line with the terms and conditions within the licence agreement. The licence will be issued with the software, on paper or in electronic form. It contains the terms and conditions of use, as set out by the software publisher or owner of the copyright. A breach of the licence conditions usually means the owners' copyright has been infringed.

8.3 Software piracy

The unauthorised copying of software is referred to as software piracy. If an organisation is using illegal copies of software, the organisation may face a civil suit, and corporate officers and individual employees may have criminal liability.

The most common type of software piracy in a business setting is referred to as Corporate Over-Use. This is the installation of software packages on more machines than there are licences for. For example if a company purchases five single-user licences of a software program but installs the software on ten machines, then they will be using five infringing copies. In the UK, the Copyright, Designs and Patents Act 1998 specifically allows the making of back-up copies of software, but only providing it is for lawful use.

Chapter Roundup

- There are many different **risks** to computer systems. Sources of risk include authorised users and staff, unauthorised users and intruders, faulty hardware, software or storage media, fire, terrorism and other major incidents and natural disasters.

- Risks should be **controlled** - as much as is practically possible.

- **Physical access controls** attempt to stop **intruders** or other unauthorised persons getting near to computer equipment or storage media. Controls include **door locks** and **card entry systems**.

- **Logical access controls** are concerned with preventing those persons who have gained physical access from gaining unauthorised access to data or software. Passwords are one example of a logical access system.

- **Hoaxes** often take the form of a warning about viruses contained in e-mail. Hoaxes waste the time of all concerned.

- In many countries, government agencies have introduced **health and safety regulations** relating to the use of computer equipment. These aim to **protect users** from risks associated with computer use.

- Risks to the **computer user** include the usual office hazards, and some particularly associated with computers such as eye strain, back strain and RSI.

- The **Data Protection Act 1998** aims to protect the rights of **individuals** in relation to information organisations hold about them.

- The **Computer Misuse Act 1990** makes it a criminal offence to attempt to access, use or change any computer system to which you do not have authorised access rights.

- In the UK most law relating to copyright is contained within the **Copyright Designs and Patents Act 1988**. Computer software is covered by copyright legislation. A breach of **software licence** conditions usually means the owners' copyright has been infringed.

Quick Quiz

1   Two statements follow about viruses:

   1.   E-mail viruses can replicate by mailing themselves to addresses held in the users contact book.
   2.   Trap doors are triggered by a certain date.

   Are the above statements true or false?

   A   Both statements are false
   B   Both statements are true
   C   Statement 1 is false but statement 2 is true
   D   Statement 1 is true but statement 2 is false

2   Which one of the following is an example of a logical access system?

   A   Door locks
   B   Card entry systems
   C   Passwords
   D   Security guards

3   One form of computer control involves scrambling data at one end of the line, transmitting the scrambled data and then unscrambling it at the receiver's end of the line. What is this called?

    A   Authentication
    B   Dial-back security
    C   Back-up
    D   Encryption

4   An e-mail containing a fictitious warning about an e-mail virus is known as a:

    A   Hoax
    B   Logic bomb
    C   Worm
    D   Trojan

5   Which of the following is data protection legislation primarily designed to protect?

    A   All private individuals and corporate entites on whom only regulated data is held
    B   All private individuals on whom only regulated data is held
    C   All private individuals on whom any data is held
    D   All private individuals and cororate entities on whom any data is held

6   In order to help prevent fraud, it is good company policy to ensure that all employees take their holidays. Is this true or false?

7   An organisation that purchases a software licence for ten users but then installs the software on fifty machines has committed what offence?

    A   Breach of copyright
    B   Hacking
    C   Breach of data protection legislation
    D   Fraud

Answers to Quick Quiz

1   D   E-mail viruses can replicate in this way. Trap doors are undocumented access points to a system allowing controls to be bypassed. (A time bomb is triggered by a certain date.)

2   C   Passwords are logical access controls because they prevent people who have gained physical access from gaining unauthorised access to data or software. Options A, B and D are examples of physical access controls.

3   D   This is known as encryption. Authentication is a technique for making sure that the message has come from an authorised sender. Dial-back security operates by requiring the person wanting access to dial into the network and identify themselves first. Back-ups are copies of data in case of damage or loss to the original copy.

4   A   Hoax. A hoax does no physical harm but it wastes people's time. Logic bombs, worms and trojans are types of virus.

5   B   Data protection legislation is intended to protect private individuals but not all data is regulated.

6   True   This is because employees who avoid holidays could be trying to hide something.

7   A   The organisation has breached the terms of the software licence and this is a breach of copyright. (Hacking usually involves circumventing logical access controls. Data protection legislation covers data about individuals and fraud usually involves theft of inventory, equipment, information or funds.)

Passwords and back-ups

5

Study guide

			Syllabus reference
2	(a)	Explain computer system access controls and procedures for individual file protection.	2(a)(i),(ii)
	(b)	Describe procedures for backing-up, archiving and storing information securely.	2(b)(i),(ii), 2(c)(iv)

1 Introduction

Two very important elements of computer system control and security are **passwords** and **back-ups**. In this chapter we discuss the role and use of passwords and back-ups. We conclude the chapter with an overview/review of the main considerations of an organisation's computer security policy.

2 Passwords

> **Passwords** are a set of characters which are required to be keyed before access is permitted. Passwords may be allocated to a person (a username), a terminal, to a function or to an individual file. Although password systems can be extremely sophisticated, they all depend on user discipline.

Key term

> A **password** is a secret series of characters that enables a user to access a computer, or a program, or a file.

Passwords are a set of characters which are required to be keyed before access is permitted. Passwords may be allocated to a person (a username), a terminal, to a system function or to an individual file.

2.1 Why require passwords?

Passwords can be applied to data files, program files and to parts of a program.

(a) One password may be required to **read a file**, and another to **write new data** to it.

(b) The user can be **restricted** to the use of certain files and programs (eg in a banking system, junior grades of staff are only allowed to access certain information and routines).

Password protected systems require users attempting to enter the system to enter a string of characters. If what is entered **matches** the password held on file for that authorised user, the system permits access. Otherwise entry is refused. The system may (and should) record the attempted unauthorised access. Keeping track of these attempts can alert managers to **repeated efforts** to break into the system.

The use of passwords to restrict access to a system, function or file is widespread and reasonably effective. Requirements for system security should be balanced against **operational requirements** for access: for example allowing only one member of staff to a certain system function could result in operations being disrupted should that person be unavailable.

2.2 Passwords, user names and user rights

> **Logical access** controls usually involve the use of usernames and passwords to perform three main checks. These are; the identification of the user, an authentication of user identity and a check on user authority.

System passwords are usually used in conjunction with a **user name**. User names are usually a code used to identify the user to the system. The use of user names allows the allocation of appropriate **user rights** to people who perform different roles within an organisation. The use of usernames/user IDs and passwords are referred to as **logical access** controls.

Logical access controls includes three main checks or operations based upon the user name and password.

- Identification of the user
- **Authentication** of user identity
- Check on user **authority**

The number of different access levels and rights required will differ depending upon the **security** and **confidentiality** requirements of the system. For example:

(a) A **payroll** system contains highly sensitive data meaning that even 'read only' access rights should be granted to identified individuals only. The right to change data in the system should require an authorisation procedure of at least two users – at least one of whom should be relatively senior.

(b) A general ledger accounts system may require a **wide range** of user access rights – for example finance staff will require the right to post journal entries (ie to 'write' data to the system rather than simply 'read' data).

(c) Some systems may identify users using used names or user IDs but allow all users to enjoy relatively **unrestricted** access. For example, a company 'bulletin board' held on an intranet.

2.3 Are passwords effective?

Passwords ought to be effective in keeping out unauthorised users, but they are **by no means foolproof**.

(a) By **experimenting** with possible passwords, an unauthorised person can gain access to a program or file by **guessing** the correct password. This is not as difficult as it may seem, as many computer users specify 'obvious' passwords. In addition **computer programs** are available that run through millions of possible combinations until the correct one is found.

(b) An authorised user may **disclose** a valid password, perhaps through carelessness, to an unauthorised person.

(c) An unauthorised person may simply **observe** someone else keying in their password. Most systems display **asterisks** (as shown below) instead of the actual characters typed, to try to prevent this. However, an observer may be able to watch the keyboard and see which keys were pressed.

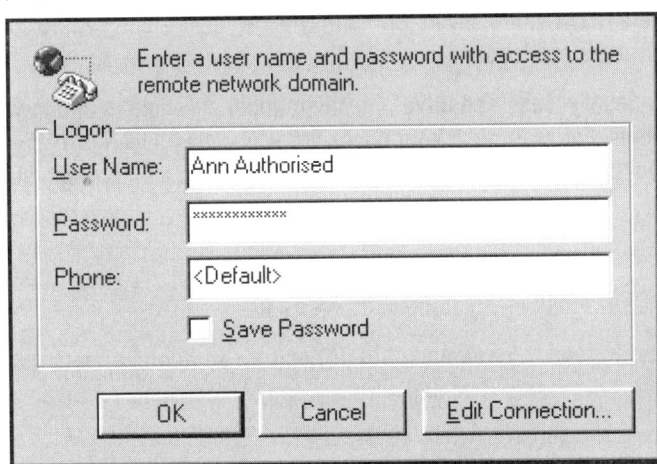

(d) Many password systems come with **standard passwords** as part of the system, such as LETMEIN. It is essential that they are removed if the system is to be secure.

(e) Password systems rely upon users to use them **conscientiously**. A password system relies on system controls and the observance of strong organisational policies if it is to be effective.

(f) The hardest to 'crack' passwords are also the most **difficult to remember**. For example, the password **f146PQzH7364** (numbers and letters, upper and lower case), would be very difficult to guess, but it is also almost impossible to remember. Valuable information may become inaccessible if someone protects a file (eg a document, spreadsheet or database) with a password that is later forgotten.

2.4 How are passwords obtained or 'broken' by unauthorised people?

> There are four main ways that passwords are obtained by **unauthorised** people. These are; using **hacking software**, guessing a password using knowledge of a user's **personal details**, encouraging users to **disclose** their password eg through a 'bogus website' and **user carelessness**, such as writing their password down in an obvious place.

There are four main ways that passwords are obtained by unauthorised people.

(a) Through the use of '**hacking software**'. 'Hackers' may download this software from various Internet sites. The software is software programmed to try all possible combinations of passwords, one after each other, until the correct one is found. This is one good reason why programs should only allow a limited number of password attempts before temporarily disabling the software.

(b) Knowledge of the **personal details** of a colleague. Many people use fairly predictable passwords, such as their middle name, their pet's name, a child's name, their favourite football team or part of their address etc.

(c) **User carelessness**. Some users write their password down in an obvious place, or reveal their password to enable a certain task to be performed.

(d) Using **deception**. For example, one scam involves someone phoning you at work and advising you that you have won a prize. The caller then requests that you provide your username and password for identification purposes to claim your prize. Another trick involves sending an e-mail to an employee containing an invitation to log onto a (bogus) website to claim a prize. The website requires user registration including a password. Many people will enter the same password as they use at work – inadvertently disclosing their password to those who set up the bogus site.

2.5 Password 'do's and don'ts'

> Passwords should be kept safe and should **not be revealed** to other users. Passwords should be **changed regularly**, or **immediately** if disclosure is suspected.

Different systems use different **password formats**. For example, some systems require a password of at least six characters, others may require seven. Some may allow spaces and symbols such as * or +, while others will allow only numbers and letters.

Password recognition is usually '**case sensitive**', meaning upper case letters and lower case letters are treated as different symbols. For example if your password was set as 'Liverpool', if you entered 'LIVERPOOL' or 'liverpool' the system would advise you have entered an incorrect password.

Password do's...

Change default system passwords when you first receive them.

Make your password **easy for you** to remember, but **difficult for someone else** to guess. Do not use a word that would appear in a dictionary (hacking software can try thousands of dictionary words in seconds).

Use a **combination** of uppercase, lowercase, digits, and punctuation characters.

Where possible, use at least six characters. Generally, the **longer** the password the **harder** it is to break.

Keep your password **secret**. Do not reveal it to anyone else.

Some people find it helpful to apply a single **theme** for all passwords they use, so they are different for all services but are memorable.

Change passwords **frequently** (as a rule of thumb, every 90-150 days), or **immediately** if you suspect disclosure.

Password don'ts...

Change or use your password while **someone is looking** at your keyboard.

Write your password(s) in a place where they may be seen or found.

Use the **same** password for all services, as if someone finds or 'cracks' your password all services will be compromised.

Use an **obvious** password, such as your name, your username, a blank password, the word 'password' or a word that could be found in a dictionary.

Disclose your password to someone else.

2.6 Taking care with passwords

System passwords are usually used in conjunction with a **username**. An **error message** indicating a failed system access attempt is often due to an incorrect username, rather than being caused by an incorrect password.

Most systems 'mask' passwords on-screen during input by representing password characters with asterisks or blobs. If you lose track of where you're up to when typing a password, delete all the characters and **retype the complete password**.

As many passwords are **case sensitive** (eg 'B' is distinct from 'b'), when typing in passwords, ensure the **Caps Lock** is not on. Also take care not to confuse 'O' (capital O) with '0' (zero) or 'l' (lower case l) with '1' (one).

If you forget your password, contact an appropriate member of staff to have your password **reset** (remember to immediately change any system allocated password). Don't repeatedly attempt to gain access using multiple passwords as this may cause staff to presume an unauthorised person is attempting to gain access.

Question

Password and user name formats

Almost all modern systems require a username and password. Think about the computer systems you use that require passwords. What formats are most common for usernames and passwords?

Answer

There are many possible formats. One format particularly popular with web based systems is to require a valid e-mail address as a username. Passwords should be at least five characters in length – preferably more.

2.7 Using passwords with Word and Excel

FAST FORWARD

One way of controlling access to information held in a **Word** document or an **Excel** spreadsheet is to allocate a **password** to the file.

One way of controlling access to information held in a Word document or an Excel spreadsheet is to allocate a password to the file. Word and Excel provide the option to assign either of two passwords:

- A password that is required to **open** the document or spreadsheet
- A password that is required to **modify** the document or spreadsheet

The options you use to set an open or modify password in a Microsoft Word document or Microsoft Excel spreadsheet vary depending upon the version you are using. To assign a password to a file, first open the document or spreadsheet you want to secure. Then, from the **File** menu, select **Save As**.

Then click on the **Tools** drop down menu and select **Security options** (or **General options**).

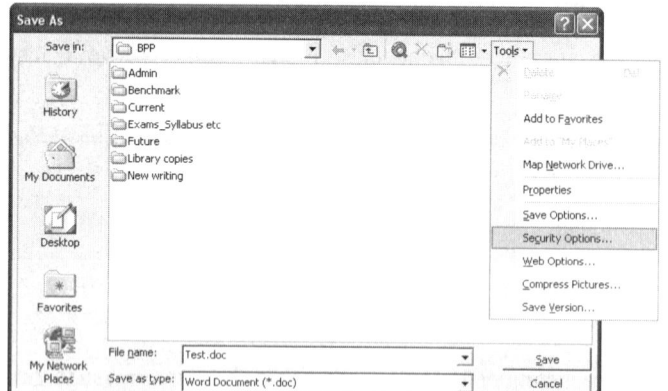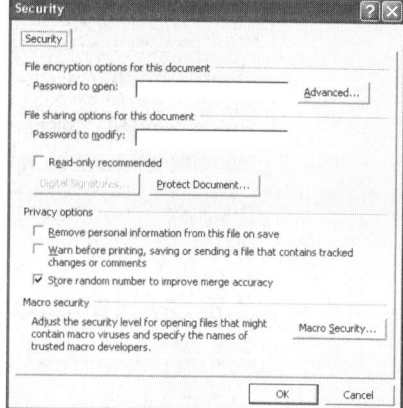

Type the password you wish to assign to either open or modify the document (or both), and then click **OK**. Confirm the one or two passwords, and then click **Save**.

Note: Passwords in Word and Excel are case-sensitive, which means it matters if you use capital letters (UPPER-CASE) or 'standard' letters (lower case). When you open a protected document, each password character must be entered using the case used when setting the password.

Question
File passwording

As part of your work you maintain a spreadsheet that holds the salary levels of all staff in the organisation. As the information held in this file is confidential, you have password protected the file. What would you do if after opening the file, by entering the password, you noticed a member of staff standing beside your desk?

Answer

You should close the spreadsheet straight away, to prevent confidential information being viewed on-screen. After the person has left the area, you should change the spreadsheet password.

3 Back-ups

3.1 What is a back-up?

FAST FORWARD

A **'back-up'** copy of computer file(s) is a duplicate copy kept separately from the main system and only used if the original fails. If the back-up copy need to be used it is **restored** to the system.

Key term

A **back-up** is a copy of a file or files held on an alternative storage medium (eg disk or tape). Back-ups are held as a precaution in case the file(s) in use become damaged or unable to be used.

Back-up means to make a copy which would enable **recovery** in the case of future failure or corruption. A back-up copy of a file is a duplicate copy kept separately from the main system and only used if the original fails.

Loss of, or damage to, a data or program file can severely disrupt computerised systems. Files can be physically **deleted**, and it is also possible for a file to become **corrupted** (changed in an unintended way).

A file might also be physically **damaged** and become **unreadable**. It is important therefore that a usable copy of a file is able to be **restored** from back-up.

3.2 Why take back-ups?

A back-up copy of computer files allows an information system to be restored to full operation following security breaches and accidents. Without a back-up, much data may be lost following system failures and security breaches.

The purpose of backing up data is therefore to enable the **most recent usable copy** of the data to be recovered and **restored**, in the event of loss or corruption on the primary storage media.

Even with a well planned back-up strategy **some re-inputting** may be required. For example, if after three hours work on a Wednesday a file becomes corrupt, the copy of the file from Tuesday night's back-up can be restored – but Wednesday's work will need to be re-input.

3.3 When should back-ups be taken?

FAST FORWARD All system and data files should be backed up on a regular basis. How regularly depends on the nature of the business. In the vast majority of organisations, **daily back-up** of data should be performed.

Creating back-up copies of all data and system files should be a regular routine in all organisations that use computers. How regularly back-ups should be taken depends on the nature of the business.

In the majority of organisations, **daily back-up of data** should be performed. In some organisations, the volume of processing and reliance on computer systems may mean that back-ups need to be performed even more frequently than this.

3.4 How is a back-up performed?

Most **operating systems** include a **back-up utility** for creating back-ups. There is also specialised back-up software available to allow easy establishment and performance of back-up routines.

With networks and larger systems the back-up utility can be set to back up everything, or certain selected files, **automatically** at a regular time each day (say, midnight).

Small systems, such as individual PC's may be backed up by simply copying all files to an appropriate external storage media, for example by using the File, Copy command from within Windows Explorer.

Some programs, such as Sage accounting software, include **back-up routines within the program**. These routines are very handy, but remember the routine will only back-up data held within that program. For example, performing a Sage back-up won't back-up any of your spreadsheet files.

Ensure you are aware of the back-up procedure used at your place if work.

3.5 Where should files be backed up to?

FAST FORWARD Backing up to **magnetic tape** is quick and convenient, although this requires a specialised tape streamer unit. It is also possible to back up onto **CD/DVD-R** or onto a **separate hard disk** or a **Zip disk**. At least some back-ups should be stored **off-site**.

Backing up to **magnetic tape** is quick and convenient, although this requires a specialised **tape streamer** unit. It is also possible to back up onto **CD/DVD-R** or onto a **separate hard disk** or a **Zip disk**. Some organisations back-up the contents of server computers to **another server computer**, possibly located in a different location.

Many back-up routines use some kind of **compression** program so that the backed-up data takes up less space than the original. If the back-up has to be used a **restore** program has to be run to **expand** the data

into useable format. Regular tests should be undertaken to verify that data backed up can be successfully restored.

3.6 Hardware arrangements

FAST FORWARD

> Organisations should also have some back-up plan for their computer **hardware**, such as an arrangement that would allow appropriate alternative equipment to be used.

Organisations should also have some **back-up plan** for their computer **hardware**. In some circumstances their premises and contents, including computer hardware, may be destroyed or be inaccessible. Arrangements should be in place that would allow appropriate alternative equipment to be used. Arrangements could involve an insurance arrangement that provides for quick replacement of equipment or agreements with hardware suppliers.

In addition, copies of all **program** disks (usually CDs) should also be kept and stored in a secure location. This will enable the re-installation of programs if required.

3.7 Storage of back-ups

At least some back-up copies should be stored **off-site.** This means that if there is a fire or a burglary at the business premises the back up copies will not be damaged. In practice many organisations keep one set of back-ups on-site (for speed of access) and a second set at a separate location.

Protecting data held on your own PC

In this section, we explain how you could back-up data held on your own PC. This advice is intended to relate to your own PC, rather than the PC you use at work. If you do wish to back-up data held on your work PC, check first that your actions wouldn't conflict with workplace policies and procedures.

Back-ups are required because the unexpected may happen. Computers get stolen, disks crash, memory sticks are lost, and files are deleted or overwritten by mistake. Your house contents insurance policy may pay for a new PC and software, but how will you restore your data? What about your CV, all your photos and the spreadsheet you've been working on for weeks?

You can minimise your losses by backing your data up. The first step to take is to decide what you want to back up. You should back-up all data files that you may need at some time in the future. A good filing structure on your hard disk will make selecting files for backing up easier. For example, some people choose to save all of their Microsoft Office files in a folder called 'My Documents'.

Let's assume you use Word and Excel, and store all data files in sub-folders off the 'My Documents' folder (eg you may have subdivided this folder into the sub-folders such as 'letters', 'CAT Paper 2' etc). Copying the contents of 'My Documents' (including all sub-folders) to another device such as a CD – DVD, magnetic tape, a Zip disk or a removable hard disk, is in effect creating a back-up copy.

To copy the files to a CD you would use CD creation software provided with the CD writer. If you then restore a file, by copying it back from the CD, the restored file may be marked as 'Read-only'. To enable you to work on the file, highlight the file within Windows explorer, then click on it with the right mouse button and select Properties. Then 'un-tick' the 'Read-only' box. Tape streamers also come with their own software. To back-up files to an external hardware device or a Zip disk, you could use the back-up utility provided by Windows, or simply highlight the files and folders to be backed up from within Windows Explorer, then 'Copy' and 'Paste' the files to the back-up storage media.

How often you should back-up depends upon how much work you are prepared to lose as a result of not having a back-up copy. In most circumstances, once a week is a minimum. If you back up your PC weekly, don't overwrite the previous back-up each week. Instead, use five sets of CDs (or tapes) numbered from 1 to 5. Use number 1 on the first Friday of the month, number 2 on the second Friday, etc, going back to number 1 at the beginning of each month. And label your CDs with 'Back-up data files taken ..... (the date)'. Why should you do this? Consider the following situation.

Suppose a file on your hard drive becomes corrupt, for example on April 10. You are unaware of the problem until you attempt to use the file on May 1. The back-up you took on April 25 contains a copy of the corrupt file – so this is of no use. However, if you still have back-up CDs from April 4 (ie you have not overwritten these with later back-ups), you are able to restore a usable copy of the file.

Keep some copies of your back-up media in a location away from your PC (eg in a different building) as an additional precaution against fire, vandalism or theft. And remember that back-ups are useful only if they are able to be restored. You should check regularly that your back-up is able to be restored (for example to a different folder so as not to overwrite your current files).

Taking back-ups can seem a pointless task, as you hope that you never need to use the result of the process. However, the feeling of relief when you are able to restore a 'lost' file will make all the effort worthwhile!

3.8 Archiving

FAST FORWARD

Archiving data is the process of moving (by copying) data from primary storage, such as a hard disk, to tape or other portable media for long-term storage.

A related concept is that of **archiving.**

Key term

Archiving data is the process of moving (by copying) data from primary storage, such as a hard disk, to tape or other portable media for long-term storage.

Archiving provides a **business history**, while freeing up **hard disk space**. If archived data is needed, it can be restored from the archived tape to a hard disk. Archived data can be used to recover from site-wide disasters, such as fires or floods, where data on primary storage devices is destroyed.

How long data should be retained will be influenced by:

- **Legal obligations** of the particular industry (eg a bank is legally required to be hold records for a longer period of time than many other businesses)
- Other business needs

Data stored for a long time should be tested periodically to ensure it is **still restorable** – it may be subject to **damage** from environmental conditions or mishandling.

Question

Backups and passwords

Anfield Tyres are looking for an accounting software package. Two of their requirements are:

- Backup and restore from inside the accounting software package
- User access controlled by user-names and passwords

Briefly describe the meaning and significance of each of these two requirements.

Answer

(a)   In the context of an accounting package, the ability to back-up and recover data from within the package refers to the ability to use a function from within the package to make a copy of the data held. This back-up copy could be used if the data held within the accounting package became damaged or corrupt.

A package such as Sage Accounts provides a back-up utility. Files should be backed up on a daily basis. Depending on the size of the files, back-ups may be stored on CDs or DVDs or maybe on a network. Some back-ups should be stored off-site.

(b)   User-names or user IDs identify a user to the computer system. User names are usually used in conjunction with passwords to help ensure only authorised users access the system. An

accounting system may be set up to allow access only to those who enter both a valid username and the password associated with that username. Only after the password has been entered correctly will the computer system start or access to the program be allowed.

With accounting systems, usernames and passwords are essential. They are needed to prevent access to potentially confidential data (for example salary details) and to prevent unauthorised amendment of data files. An appropriate password system will have to be implemented, with users being given access to those parts of the system they need. For example, a receivables ledger clerk will need access to the ordering, inventory and sales systems, but not the cash receipt or salary systems.

Exam focus point

Back-up procedures are important and questions on this area are likely.

Chapter Roundup

- **Passwords** are a set of characters which are required to be keyed before access is permitted. Passwords may be allocated to a person (a username), a terminal, to a function or to an individual file. Although password systems can be extremely sophisticated, they all depend on user discipline.

- The restriction of access to a system with passwords is effective and widely used. Requirements for **system security** should be balanced by the **operational requirements.**

- **Logical access** controls usually involve the use of usernames and passwords to perform three main checks. These are; the identification of the user, an authentication of user identity and a check on user authority.

- There are four main ways that passwords are obtained by **unauthorised** people. These are; using **hacking software**, guessing a password using knowledge of a user's **personal details**, encouraging users to **disclose** their password eg through a 'bogus website' and **user carelessness**, such as writing their password down in an obvious place.

- Passwords should be kept safe and should **not be revealed** to other users. Passwords should be **changed regularly**, or **immediately** if disclosure is suspected.

- One way of controlling access to information held in a **Word** document or an **Excel** spreadsheet is to allocate a **password** to the file.

- A **'back-up'** copy of computer file(s) is a duplicate copy kept separately from the main system and only used if the original fails. If the back-up copy need to be used it is **restored** to the system.

- All system and data files should be backed up on a regular basis. How regularly depends on the nature of the business. In the vast majority of organisations, **daily back-up** of data should be performed.

- Backing up to **magnetic tape** is quick and convenient, although this requires a specialised tape streamer unit. It is also possible to back up onto **CD/DVD-R** or onto a **separate hard disk** or a **Zip disk**. At least some back-ups should be stored **off-site**.

- Organisations should also have some back-up plan for their computer **hardware**, such as an arrangement that would allow appropriate alternative equipment to be used.

- **Archiving** data is the process of moving (by copying) data from primary storage, such as a hard disk, to tape or other portable media for long-term storage.

Quick Quiz

1. Which one of the following is NOT a main check of logical access controls?

    A   The identification of the user
    B   An authentication of user identity
    C   The authority of the user
    D   The time of the access

2. Which one of the following passwords would be most secure?

    A   pAsSwOrd
    B   p@55wORD
    C   p5ssWoRD
    D   pa44WOrd

3. Many back-up routines use a compression program so that data takes up less space than the original. When the back-up copy has to be copied back to the primary storage media, the process performed is known as:

    A   Back-up reversal
    B   Anti-compression
    C   Corrupt
    D   Restore

4. Moving or copying data from primary storage to tape or other portable media for long-term storage is known as :

    A   Back-up
    B   Archiving
    C   Streaming
    D   Dumping

5. A system that requires a valid user-name and password to gain entry is 100% secure from unauthorised intruders. Is this true or false?

Answers to Quick Quiz

1. **D**   Logical access controls usually involve the use of user names and passwords to perform three main checks. These checks are options A, B and C.

2. **B**   Option B is the most secure as it contains a combination of upper case, lower case, digits and symbols. Choosing the word 'password', however, is not particularly sensible! Using the first letters of the words in a line of a song would be more secure. For example the line 'Old McDonald had a farm' could become OMcDh@7arm.

3. **D**   If the back-up has to be used, a restore program has to be run to expand the data into a useable format.

4. **B**   Archiving. Be careful not to confuse back-up and archiving. Back-up files are only intended to be used in case of a problem on the system. Archived files are used to provide long-term storage of records no longer required on the primary storage system.

5. **False**   Unauthorised personnel could obtain somebody's password through the use of hacking software, by guessing a password using knowledge of a user's personal details, by encouraging a user to disclose their password or through user carelessness.

5: Passwords and back-ups | Part A Computer systems

P
A
R
T

B

Management information

Introduction to management information

Study guide

			Syllabus reference
3	(a)	Discuss the purpose of management information: planning, control and decision-making	3a
	(b)	Distinguish between data and information	6b
	(c)	Describe the features of useful management information	3a
	(d)	Describe and identify sources and categories of information	6b
	(e)	Compare cost and management accounting with external financial reporting	3a
	(f)	Explain the limitations of cost and management accounting information	6b
	(g)	Describe the accounting technician's role in a cost and management accounting system	6b

1 Introduction

The main aim of this chapter is to introduce you to the subject of **management information** and, in particular, explain what management information is and why it is needed. Let's start from basics.

2 Data and information

FAST FORWARD

Raw **data** may be processed to produce meaningful **information**.

2.1 What is data?

Key term

> **Data** is a 'scientific' term for facts, figures, information and processing. Data are the raw materials for data processing.

Examples of data include the following.

* The number of tourists who visit Hong Kong each year
* The sales turnovers of all restaurants in Zambia
* The number of people (with black hair) who pass their driving test each year

2.2 What is information?

Key term

> **Information** is data that has been processed in such a way as to be meaningful to the person who receives it. Information is anything that is communicated.

Information is sometimes referred to as processed data. The terms 'information' and 'data' are often used interchangeably. Let us consider the following situation in which data is **collected** and then **processed** in order to produce meaningful information.

Many companies providing a product or service research consumer opinion to ensure they provide what customers and potential customers want and will buy. A typical market research survey employs a number of researchers who request a sample of the public to answer questions relating to the product. Several hundred questionnaires may be completed. The questionnaires are usually input into a computer system for analysis.

Individually, a completed questionnaire would not tell the company very much, only the views of one consumer. In this case, the individual questionnaires are **data**. Once they have been processed, and analysed, the resulting report is **information**. The people who run the business can consider the report

and use the information to make decisions regarding the product, such as whether to improve it or scrap it.

Management is the term used for the people in charge of running a business (managers) or other organisation.

Management information can therefore be described as information that is given to the people who are in charge of running an organisation. The report described above is one example of management information.

To run a business successfully depends upon making the right decisions. Information is vital to enable good decisions to be made. Examples of the some of the questions that management might wish to have answers to include:

- How much does it cost to produce the product(s) or service(s) they supply.
- How many product(s)/service(s) they sold last month.
- How much was spent on wages last year.
- How many staff the company currently employs.

Management information is often classified into two types:

- Financial information (measured in terms of money)
- Non-financial information (not measured in terms of money)

3 The purpose of management information

FAST FORWARD

The purpose of **management information** is to help managers to manage resources efficiently and effectively, by planning and controlling operations and by allowing informed **decision-making**.

3.1 Introduction

In order to manage their resources, managers in any organisation need to know on a regular basis how their particular department or section is performing. They will also wish to know whether activities are going as planned and whether any problems have arisen.

Management information has the following purposes.

- **Planning**
- **Control**
- **Decision making**

Planning. Management needs to decide what the objectives of the company are and how they can be achieved. Management information is used to help management **plan** the resources that a business will require and how they will be used.

Control. Once management puts a plan of action into operation, there needs to be some **control** over the business's activities to make sure that they are carrying out the original plans.

Decision making. Management at all levels within an organisation take decisions. Decision making always involves a **choice between alternatives.** Information is required that enables management to reach an informed decision.

The information required by a manager will vary according to the nature of the organisation and their individual responsibilities. Look at the following examples.

(a) Senior management will usually be interested in the financial statements (statement of financial position and income statement), on a monthly basis.

(b) A supervisor in a large factory may want a daily output report for every production shift.

(c) A sales manager may want a weekly report of orders achieved by the sales team.

Management information is used for a wide variety of purposes. In a management accounting context, **planning**, **control** and **decision making** activities include:

- Pricing
- Valuing inventory
- Assessing profitability
- Deciding on the purchase of capital assets

In the present business environment where the rate of change is increasing, good management information systems are seen by many as the key to success. Although such systems give a basis for improved management decisions they do not guarantee good management. Poor information, however, is likely to reduce a manager's chances of success.

If we take a wider view, and look at information in general rather than just information used specifically by management, we could say that organisations require information for five purposes. We have already looked at planning, controlling and decision making. The other two purposes are for **recording transactions** and **measuring overall performance**.

3.1.1 Recording transactions

Information about **each transaction or event** is required for a number of reasons. Documentation of transactions can be used as **evidence** in a case of dispute. There may be a **legal requirement** to record transactions, for example for accounting and audit purposes. Detailed information on production costs can be built up, allowing a better **assessment of profitability**.

3.1.2 Overall performance measurement

Just as individual operations need to be controlled, a wider picture of performance is also required, for example to enable **comparisons against budget** to be carried out. This requires information on, for example, costs, revenues, volumes, time-scale and profitability.

Key term

> **Management information** is information supplied to managers for the purposes of planning, control and decision making.

Question

Helping management

The management accountant compares the profitability of two products, P and Q, and concludes that P is the best product to make. He writes a report of his findings for the board of directors. This report will primarily aid management in

A   Decision-making
B   Planning
C   Controlling
D   Implementing

Answer

Answer A. A decision can be made as to which product should be made using this information.

Exam focus point

> You need to make sure that you understand the role of management and the purpose of management information.

4 Reports for management

Producing **useful management information** such as a report depends on understanding the **needs** of the end **user** and of the organisation.

Reports to managers should enable them to manage the resources for which they are responsible, and give the required level of detail.

If management information does not contain enough detail, it may fail to highlight problems within the organisation. On the other hand, too much detail may mean that the most important information is not seen.

Numbers are often rounded to make reports easier to read, eg money may be expressed to the nearest $100, $1,000 or $10,000 depending on the size of the organisation.

The **time periods** covered by reports will also vary for different organisations and for different managers within them. Some computer systems allow managers access to information on a **real time basis** and/or to construct their own reports as necessary.

It is more common for reports to be provided by the accounting department of an organisation every week or month (or any specified period).

Reporting information requires the active **co-operation** of the following groups.

- **End users**: managers and supervisors
- **The accounts department**: which usually processes the information
- **The information technology department**: which usually sets up and makes changes to the computer system

Difficulties may arise when these groups **fail to communicate effectively** or when the system itself is **not flexible** enough to respond to changing needs. Information requirements must be clearly specified.

4.1 Example: management report

SUMMARY MONTHLY REPORT TO TRUSTEES OF A CHARITY FOR THE HOMELESS

	Fund raising activities $'000	*Donations* $'000	*Interest on investments* $'000	*Total* $'000
Income	15.1	9.8	5.4	30.3
Associated costs	2.1	1.0	n/a	3.1
	13.0	8.8	5.4	27.2
Expenditure				
Mobile catering project				6.2
Medical services				2.1
Warm clothing				3.7
Hostel costs				16.0
				28.0
Shortfall for the month				0.8

This type of report is often backed up with appendices. An appendix would give more details of costs and income to help the trustees decide what to do about the shortfall for the month. The charity has spent $800 more than it received in the month under consideration. Individual managers (for fund raising, the catering project, the hostel etc) will need to receive more detailed reports for their own activities.

4.2 Management information

Management information reports might also show the following.

- Comparisons between planned results (budgets) and actual results
- Year-to-date (cumulative information)
- Comparison of company results and competitor results
- Comparison between current year and previous year's results
- The profitability of a product or service or the whole organisation
- The value of inventories that are still held in store at the end of a period

5 Sources and categories of information

5.1 The qualities of good information

Good management information should be:

Accurate
Complete
Cost-beneficial
User-targeted
Relevant
Authoritative
Timely
Easy to use

Good management information helps managers makes informed decisions. The **qualities of good information** are outlined below - in the form of a mnemonic 'accurate'.

Quality		Example
A	ccurate	Figures should **add up**, the degree of **rounding** should be appropriate, there should be **no mistakes**.
C	omplete	Information should include all relevant information – information that is correct but excludes something important is likely to be of little value. For example external data or comparative information may be required.
C	ost-beneficial	It should not **cost more** to obtain the information than the **benefit** derived from having it.
U	ser-targeted	The **needs of the user** should be borne in mind, for instance senior managers may require summaries.
R	elevant	Information that is **not relevant** should be omitted.
A	uthoritative	The **source** of the information should be reputable and reliable.
T	imely	The information should be available **when it is needed**.
E	asy to use	Information should be **clearly presented**, **not excessively long**, and sent using the **right communication channel** (e-mail, telephone, intranet, hard-copy report etc).

5.2 Internal information

Data and information come from sources both inside and outside an organisation. An information system should be designed so as to obtain - or **capture** - relevant information from whatever source. Capturing data/information from **inside** the organisation involves the following.

(a) A **system** for collecting and/or measuring **transaction** data - for example sales, purchases, inventory turnover etc.

(b)   **Informal communication** of information between **managers and staff** (for example, by word-of-mouth or at meetings).

(c)   **Communication** between staff at all levels.

5.3 Internal data sources

There are many **sources** of information (both internal and external) including accounting records, websites, staff, the staff of competitors, the government, the media and many others.

5.3.1 The accounting records

Receivables ledgers, payables ledgers, general ledgers, cash books etc hold information that may be of great value outside the accounts department, for example, sales information for the **marketing** function.

To maintain the integrity of its accounting records, an organisation requires **controls** over transactions. These also give rise to valuable information. An inventory control system for example will include details of purchase orders, goods received notes, goods returned notes and so on, which can be analysed to provide management information about speed of delivery, say, or the quality of supplies.
Other internal sources

Organisations record information to enable them to carry out operations and administrative functions.

(a)   Information about **personnel** will be held, possibly linked to the **payroll** system. Additional information may be obtained from this source if, say, a project is being costed and it is necessary to ascertain the availability and rate of pay of different levels of staff, or the need for and cost of recruiting staff from outside the organisation.

(b)   Much information will be produced by a **production** department about machine capacity, fuel consumption, movement of people, materials, and work in progress, set up times, maintenance requirements and so on.

(c)   Many **service** businesses, notably accountants and solicitors, need to keep detailed records of the **time spent** on various activities, both to justify fees to clients and to assess the efficiency and profitability of operations.

Staff themselves are one of the primary sources of internal information. Information may be obtained either informally in the course of day-to-day business or through meetings, interviews or questionnaires.

5.4 External information

Capturing information from **outside** the organisation might be a **routine** task entrusted to particular individuals, or might be collected on an 'informal' **non-routine** basis.

Routine formal collection of data from outside sources includes the following.

(a)   A company's **tax specialists** will be expected to gather information about changes in tax law and how this will affect the company.

(b)   Obtaining information about any new legislation on health and safety at work, or employment regulations, must be obtained - for example by the company's **legal expert** or **company secretary** - who must then pass on the information to other managers affected by it.

(c)   Research and development (R & D) work often relies on information about other R & D work being done by another organisation.

(d)   **Marketing managers** need to know the attitudes and opinions of current and potential customers. To obtain this information, they might carry out market research exercises.

Non-routine, informal gathering of information from the environment **goes on all the time, both consciously and unconsciously.** For example, employees are exposed to newspapers, television reports, websites, meetings with business associates and trade publications.

5.5 External data sources

An organisation's files (paper and/or computerised) include information from external sources - such as invoices, e-mails, letters, advertisements and so on **received from customers and suppliers**. Sometimes additional external information is required – meaning an active search outside the organisation is necessary. The following sources may be identified.

(a) The government.

(b) Advice or information bureaux.

(c) Consultancies of all sorts.

(d) Newspaper and magazine publishers.

(e) There may be specific reference works which are used in a particular line of work.

(f) Libraries and information services.

(g) Increasingly businesses can use each other's systems as sources of information, for instance via electronic data interchange (EDI).

(h) Electronic sources of information are becoming ever more important, for example companies like **Reuters** offer access to a range of business related information.

(i) Many information provision services are now provided via the **Internet**. As the rate of Internet use increases, greater numbers of people and organisations are using it to source information on a vast range of topics.

Exam focus point

Internal and external sources of information could easily be examined in a MCQ.

Question

Good management information

Good management information is

A Relevant, regular and reliable
B Timely, regular and sufficient
C Reliable, timely and relevant
D Relevant, convenient and material

Answer

C provides the most appropriate description

6 Management accounting and financial reporting

FAST FORWARD

Computer systems and **coding structures** help to sort the information into the categories and formats required for both financial and management accounting.

Basic (prime) sources of management information include sales invoices and purchase invoices. These will also provide information for the financial accounts of a company.

In most organisations, this accounting information will be keyed into a **computer system** and the **coding structure** (also called the **chart of accounts**) for this system should be set up to provide information in the categories required.

For example, if the organisation is divided into different business units, costs and income must be coded to the correct unit. In a factory which makes different products, raw materials must be coded to the product which uses them. Errors in coding will lead to inaccurate information.

We will look at the **recording** of income and expenditure in more detail in Chapter 8. In Chapters 9 to 11 we will go on to look at how income and expenditure is **coded**.

Other **sources of information** may include reports from various departments of the organisation.

- Timesheets, employee and wage information from the personnel department
- Goods received notes and material requisition notes from the warehouse
- Price lists (in-house and suppliers)
- The organisation's policy manual (to ensure that consistent procedures are followed)

Information will be sorted and amalgamated through the **coding structure** so that the reports required by management can be produced. Ways in which information can be collected include the following.

- **Cost centres** (physical locations which use resources, for example a department, a machine).
- **Profit centres** (sections of the business which use resources and generate income to match against them).
- **Projects,** for example, research projects, activities (for example invoice processing) or other outputs (for example a job for a specific customer).

Key term

- A **cost centre** is a production or service location, function, activity or item of equipment for which costs are accumulated.
- A **cost code** is a 'shorthand' description of a cost using numbers, letters, or a combination of both.

6.1 Example: a typical computer cost code structure

An example of the outline for an 8 digit code is shown as follows.

01	172	301
Originating department	Type of cost or income	End product/service
Cost centre or location		Eg project, contract, job, service, product

Therefore the code 01172301 will tell us where the cost came from, what type of cost (or income) it was and which end product or service it should be charged to. For example, it could be from factory department 1, wages, chargeable to product 301. We will be looking at coding in more detail in Chapter 11.

As you have seen, the purpose of **management accounting** is to provide managers with whatever information they need to help them manage their resources efficiently and take sensible decisions. There are **no externally imposed rules** about how this is done: it depends on the needs of the organisation.

The purpose of financial accounting is to provide **accurate financial information** for the company accounts, which will be used by both senior management and external parties (for example investors). The data used to prepare financial accounts and management accounts are the same. The differences between the financial accounts and the management accounts arise because the data is **analysed in a different way**.

6.1.1 Management accounts

- They are distributed **internally** for use within a business only
- They are recorded and presented in a way that is decided by management
- They look at **past** data and also **future** data (for planning purposes)
- They are used to help management in **planning**, **control** and **decision making**
- There is no legal requirement to prepare them
- They include both **financial** and **non-financial** information

6.1.2 Financial accounts

- They are used for **external** reporting
- There is a **legal requirement** for limited companies to prepare them

- They are concerned with **past data** only
- They usually include only **financial information**
- They detail the results of an organisation over a **defined period** (usually a year)

Question

A computer coding structure is useful in

A Cost and management accounting
B Financial accounting
C Both cost and management accounting and financial accounting
D Neither cost and management accounting or financial accounting

Answer

Answer C. A computer coding structure allows information to be sorted and grouped for both the provision of management information and for financial accounting purposes.

7 The limitations of cost and management accounting information

FAST FORWARD

There are no external rules governing the format or content of management information, unlike the financial accounts.

We have already seen that for cost and management accounting information to be useful it must have certain characteristics. If these characteristics are not present then this will limit the usefulness of such information.

Cost and management information does not necessarily need to be accurate to the cent but the information itself will only be useful if the underlying figures that make it up are **reliable**. For example if costs have been coded to the wrong products then any management information on product profitability will be of little use.

It is not normally possible to provide management with all of the information they need every minute of the day and therefore decisions will be taken as to how frequently cost and management information is produced. Suppose that a report comparing actual production costs to budgeted production costs is prepared every month although any problems that this report highlights can be addressed for the next month it has not been helpful in addressing the problems in the current month.

It is often the case that managers **do not necessarily communicate** with the cost and management accountant and therefore the information that is provided to the manager is not **of the type or in the format** that he/she requires.

Many types of cost and management accounting information take the form of comparison of figures over time. Care must be taken here as if prices are changing then the **comparison may not be valid** and will therefore limit the use of the information.

The information that the cost and management accountant provides for management may be reliable and timely but if it is not **complete** then it will be of limited use. For example if management are taking a decision about the future of a product they will require **information on its profitability**. However if the sales manager has provided sales forecast figures but omitted to mention that these are dependent upon $50,000 being spent on advertising then the information will not be complete and will be of limited use for management decisions.

Many managers are not accountants and therefore the form in which cost and management information is provided, normally in accountant's terms, **will limit its use**. Care should be taken, as an accountant, when providing information to **avoid accountancy jargon** and to explain matters in non-accountant terms whenever possible.

By its very nature, cost and management accounting information comes from the cost and income records. However in many cases there will be **non-financial** matters that are relevant to planning, decision-making and control and these may not be included in the cost and management information that is provided. For example the future sales of a product may be extremely dependent upon the level of customer satisfaction with the product or the service that is provided and the cost and **management information may well not include such non-financial factors as customer satisfaction**.

8 The accounting technician's role in a cost accounting system

FAST FORWARD

In a cost accounting system, the role of the accounting technician is to provide answers to questions on costs and revenues. The organisation must have a cost accounting system capable of analysing cost information quickly and easily.

You have now had a brief introduction to cost accounting and cost information. Let us now consider the role of the accounting technician in a cost accounting system.

Remember that the accounting technician will have access to a **large amount of information** which is all recorded in the **cost accounting records**. With so much information at his/her fingertips, it is inevitable that **many people** are going to want to ask him/her **lots of questions**!

So, what sort of questions is the accounting technician going to provide answers for? Well, here are a few examples.

(a)   What has the **cost of goods produced** or services provided been?
(b)   What has the **cost of operating a department** been?
(c)   What have **revenues** been?

All of these questions may relate to **different periods**. For example, if someone wants to know what revenues have been for the past ten years, the accounting technician will need to extract this information from the cost accounting records. It is important therefore that the cost accounting system is capable of analysing such information.

If the accounting technician knows all about the costs incurred or revenues earned, he may also be asked to do the following types of task.

(a)   To assess **how profitable** certain products or departments are.
(b)   To **review the costs** of products, and to use this information to enable him/her to **set suitable selling prices**.
(c)   To put **a value to inventories** of goods (such as raw materials) which are unsold at the end of a period. As you will learn later on in your studies, the **valuation of inventory** is a **very important part of cost accounting**.

The accounting technician may also need to provide information on **future costs** of goods and services. This is an integral part of the planning or budgeting process.

By comparing current costs with budgeted costs, the accounting technician should be able to highlight areas which show **significant variances**. These variances should then be **investigated**.

Most cost accounting systems should be capable of producing regular performance statements, though the accounting technician is likely to be the person producing them, and distributing them to the relevant personnel.

The role of an accounting technician in a cost accounting system is therefore fairly **varied**. The role is likely to include spending much time providing answers to the many questions which may be directed at the accounting technician (such as those that we have considered here).

Chapter Roundup

- Raw **data** may be processed to produce meaningful **information**.

- The purpose of **management information** is to help managers to manage resources efficiently and effectively, by planning and controlling operations and by allowing informed **decision-making**.

- Producing **useful management information** such as a report depends on understanding the **needs** of the end **user** and of the organisation.

- Good management information should be:

    Accurate
    Complete
    Cost-beneficial
    User-targeted
    Relevant
    Authoritative
    Timely
    Easy to use

- There are many **sources** of information (both internal and external) including accounting records, websites, staff, the staff of competitors, the government, the media and many others.

- **Computer systems** and **coding structures** help to sort the information into the categories and formats required for both financial and management accounting.

- There are no external rules governing the format or content of management information, unlike the financial accounts.

- In a cost accounting system, the role of the accounting technician is to provide answers to questions on costs and revenues. The organisation must have a cost accounting system capable of analysing cost information quickly and easily.

Quick Quiz

1   Two statements follow about information:

    1.   Information is the scientific term for facts, figures and processing.

    2.   Management information is information that is given to the people who are in charge of running an organisation.

    Are the above statements true or false?

    A   Both statements are true
    B   Both statements are false
    C   Statement 1 is false but statement 2 is true
    D   Statement 1 is true but statement 2 is false

2   Which one of the following is not usually considered to be one of the purposes of management information?

    A   Implementing
    B   Planning
    C   Control
    D   Decision making

3   What is the main factor to consider when designing a management report?

    A   The needs of the user
    B   The length of the report
    C   Confidentiality
    D   Neat handwriting

4   Which one of the following 'qualities of information' does not appear in the mnemonic 'accurate'?

    A   Accurate
    B   Communication
    C   Complete
    D   User-targeted

5   Which one of the following sources of information would usually be an internal source of information for a business?

    A   The government
    B   Tax consultants
    C   The internet
    D   The receivables ledger

6   Which one of the following options describes a cost centre?

    A   A production or service location, function, activity or item of equipment for which costs are accumulated

    B   A shorthand description of a cost using numbers, letters or a combination of both

    C   A section of the business which uses resources and generates income to match them

    D   An activity or other output, for example a job for a specific customer

7   Two statements follow about the format and content of information.

    1.   There are no external rules governing the format and content of management information
    2.   There are no external rules governing the format and content of financial information

    Are the above statement true or false?

    A   Both statements are true
    B   Both statements are false
    C   Statement 1 is false but statement 2 is true
    D   Statement 1 is true but statement 2 is false

8   Which one of the following questions would not normally be answered by the accounting technician?

    A   What has the cost of goods produced been?
    B   What have revenues been?
    C   What should our business strategy be for the next five years?
    D   What has the cost of operating department A been?

1   C   Statement 1 is false. It is **data** which is the term for facts, figures and processing. Statement 2 is true.

2   A   Implementing. The purpose of management information is to help managers to manage resources efficiently and effectively by planning and controlling operations and by allowing informed decision making.

3   A   The needs of the user. When considering the needs of the user you may also want to consider the length of the report and confidentiality but the first consideration should be the user's needs.

4   B   Communication. Communication is not a 'quality of information'. It is worth memorising the mnemonic for the exam.

5   D   The receivables ledger. The question says 'usually' because a tax specialist company would probably not need to use external tax consultants so their source of tax information would be internal.

6   A   Option B is a cost code. Option C is a profit centre. Option D is a project.

7   D   Statement 1 is true, management information has no external rules. Statement 2 is false as financial information is subject to external rules and regulations

8   C   The accounting technician is likely to provide answers to questions on costs and revenues. Questions on business strategy would normally be discussed at board level. The accounting technician may well be told what the business strategy is, but would not be expected to decide on the strategy himself/herself.

Reporting management information

7

Study guide

			Syllabus reference
4	(a)	Discuss methods of analysing, presenting and communicating information	3(b)(i)
	(c)	Identify suitable formats for communicating management information according to purpose	3(b)(i)
	(d)	Identify the general principles of distributing reports (eg procedures, timing, recipients) including the reporting of confidential information	3(b)(i), (ii)
	(e)	Interpret information presented in management reports	3(b)(i)

1 Introduction

In the last chapter we discussed how you obtain and code management information. In the rest of this Text we focus on what information that has been produced tells us, and how it maybe used.

In this chapter we shall talk about **different ways** of communicating and presenting information. We also discuss when you should not communicate information – when you should keep it confidential.

2 Deciding who needs what

FAST FORWARD

> Management information should be **relevant to** and **understood** by the individual who receives it.

You learnt in Chapter 6 that management information should be **relevant** to the organisation and the individual.

The person receiving management information should be able to understand it. Understandability can be helped by:

- Avoiding unexplained technical terms
- Cutting out unnecessary detail
- Using charts, diagrams, tables and good report layouts
- Asking the users' views on required information and presentation

In many organisations standard reports are issued regularly. The information system may produce the reports directly. Alternatively the reports may need special preparation. They will tell the managers responsible for various activities how they are performing. They may be used as a basis for extra rewards such as bonuses, promotions etc.

Ideally the reports should distinguish between **controllable** and **non-controllable** factors. This is not always easy in practice however.

Managers may also need **ad hoc** reports to help them with particular problems. For example they may want more detail than is given by the regular reports on a particular aspect of the business. If you have to provide this type of information you must understand **exactly what is required**, including the **format** required for presenting it.

3 Types of communication

FAST FORWARD

> **Types of communication** include:
>
> - Letters
> - Memos
> - E-mails
> - Formal reports
>
> It is important to choose the right one for a given purpose.

Choosing the right method of communication is important. Many organisations have standard sets of regular reports in prescribed formats. Many also have a standard **house style** for other documents, that is a particular way of setting things out. The aim of this is to:

- Make it easier for employees to read, locate and produce information
- Present a consistent image to people outside the organisation

Different situations suit different methods of communication. Some relevant considerations are outlined in the following table.

Choosing a communication method	
Factor	**Considerations**
Time	How long will be needed to prepare the message, and how long will it take to transmit it in the chosen form? This must be weighed against the urgency with which the message must be sent.
Complexity	The method used for relaying a complex piece of information must be chosen carefully. A written document may make it easier for the reader to take their time over digesting the information. On the other hand, a conversation would allow for instant clarification where necessary.
Distance	How far is the message required to travel? Must it be transmitted to an office on a different floor of the building, or across town, or to the other end of the country?
Written record	A written record may be needed as proof, confirming a transaction, or for legal purposes, or as an aid to memory. It can be duplicated and sent to many recipients. It can be stored and later retrieved for reference and analysis as required.
Feedback/ interaction	How quickly is the feedback required? If an instant response is needed then a conversation may be appropriate. How many responses are required? If there are many responses needed then talking to each individual may take too long.
Confidentiality	Telephone calls may be overheard; faxed messages can be read by whoever is standing by the fax machine; internal memos may be read by colleagues or by internal mail staff; highly personal letters may be read by the recipient's secretary. On the other hand a message may need to be spread widely and quickly to all staff: the notice-board, or a public announcement or the company newsletter may be more appropriate.
Recipient	It may be necessary to be reserved and tactful, warm and friendly, or impersonal, depending upon the desired effect on the recipient. If you are trying to impress him, a high quality document may be needed.
Cost	Cost must be considered in relation to all of the above factors. The aim is to achieve the best possible result at the least possible expense.

3.1 Letters

You are most likely to use a letter when communicating with someone **outside your organisation.**

Letters should be polite, accurate, clear, logical and concise; and should give appropriate references. Spelling and punctuation should, of course, be impeccable! Also, if your company has a house-style, your letter should conform to that.

3.2 Example: a letter

Brown Bros

24 Croxley Road

Coulton

Surrey

RH3 9BZ

Tel: 0192 730 1933

Fax: 0192 730 1934

> Required so that letter can be filed and retrieved

Date: 11 May 20X1

Our ref: ACF/pj

> Always use this if you have it from previous correspondence

Your ref: LRS/NP

> If possible, address to a specific individual

The Invoice Clerk

Pebble and Sons

16 Rowe Street

Lambourn

Berks

MA6 3AJ

> Body of letter

> Yours faithfully goes with 'Dear Sir'. 'Yours sincerely' when writing to a named person (Mr Smith)

Dear Sir

Re: ....(subject of letter)....................................

Yours faithfully

C Ford

> Type name and title under signature

Carol Ford, Accounts Supervisor

Question

If you begin a letter 'Dear Sir', you should sign the letter

A   Yours sincerely
B   Yours faithfully
C   Yours truly
D   Yours gratefully

Answer

B   Yours faithfully is the formal ending if the recipient's name is not used. A would be used if the recipients name had been referred to, e.g. 'Dear Mr Jackson'. C and D are not generally used in business letters.

3.3 Memos

Key term

> The **memorandum** or **memo** performs internally the same function as a letter does in communication externally. It can be used for any kind of communication that is best conveyed in writing such as reports, brief messages or notes.

Memos need less detail than a formal letter.

3.4 Example: a memo

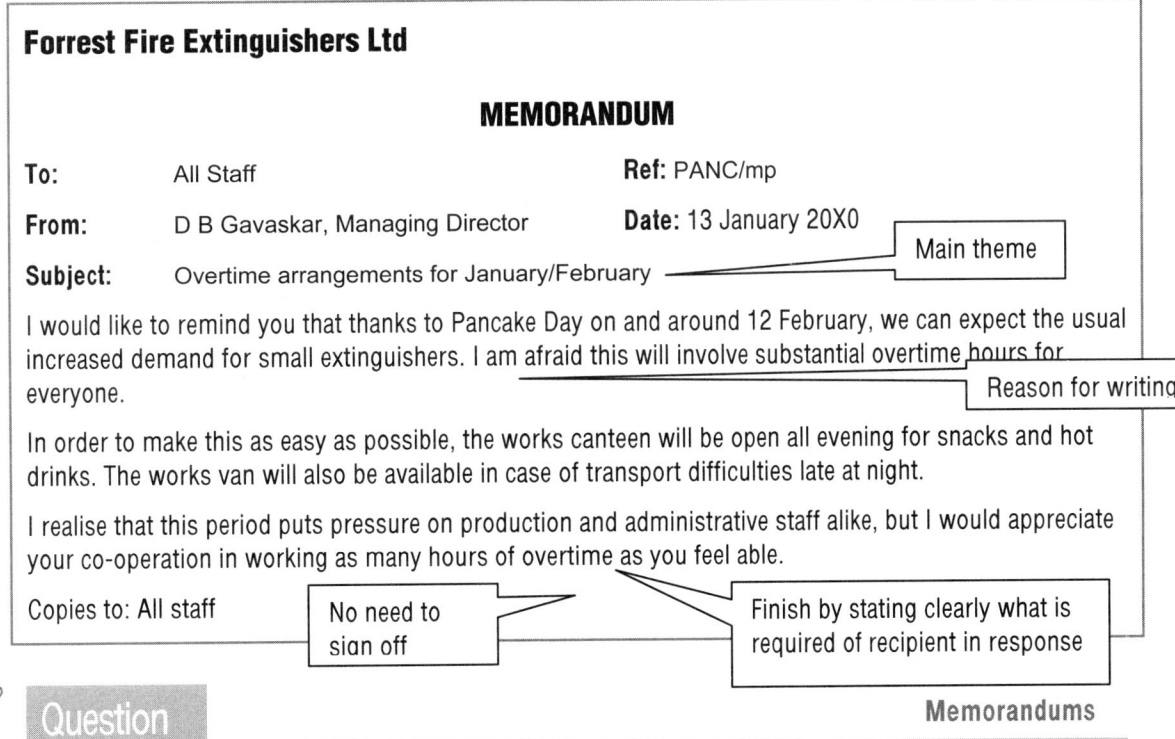

Question

Memorandums

A memorandum is

A   Signed by the person sending it
B   Generally used for the communication of short messages between different organisations
C   Not used if important information is to be communicated
D   For any written communication within an organisation

D   A memo can be used for internal communication of information that is presented in writing, so B and C are incorrect. A is incorrect as it does not have to be signed.

3.5 E-mails

If available, you can use **e-mails** in the same way as a memo, or for external communications where signatures are unnecessary. An e-mail would therefore not be suitable for confirming a contract, but you can use it to respond to a price query.

We covered the advantages and dangers of e-mail in section 4 of Chapter 2. Re-read this section now to refresh your memory.

3.6 Reports

FAST FORWARD

Standard reports are a regular part of the management information system.

Ad-hoc reports deal with a one-off issue or problem.

A formal **report** may be needed where a comprehensive investigation has taken place.

ELEMENTS OF A FORMAL REPORT	
Title	Subject of report
Terms of reference	Clarify what has been requested
Introduction	Who the report is from and to How the information was obtained
Main body	Divided into sections with sub-headings to aid reader Logical order
Conclusions	Summarises findings
Recommendations	Based on information and evidence May be combined with conclusion
Signature	Of writer
Executive summary	Saves time for managers receiving a long report No more than one page

One example of a short formal report is shown on the next page.

3.7 Example: short formal report

REPORT ON PROPOSED UPDATING OF COMPANY POLICY MANUAL

To: Board of Directors, BCD Ltd
From: J Thurber, Opus Management Consultants
Status: Confidential
Date: 3 October 20X8

I   INTRODUCTION AND TERMS OF REFERENCE

This report details the results of an investigation commissioned by the Board on 7 September 20X8. We were asked to consider the current applicability of the company's policy manual and to propose changes needed to bring it into line with current practice.

II   METHOD

The following investigatory procedures were adopted:

1   Interview all senior staff regarding use of the policy manual in their departments
2   Observe working practices in each department

III   FINDINGS

The manual was last updated 10 years ago. From our observations, the following amendments are now needed:

1   The policy section on computer use should be amended. It deals with safe storage of disks, which is no longer applicable as data is now stored on a server. Also, it does not set out the company's e-mail policy.

2   The company's equal opportunities policy needs to be included.

3   The coding list in the manual is now very out of date. A number of new cost centres and profit centres have been set up in the last 10 years and the codes for these are not noted in the manual.

4   There is no mention of the provisions of the Data Protection Act as they relate to the company.

IV   CONCLUSIONS

We discovered upon interviewing staff that very little use is made of the policy manual. When it has been amended as above, it can be brought back into use, and we recommend that this should be done as soon as possible.

Signed J Thurber, Opus Management Consultants

A formal report like this will of course be **word-processed**.

Question   Communication methods

In each of the cases below, select the form of communication which will generally be the most appropriate.

1   A complaint to a supplier about the quality of goods supplied.

        A   Letter
        B   Memo
        C   Formal report
        D   E-mail

2   A query to a supervisor about the coding of an invoice.

    A   E-mail
    B   Memo
    C   Face-to-face
    D   All of the above are equally suitable if available

3   An investigation into the purchasing costs of your company.

    A   Letter
    B   Memo
    C   Formal report
    D   E-mail

4   Notification to customers of a change of the company's telephone number.

    A   Letter
    B   Memo
    C   E-mail
    D   All of the above are equally suitable if available

5   Reply to an e-mail.

    A   Letter
    B   Memo
    C   E-mail
    D   Face-to-face

6   Query to the sales department about an expenses claim.

    A   Memo
    B   E-mail
    C   Telephone
    D   All of the above are equally suitable if available

Answer

1	A
2	D
3	C
4	A
5	C
6	D

Exam focus point

In the exam you might be required to determine the most appropriate form of communication as in the activity above.

4 Confidentiality

FAST FORWARD

Some information will be **confidential**, maybe because of the Data Protection Act or because of company policy. Access to it will be restricted.

Keeping some information confidential is an important **legal requirement.** It may also be part of your organisation's **policy**.

Some requirements are pure common sense. For example most of us would expect details of our wages, salaries, health etc to be kept confidential. Others are less obvious. For example some information about your organisation may be valuable to competitors. This is known as **commercially sensitive information.**

4.1 Data Protection Act 1998

We covered The Data Protection Act in Chapter 4. The main points are recapped below.

The Act lays down strict rules about the:

- Storage
- Purposes or uses
- Accuracy
- Processing and
- Transfer of personal data

The Act applies to information held in any form. Therefore it does not matter whether the information is held on paper, in computer files or in another form – it is all covered by the Act.

The strictest requirements of the Act apply to **'sensitive data'** such as racial origin, health, sexual orientation or political or religious beliefs. The processing of sensitive data is generally forbidden without the consent of the subject.

Key term

> **Data users** are organisations or individuals which use personal data covered by the Act.

The most obvious use is actually **processing the data**. However use also includes **controlling** the **contents** of **personal data files**.

Data users must apply to the Data Protection Registrar to be **registered** for holding personal data for a particular purpose. Registered users are only allowed to hold and use personal data for the registered purposes.

Key term

> **Data subjects** are individuals on whom personal data is held.

Data subjects can **sue** data users for **damage** or **distress** caused by inaccurate data, loss of data or unauthorised disclosure. They also have a legal right to see their own personal data.

4.2 Internal requirements

Within an organisation, the policy manual will often lay down other confidentiality rules. For example some organisations forbid employees to talk to the press without authorisation, or to publish their research results. You can imagine that businesses planning large redundancies or the launch of a new product will not want the information to become public prematurely.

Paper files with **restricted access** should be

- Listed
- Stored securely
- Only accessible by specific people

Computer systems often use **passwords** to restrict access to information that is held on computer. You should never divulge your password to an unauthorised person or keep it in view on your desk. Think of your password as needing as much secrecy as your bank PIN number.

Use of the **Internet** can pose particular problems in maintaining confidentiality. Many companies have a policy on the purposes for which the Internet should and should not be used. The law surrounding Internet information and its protection is still developing.

If you have access to restricted information in any form, you are responsible for protecting it to comply with company policy and the law. You should lock confidential papers or computer disks away when you are not using them. You should not leave them lying around on your desk (or in the photocopier!).

You should also **not provide confidential information** to **others** outside your department without checking with a supervisor.

Question

Your company's planning department asks for a copy of the monthly research cost reports for the last six months. Your computer password does not give you access to this information. What should you do?

A   Refer the query to your supervisor
B   Ask someone what the password is that will access the information
C   Ask for your password to be changed so that it will access the information
D   Try and find a hard copy of the information

Answer

A   Access to this information is restricted. B, C and D are therefore not appropriate.

5 Charts, graphs and tables

FAST FORWARD

Charts and **graphs** and tables are often excellent ways of communicating information.

In many cases, communication may best be achieved if information is presented in a visual form such as a chart or a graph.

Graphs and charts can be complex and highly technical, so they should, like any other medium of communication, be adapted to suit the understanding and information needs of the intended recipient: they should be simplified and explained as necessary, and include only as much data as can clearly be presented and assimilated.

5.1 Charts

The **bar chart** is one of the most common methods of presenting data in a visual display. It is a chart in which data is shown in the form of a **bar** (two dimensional, or three dimensional for extra impact), and is used to **demonstrate and compare amounts or numbers of things**. The bars are the same width but variable in height and are read off a vertical scale as you would read water levels or a thermometer. A horizontal presentation is also possible.

The bar chart is very **versatile**. Each block may represent a different (identified) item, for example the annual production cost of a different product (to compare costs of a range of products), or the total sales turnover of a company for a year (to compare success over a period of years), or the number of hours required to produce a product in a particular country (to compare efficiency in a group of industrial nations).

Key term

> A **simple barchart** is a chart consisting of one or more bars, in which the length of each bar indicates the magnitude of the corresponding data item.

A simple bar chart is a visually appealing way of illustration.

5.2 Example: simple bar chart

A company's total expenditure for the years from 20X4 to 20X9 are as follows.

Year	$'000
20X4	800
20X5	1,200
20X6	1,100
20X7	1,400
20X8	1,600
20X9	1,700

The data could be shown on a simple bar chart as follows.

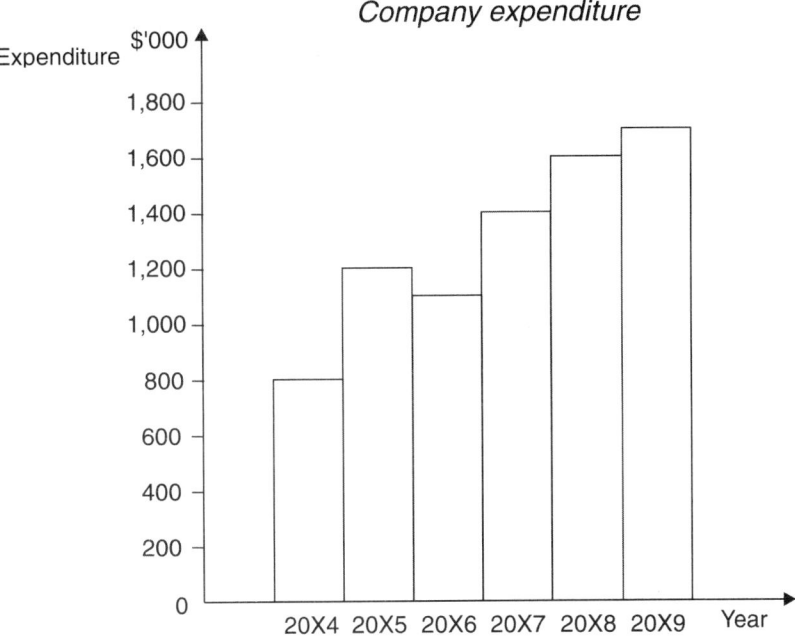
Company expenditure

5.3 Line graphs

Line graphs are often used in commercial contexts, to display a wide variety of information. They are particularly useful for **demonstrating trends**: the progress of events or the fluctuation over time of variables such as profits, prices, sales totals, customer complaints.

This is done by plotting points of information on a grid, usually something like this.

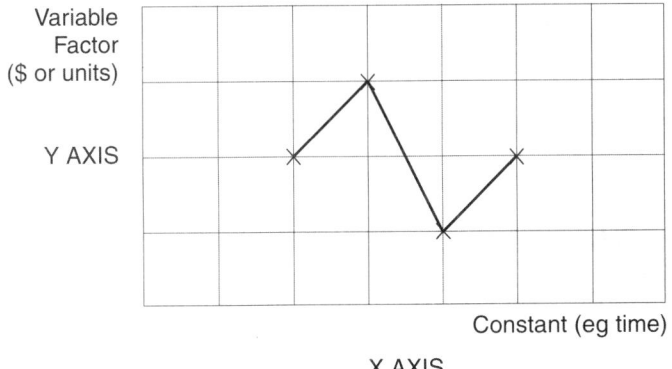

The points are joined by a line which thus reflects the 'ups and downs' of the variable, over a period of time. Two or three such lines may comfortably be drawn on a spacious graph before it gets too overcrowded, allowing several trends (for example the performance of several competing products over a period of time) to be compared. An example is shown below.

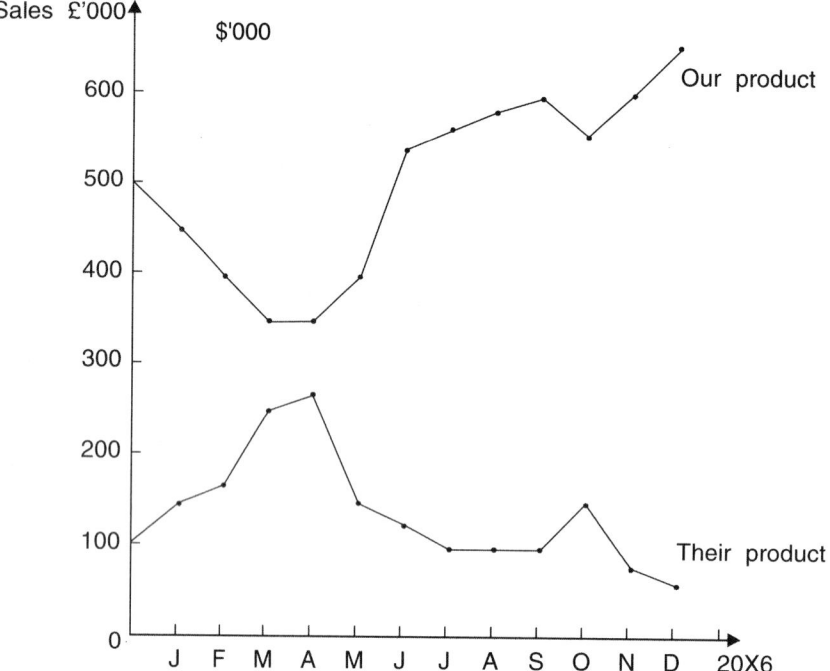

It is easy to see the progression of share prices in the following graph.

British Airways

Share price relative to the
FT~A All~Share Index

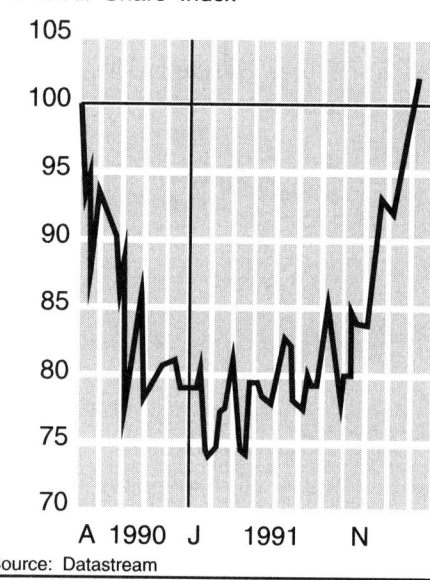

Source: Datastream

The scale of the vertical axis is large enough for you to tell with reasonable accuracy the price at any given point during the period. (This is important, because the eye cannot distinguish fractions of inches which might represent a large leap on a scale marked for example by units of ten or a hundred).

Despite peaks and troughs, the overall trend is also obvious, in a way that would not be possible in a table of fluctuating figures. This will be helpful, for example, in demonstrating the success of a productivity scheme to encourage employees, or in spotting potentially disastrous declines in sales (or increases in absenteeism).

Exam focus point	You will not be required to prepare a graph in the exam but there may be a question about how you would prepare one.

5.4 Tables

Tables are a simple way of presenting **numerical information**. Figures are displayed, and can be compared with each other: relevant totals, subtotals, percentages can also be presented as a summary for analysis.

A table is **two-dimensional** (rows and columns): so it can only show two variables: a sales chart for a year, for example, might have rows for products, and columns for each month of the year. (We looked at how tables may be produced using word processing software in Chapter 3.)

SALES FIGURES FOR 20--													
Product	Jan	Feb	Mar	Apr	May	Jun	Jul	Aug	Sep	Oct	Nov	Dec	Total $'000
A													
B													
C													
D													
Total													

You are likely to be presenting data in tabular form very often, in doing so, be aware of the following guidelines.

- The table should be given a **clear title**.
- All columns should be **clearly labelled**.
- Where appropriate, there should be **clear sub-totals** and a right-hand **total column** for comparison.
- A **total figure** is often advisable at the bottom of each column of figures also, for comparison.
- Tables should not be packed with too much data so that the information presented is difficult to read.

6 Using Excel to produce charts and graphs

Using Microsoft Excel, it is possible to use data held in a spreadsheet to generate a variety of charts and graphs.

Today, the vast majority of **charts** and **graphs** produced in a business setting are prepared using **spreadsheet software**.

This section assumes you are reasonably competent in the basics of Microsoft Excel.

6.1 Using Microsoft Excel to produce charts and graphs

Using Microsoft Excel, it is possible to display data held in a range of spreadsheet cells in a variety of charts or graphs. We will use the Discount Traders Ltd spreadsheet shown below to generate a chart.

	A	B	C	D	E
1	**Discount Traders Ltd**				
2	*Sales analysis – April 200X*				
3	Customer	Sales	5% discount	Sales (net)	
4		£	£	£	
5	Arthur	956.00	0.00	956.00	
6	Dent	1423.00	71.15	1351.85	
7	Ford	2894.00	144.70	2749.30	
8	Prefect	842.00	0.00	842.00	
9					

The data in the spreadsheet could be used to generate a chart, such as those shown below. We explain how later in this section.

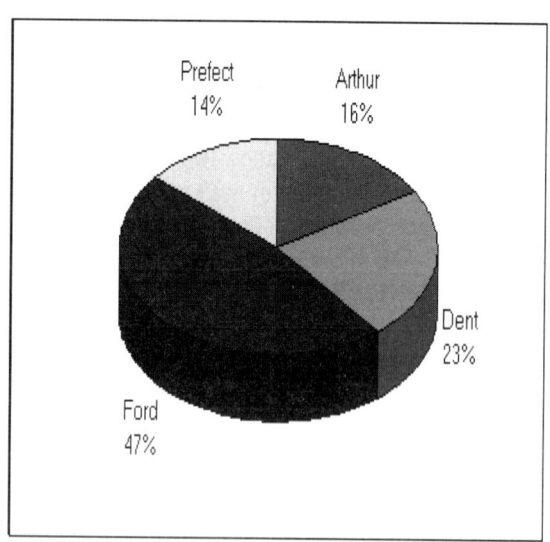

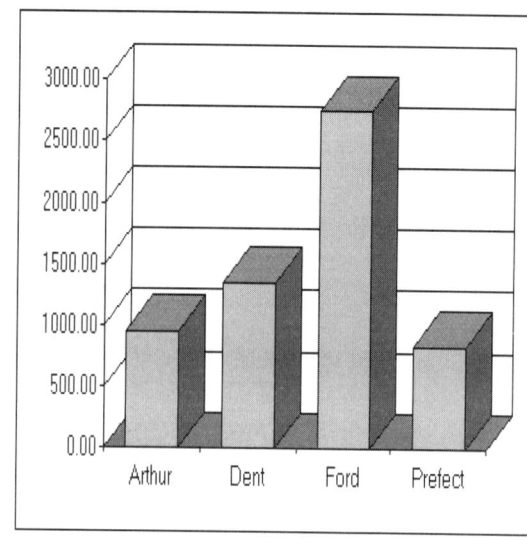

The Chart Wizard, which we explain in a moment, may also be used to generate a line graph. A line graph would normally be used to track a tend over time. For example, the chart below graphs the Total Revenue figures shown in Row 7 of the following spreadsheet.

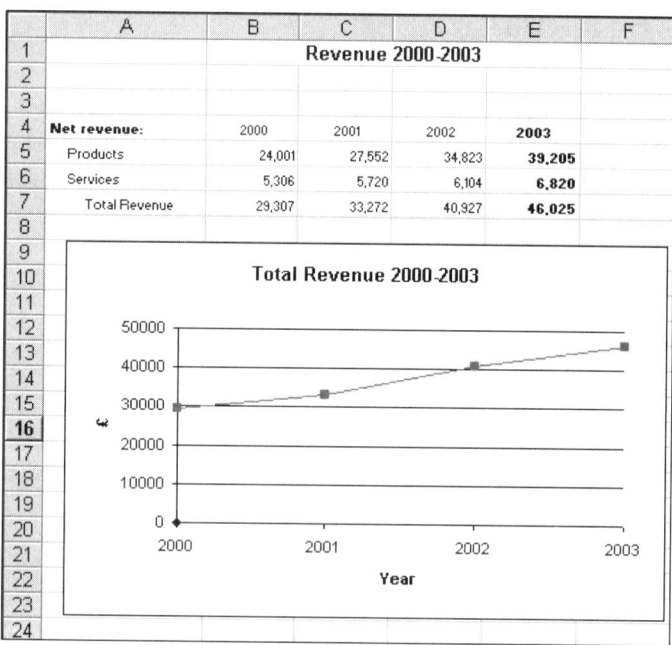

6.2 The Chart Wizard

Charts and graphs may be generated simply by **selecting the range** of figures to be included, then using Excel's Chart Wizard. The Discount Traders spreadsheet referred to earlier is shown again below.

	A	B	C	D	E
1	Discount Traders Ltd				
2	Sales analysis - April 200X				
3	Customer	Sales	5% discount	Sales (net)	
4		£	£	£	
5	Arthur	956.00	0.00	956.00	
6	Dent	1423.00	71.15	1351.85	
7	Ford	2894.00	144.70	2749.30	
8	Prefect	842.00	0.00	842.00	
9					

To chart the **net sales** of the different **customers**, follow the following steps.

Step 1   Highlight cells A5:A8, then move your pointer to cell D5, hold down **Ctrl** and drag to also select cells D5:D8.

Step 2   Look at the **toolbar** at the top of your spreadsheet. You should see an **icon** that looks like a small bar chart. Click on this icon to start the 'Chart Wizard'.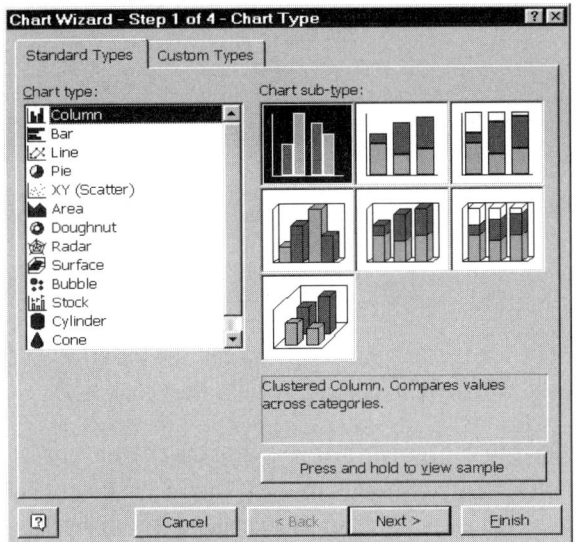

The following steps are taken from the Excel 2000 Chart Wizard. Other versions may differ slightly.

Step 3   Pick the type of chart you want. We will choose chart type **Column** and then select the sub-type we think will be most effective. (To produce a graph, select a type such as **Line**).

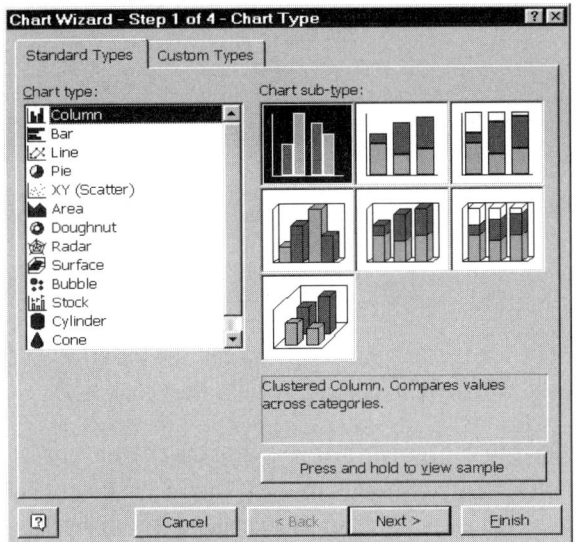

Step 4   This step gives us the opportunity to confirm that the data we selected earlier was correct and to decide whether the chart should be based on **columns** (eg Customer, Sales, Discount etc) or **rows** (Arthur, Dent etc). We can accept the default values and click Next.

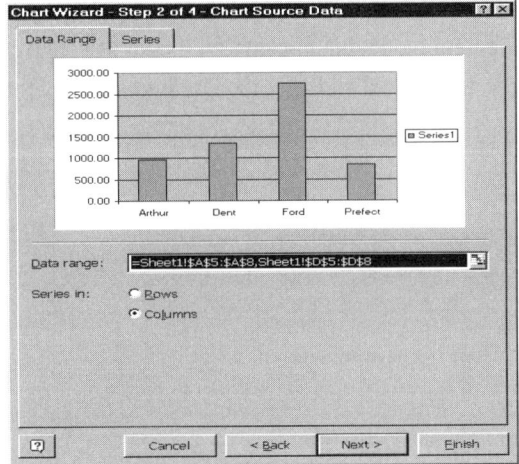

Step 5   Next, specify your chart **title** and axis **labels**. Incidentally, one way of remembering which is the **X axis** and which is the **Y axis** is to look at the letter Y: it is the only letter that has a vertical part pointing straight up, so it must be the vertical axis! Click Next to move on.

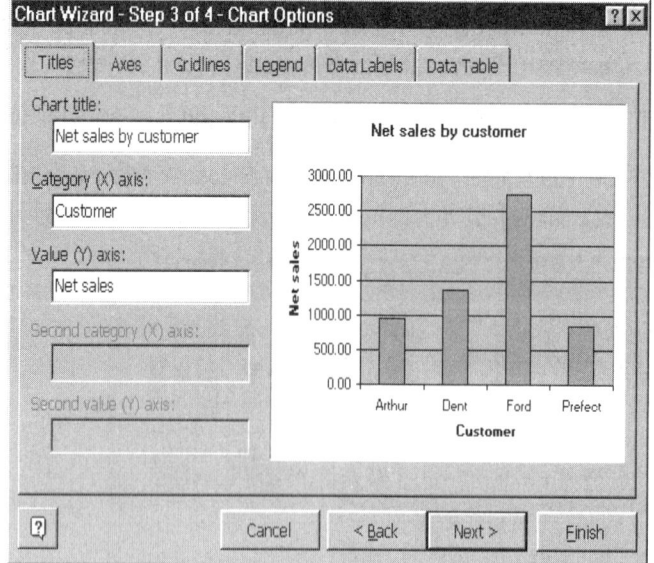

As you can see, there are other index tabs available. You can see the effect of selecting or deselecting each one in **preview** – experiment with these options as you like then click Next.

Step 6   The final step is to choose whether you want the chart to appear on the same worksheet as the data or on a separate sheet of its own. This is a matter of personal preference – for this example choose to place the chart as an object within the existing spreadsheet.

6.3 Changing existing charts

Even after your chart is 'finished', you can change it.

(a)   You can **resize it** simply by selecting it and dragging out its borders.

(b)   You can change **each element** by **double clicking** on it then selecting from the options available.

(c)   You could also select any item of **text** and alter the wording, size or font, or change the **colours** used.

(d)   In the following illustration, the user has double-clicked on the Y axis to enable them to **change the scale**.

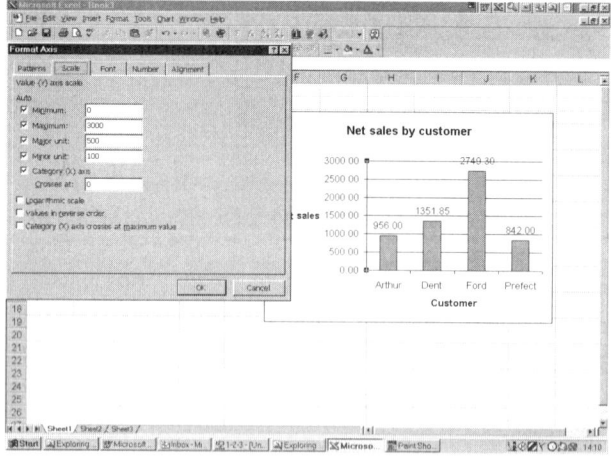

Chapter Roundup

- Management information should be **relevant to** and **understood** by the individual who receives it.
- **Types of communication** include:
  - Letters
  - Memos
  - E-mails
  - Formal reports

  It is important to choose the right one for a given purpose.
- **Standard reports** are a regular part of the management information system.
- **Ad-hoc reports** deal with a one-off issue or problem.
- Some information will be **confidential**, maybe because of the Data Protection Act or because of company policy. Access to it will be restricted.
- **Charts** and **graphs** and tables are often excellent ways of communicating information.
- Using Microsoft Excel, it is possible to use data held in a spreadsheet to generate a variety of charts and graphs.

Quick Quiz

1   Which one of the following options would **not** help management information to be understood?

   A   Avoiding unexplained technical terms
   B   Using charts, diagrams and tables
   C   Asking the users' view on required information and presentation
   D   Lots of detail

2   Which one of the following is **not** an aim of house style for documents?

   A   To make it easier to read the documents
   B   To make it easier to locate information
   C   To control costs
   D   To present a consistent image to people outside the organisation

3   Information about an organisation which may be valuable to competitors is known as:

   A   Cost sensitive information
   B   Commercially sensitive information
   C   Commercially secure information
   D   Cost secure information

4   Data users are individuals on whom personal data is held. Is this true or false?

5   What would be the most effective way of demonstrating the trend in new car sales from January to December 20X8?

   A   Line graph
   B   Bar chart
   C   Table
   D   Pie chart

1   D   Cutting out unnecessary detail can greatly benefit understandability

2   C   Controlling costs is not one of the aims of house style

3   B   This is known as commercially sensitive information

4   False   Data subjects are individuals on whom personal data is held. Data users are organisations or individuals which use personal data.

5   A   Line graph. Line graphs are particularly useful for demonstrating **trends.**

8

Business organisation and accounting

Study guide

			Syllabus reference
5	(a)	Describe the organisation and main functions of an office as a centre for information and administration.	3(b)(iv)
	(b)	Describe the function and use of a manual of policies, procedures and best practices.	4(c)(iii)
	(c)	Identify the main types of transactions undertaken by a business and the key personnel involved in initiating, processing and completing transactions	3(b)(iv)
	(d)	Discuss the need for effective control over transactions.	3(b)(iv)
	(e)	Explain and illustrate the principles and practice of double-entry book-keeping.	3(b)(iv)
	(f)	Describe and illustrate the use of ledgers and prime entry records in both integrated and interlocking accounting systems.	3(b)(iv)
	(g)	Identify the key features, function and benefits of a computerised accounting system.	3(b)(iv)

1 Introduction

Businesses come in all shapes, sizes and forms. There are manufacturers, retailers, wholesalers and providers of services such as accountants and solicitors. However, whatever the function of the business, all require an effective and efficient system of administration and accounting.

2 Office organisation and functions

FAST FORWARD

The **office** in an organisation is a centre for information and administration.

The most common functions in an office are **purchasing**, personnel **(human resources)**, general **administration**, **finance** and **sales** and **marketing**.

There are a number of areas or functions to be administered and managed within a business. For example, the 'head office' of say a manufacturing, retailing or service business may cover the following areas:

- Purchasing
- Personnel/human resources
- General administration
- Finance
- Selling and marketing

Whether a business manufactures products or sells 'bought in' products, there will be a large purchasing function, either purchasing raw materials for manufacture or purchasing finished goods for resale. The function of the purchasing department will be to ensure that the business purchases from suppliers providing the best overall deal in terms of price, service, delivery time and quality. The purchasing department will also be responsible for ensuring that only necessary purchases are made by the business.

Any business that employs a significant number of people is likely to have a personnel function or human resources function as it is often called in larger organisations. This area of the office will be responsible for the hiring and firing of staff, for training of staff and for the general welfare of the employees.

General administration functions are very wide-ranging but might include secretarial support, dealing with telephone queries and arranging matters such as rent of properties.

The finance function is also very wide-ranging. On a day to day level the accounts department will deal with sending invoices to customers, receiving invoices from suppliers, payment of suppliers, receiving money from customers and making other payments such as purchases of non-current assets and

payment of employees. The higher levels of management in the accounting function may also be responsible for management of the cash balances and for the overall financing of the organisation.

The selling and marketing function will deal with all aspects of taking sales orders, advertising, and any sales personnel.

In many organisations administrative functions are carried out at head office as much as is possible. When this is the case, the administration function is said to be **centralised**.

Key term

> A **centralised** administration department involves as many administrative tasks as possible being carried out at a single central location, such as head office.

Advantages of a centralised administration office include the following.

(a) Consistency – for example the same account codes are likely to be used no mater which part of the organisation submits an invoice. Everyone uses the same data and information.

(b) It gives better security/control over operations and it is easier to enforce standards.

(c) Head office is in a better position to know what is going on.

(d) There may be economies of scale available, for example in purchasing computer equipment and supplies.

(e) Administration staff are in a single location and more expert staff are likely to be employed. Career paths may be more clearly defined.

Disadvantages of a centralised administration office include the following.

(a) Local offices might have to wait for tasks to be carried out.

(b) Reliance on head office. Local offices are less self-sufficient.

(c) A system fault or hold-up at head office will impact across the organisation.

Procedures may not suit all local offices.

Question

The purchasing department

Which of the following is not a function of the purchasing department?

A   Ensuring that only required goods are purchased
B   Ensuring that suppliers used give the best price
C   Paying suppliers' invoices
D   Negotiating discounts with suppliers

Answer

C   Normally the accounts department will pay suppliers' invoices

3 Policy manual

FAST FORWARD

A **policy manual** should help to ensure that all personnel follow procedures and best practices

As you will be starting to realise in any reasonable sized business there will be a lot of different transactions and roles being carried out by many different people in the organisation. As with any entity, in order for the management to keep control of the activities there will have to be some form of rules and procedures.

For example there must be authorisation policies for the purchase of non-current assets, procedures for choosing new suppliers, procedures for accepting new customers etc.

In smaller organisations where only a handful of individuals are involved in the transactions of the business such procedures and best practices can be communicated orally by management. However in larger organisations where there are very many people carrying out functions possibly at a number of different geographical locations then a more formal procedure is needed to ensure that the correct procedures and practices are followed.

This often takes the form of a policy manual which will set out the required procedures for all of the various functions of the business. Every employee will be expected to have read the areas relevant to their functions and the policy manual should always be readily available for easy reference.

Although a policy manual is to be recommended as a form of control over the activities of employees care must be taken that strict adherence to the rules does not create inflexibility and in cases of doubt a more senior member of the staff should be consulted.

4 Main types of transactions of a business

FAST FORWARD

The main types of transactions that most businesses enter into are **sales**, **purchases**, **paying expenses**, **paying employees** and purchasing **non-current assets**.

It was mentioned earlier that businesses come in all shapes and forms however there will be a number of types of transactions which will be common to most businesses:

- Making sales
- Making purchases
- Paying expenses
- Paying employees
- Purchasing non-current assets

For each of these functions we will consider the key personnel involved in initiating, processing and completing the transaction.

In a **retail organisation sales** are of course made **on the shop floor**. However in a **manufacturing organisation** there will normally be a **sales and marketing function** whose responsibility is to market the organisation's products and take orders from customers. Often the day to day responsibility for taking orders will be with the **salesmen and women**. This may be done over the telephone or may be via personal visits to customers or potential customers.

If a sale is being made to an **existing customer**, provided that customer has **not exceeded their credit** balance then the procedure will be for the sales person to take **details of the order** and pass those details to the stores department for despatch and to the accounts department for invoicing of the customer.

However **if the sale is to a new customer** then a more senior level of management will have to be involved because if the sale is to be on credit, **the credit status of the new customer must be determined** and a decision made as to whether sales on credit should be made to this customer.

Once the goods have been despatched to the customer, responsibility then passes to the accounting function to invoice the customer for the goods and to ensure that payment is received.

The making of purchases will initially be started by either the purchasing department or the stores department. The need for the purchase of more goods will be recognised by, for example, the stores manager when he realises that an item of inventory is running low. He will then complete a **purchase requisition which must be authorised** and then the purchasing function will determine the most appropriate supplier on the basis of price, delivery and quality. An order will be placed by the purchasing function and the goods will normally be received by the stores department (see Chapter 11).

After this, **responsibility then goes to the accounting department** which will await the arrival of the invoice for the goods from the suppliers, will check that the invoice is accurate and for goods that have in fact been received and then **in due course pay the amount due to the supplier**.

Organisations will incur a variety of expenses such as rent and rates, insurance, telephone bills, energy bills, advertising expenses etc. In some cases these will be incurred by a specific department of the

business such as the marketing department entering investing in an advertising campaign or alternatively the receipt of the telephone bill will be part of the general administration of the business.

When bills for expenses are received they will be passed to the accounting function which will check that the expense has been incurred or is reasonable and then will process the expense for payment.

Every week and/or every month the **employees of the business must be paid**. For this process to take place there are a lot of calculations to be made and a lot of paperwork to be filled out. In larger organisations there will be payroll department which will deal with this otherwise it will be the responsibility of the payroll clerk in the accounting function.

The payroll function will determine the **gross pay** for each employee, based upon a variety of different remuneration schemes (see Chapter 12), and then will calculate the statutory and other deductions that must be made and will then calculate the net pay due to the employee. Finally the payroll function must then organise the method of payment to the employees.

From time to time an **organisation will need to purchase non-current assets**. These are assets that are to be used in the business for the medium to long term rather than being purchased for resale. This will include items such as machinery, cars, computer equipment, office furniture etc.

In order for the purchase of non-current assets to be put in motion the manager of the department which requires the asset must firstly fill out a **purchase requisition**. As most non-current assets are relatively expensive this will probably have to be **authorised** by more senior management. Once the requisition has been authorised the **purchasing function** will then find the most **appropriate supplier** for the assets.

Once a purchase order has been placed the details will then be passed to the accounting function which will then process and pay the invoice when it is received.

Question   Business personnel

Which of the following personnel in an organisation would **not** be involved in the purchase of materials?

A   Credit controller
B   Stores manager
C   Account
D   Purchasing manager

Answer

A   The credit controller deals with credit customers not the purchase of materials

5 Control over transactions

FAST FORWARD

In order for management to control the transactions of the business there must be a system of **authorisation** of transactions in place.

As you may have noticed in the last section any transaction that a business is involved in will tend to involve a number of different people within the organisation. You will have also noticed the requirement for transactions to be authorised.

The management of a reasonably large business cannot have the time to personally be involved in every transaction of the business. However in order to keep control of the sources of income of the business and the expenditure that the business incurs it is important that transactions are authorised by a responsible member of the management team.

In particular this means that management must have control over the following areas:

(a) Sales on credit made to new customers. If a sale is made on credit the goods are sent out with a promise from the customer to pay in the future therefore the management of the business must be as certain as they can be that this new customer can, and will, pay for the goods which means that the credit controller must be happy that the new customer has a good credit rating and is fairly certain to pay for the goods.

(b) Purchases of goods or non-current assets and payments for expenses. This is money going out of the business therefore it is essential that these are necessary and valid expenditures so a responsible official must authorise them.

(c) One of the largest payments made by most organisations is that of the wages bill for their employees. It is essential that only bona fide employees are paid for the actual hours that they have worked therefore authorisation of the payroll is a very important part of any business.

6 Double entry bookkeeping – basic principles

FAST FORWARD

The basic principle of **double entry bookkeeping** that for every debit entry there must be a corresponding credit entry.

Debit entries in ledger accounts are increases in assets or expenses and decreases in liabilities and income.

Credit entries in ledger accounts are increases in liabilities and income and decreases in assets and expenses.

In later chapters we will be dealing with the accounting entries for materials, labour and expenses. Therefore, in this chapter we remind ourselves of basic double entry bookkeeping and give an overview of how this is used in cost accounting.

You will have covered double-entry bookkeeping in detail in Paper 1, Recording Financial Transactions. You should remember that one of the basic principles of double entry is that for every debit entry there is an equal and opposite credit entry. Remember also that the owner of the business is treated as a separate entity to the business itself and the amount that the owner puts into the business is a special payable of the business known as capital. These two points together mean that the accounting equation will always be:

Assets – liabilities = Capital + profit – drawings

For cost accounting purposes we will be concerned largely with the sales of goods, purchases of materials, the payment of wages and the treatment of expenses. So here is a brief reminder of the basic double-entry that you are likely to come across.

Sales of goods

DEBIT   Bank/receivables
CREDIT   Sales

Receipts from receivables

DEBIT   Bank
CREDIT   Receivables

Purchases of materials

DEBIT   Materials control
CREDIT   Bank/payables

Payment of payables

DEBIT   Payables
CREDIT   Bank

Payment of wages

DEBIT   Wages expense
CREDIT   Bank

This is for the net wages – the full picture is slightly more complicated and this will be dealt with in Chapter 12.

Payments of expenses or overheads

DEBIT   Expenses/overheads
CREDIT   Bank/payables

If in doubt with double entry remember the following rules:

Debit entry: increase in an asset
               decrease in a liability
               increase in an expense
               decrease in income
Credit entry: increase in a liability
               decrease in an asset
               increase in income
               decrease in an expense

Question   Double entry

Which of the following is the correct double entry for a sale on credit?

A   DEBIT   Payables
        CREDIT   Sales

B   DEBIT   Sales
        CREDIT   Payables

C   DEBIT   Receivables
        CREDIT   Sales

D   DEBIT   Sales
        CREDIT   Receivables

Answer

C

Exam focus point

A question on double entry in the costing system is highly likely in the exam.

7 Cost ledger accounting

FAST FORWARD

Transactions are initially recorded in **books of prime entry** which are totalled and the totals posted to the ledger accounts.

Again from your studies of Paper 1, Recording Financial Transactions, you should remember that in practice a business will not enter every individual transaction to the ledger accounts. Instead each type of transaction will be recorded initially in its own primary entry record or book of prime entry. As a reminder the main types of transaction and their related books of prime entry are given below:

Sales invoices sent out   –   Sales day book
Credit notes sent out   –   Sales returns day book

Purchase invoices received   –   Purchases day book
Credit notes received   –   Purchases returns day book

Cash/cheque receipts   –   Cash received book
Cash/cheque payments   –   Cash payments book

Which of the following is not a book of prime entry?

A   Petty cash book
B   Journal
C   Non-current asset register
D   Purchase returns day book

Answer

C

An **integrated system** is one which combines the cost accounting and financial accounting functions in one system of ledger accounts.

An **interlocking system** has a cost ledger for the cost accounting function and a financial ledger for the financial accounting function.

From the summaries of transactions in the day books, double entry bookkeeping takes place. For example, in the sales day book (a book of prime entry) there will be a list of sales invoices totalling $1,487. This total will then be posted to the ledger accounts as follows:

Debit receivables account	$1,487
Credit sales account	$1,487

In a similar way purchase invoices are posted from the purchases day book. In the ledger accounts there are always **two sides** to every transaction. It is only after the books of prime entry have been totalled that they are then posted to the ledger accounts. For cost accounting purposes there are two possible methods of structuring the ledger accounts – an **integrated system** and an **interlocking system**.

An integrated system combines the cost accounting and financial accounting functions into one system of ledger accounts. This gives a saving in terms of time and cost. However it has the disadvantage of trying to fulfil two purposes with one set of ledger accounts despite the differences already considered between financial accounting and management accounting requirements.

An interlocking system is one where separate ledgers are kept for the cost accounting function (the cost ledger) and the financial function (the financial ledger). The cost ledger will include a cost ledger control account which is essentially there to provide a place for items of a financial nature.

For example when an invoice is received for materials, the materials control account will be debited but instead of crediting the payables account, as this is a financial item, the credit is to the cost ledger control account.

In a similar manner in the financial ledger, a financial ledger control account is used to maintain the integrity of the double entry system.

Although an interlocking system allows easier access to cost accounting information, it is more time consuming to prepare two sets of ledger accounts and the two ledgers will need reconciling on a regular basis.

 Question   Integrated and interlocking systems

Which of the following statements is correct?

A   An interlocking system is a single system for cost and financial accounting
B   In an integrated system there will be a financial ledger control account
C   In an interlocking system there will be a cost ledger control account
D   In an integrated system there are separate ledgers for cost and financial accounting

C

8 Computerised accounting systems

FAST FORWARD

A computerised accounting system will allow much quicker and more accurate entries to the accounting system.

Almost all businesses now use some form of computerised accounting system.

In a full ledger computerised system the computer system will normally maintain the following ledgers:

- General or main ledger (for all asset, liability, income and expense accounts)
- Receivables ledger – accounts for each customer
- Payables ledger – accounts for each supplier
- Cash books – including the main cash book and the petty cash book

The system may also contain detailed inventory records and a programme for dealing with payroll.

Accounting using a computerised system involves inputting data, processing it according to accounting rules contained in the software, and producing output ('the accounts' or other management reports). Computerised accounting therefore follows a data processing **cycle** of **input**, **process**, and **output**.

(a) Data is **collected**. There has to be a system or procedure for ensuring that all the data required is collected and made available for processing. The quality, accuracy and completeness of the data will affect the quality of information produced.

(b) Data is **processed** into information, perhaps by summarising it, classifying it and/or analysing it. For example, a receivables ledger system may process data relating to customer orders so as to:
- Produce a report of the total sales for the day/week
- Record the total value of invoices issued in the receivables control account in the general ledger

(c) Files are **updated** to incorporate the processed data. Updating files means bringing them up to date to record current transactions. Updating the personal ledgers and the receivables control account are file updating activities to keep the receivables ledger records up to date.

(d) Data is **communicated**. Continuing the example of the receivables ledger system, output may consist of **customer statements** and **management reports**.

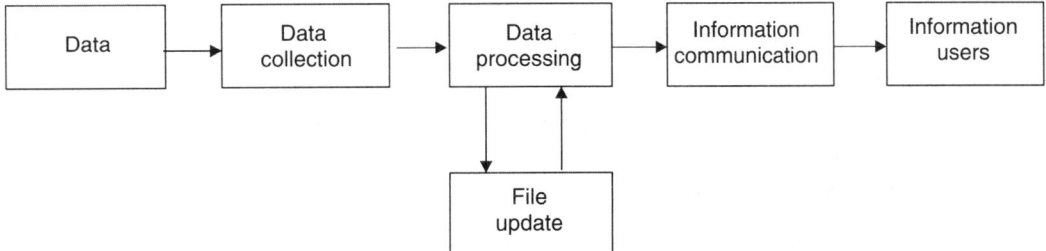

In terms of **accounting** systems and databases, a data **file** is a collection of **records** with similar characteristics. Examples of data files include the receivables ledger, the payables ledger and the general ledger.

A **record** in a file consists of data relating to one logically definable unit of business information. A collection of similar records makes up a file. For example, one record in the receivables ledger file would be one customer account.

A record is made up of several **fields**. A field is an item of data relating to a record. For example, a customer record would include a field for the customers account number, another for the customer name, another for their credit limit, and so on.

Records on a file should contain at least one key field. This is an item of data within the record by which it can be **uniquely identified**. An example would be a unique **code** for each customer.

In older systems, files may be conventionally classified into **transaction** files, and **master** files. These distinctions are particularly relevant in **batch** processing applications, described in a moment.

A transaction file is a file containing records that relate to **individual transactions.** For example, when a company sells goods, the sales for each day may be recorded in the **sales day book**. The sales day book entries are examples of **transaction records** in a **transactions file**.

A master file in such a system is a file containing **reference data**, such as customer names and addresses, and also **cumulative transaction data** such as 'year to date' sales.

For example, in a payables ledger system, master file data would include:

(a)   **'Standing' reference data** for each supplier (supplier name and address, reference number, amount currently owed etc), and

(b)   **Transaction totals for each supplier** showing purchases, purchase returns and payments.

The terms transaction file and master file are not used much in modern processing, which prefers to talk in terms of **'databases'**.

Files are used to **store** data and information. The main types of data processing operations involving files are file **updating**, file **maintenance** and **file enquiry.**

Both manual and computer data processing can be divided into two broad types: **batch** processing and **real-time** processing.

8.1 Batch processing

Key term

> **Batch processing** involves transactions being **grouped** and **stored** before being processed at regular intervals, such as daily, weekly or monthly. Because data is not input as soon as it is received the system will not always be up-to-date.

For example, **payroll** processing for salaried·staff is usually done in one operation once a month. To help with organising the work, the payroll office might deal with **each department separately**, and do the salaries for department 1, then the salaries for department 2, and then department 3, and so on. If this is the case, then the batch processing would be carried out by dividing the transaction records into smaller batches eg **one batch per department**.

Transactions will be collected up over a period of time, and will then be dealt with together in a batch. Some **delay** in processing the transactions must therefore be acceptable.

Batch input allows for good **control** over the input data, because data can be grouped into **numbered batches**. The batches are dispatched for processing and processed in these batches, and printed output **listings** of the processed transactions are usually organised in **batch order**.

If any records 'go missing' it is possible to locate the batch in which the missing record should belong. Errors in transaction records can be located more quickly by identifying its **batch number**. A check can be made to ensure that every batch of data sent off for processing is eventually received back from processing, so that entire batches of records do not go missing.

The lack of up-to-date information means batch processing is usually not suitable for systems involving customer contact. Batch processing is suitable for internal, regular tasks such as payroll.

Example: batch processing of receivables ledger application

A company operates a computerised receivables ledger using batch processing based on paper records. The main stages of processing are as follows.

Step 1	Sales invoices are hand-written in a numbered invoice book (in triplicate ie three copies per invoice). At the end of the day all invoices are clipped together and a batch control slip is attached. The sales clerk allocates the next unused batch number from the batch control book. He or she enters the batch number on the control slip, together with the total number of documents and the total value of the invoices. These details are also entered in the control book.
Step 2	The batch of invoices is then passed to the accounts department for processing. An accounts clerk records the batch as having been received.
Step 3	The relevant account codes are written on the invoices and control slip. Codes are checked, and the batch is keyed into the computerised receivables ledger system.
Step 4	The clerk reconciles the totals on the batch control slip with the totals for valid and rejected data.
Step 5	The ledger update program is run to post data to the relevant accounts.
Step 6	A report is printed showing the total of invoices posted to the ledger and the clerk reconciles this to the batch totals.
Step 7	All rejected transaction records are carefully investigated and followed up, usually to be amended and then re-input with the next processing run.

8.2 Real-time, on-line processing

Key term

> **Real time, on-line processing** involves transactions being input and processed immediately, in 'real time'.

On-line refers to a machine which is under the **direct control** of the main **central processor** for that system. A terminal is said to be on-line when it communicates with the central processor. PCs have their own processor, so are on-line by definition. (However, the term 'on-line' is increasingly being used to describe an active Internet connection.)

On-line, real time processing is appropriate when immediate processing is required, and the delay implicit in batch processing would not be acceptable.

On-line systems are the **norm** in modern business. **Examples** include the following.

(a) As a sale is made in a department store or a supermarket, the item barcode is scanned on the **point of sale terminal** and the inventory records are updated immediately.

(b) In **banking and credit card** systems whereby customer details are often maintained in a real-time environment. There can be immediate access to customer balances, credit position etc and authorisation for withdrawals (or use of a credit card).

(c) **Travel agents**, **airlines** and **theatre ticket** agencies all use real-time systems. Once a hotel room, plane seat or theatre seat is booked up everybody on the system must know about it immediately so that they do not sell the same holiday or seat to two (or more) different customers.

The workings of both batch and on-line processing methods are shown in the following diagram.

Batch processing and on-line processing

Batch Processing

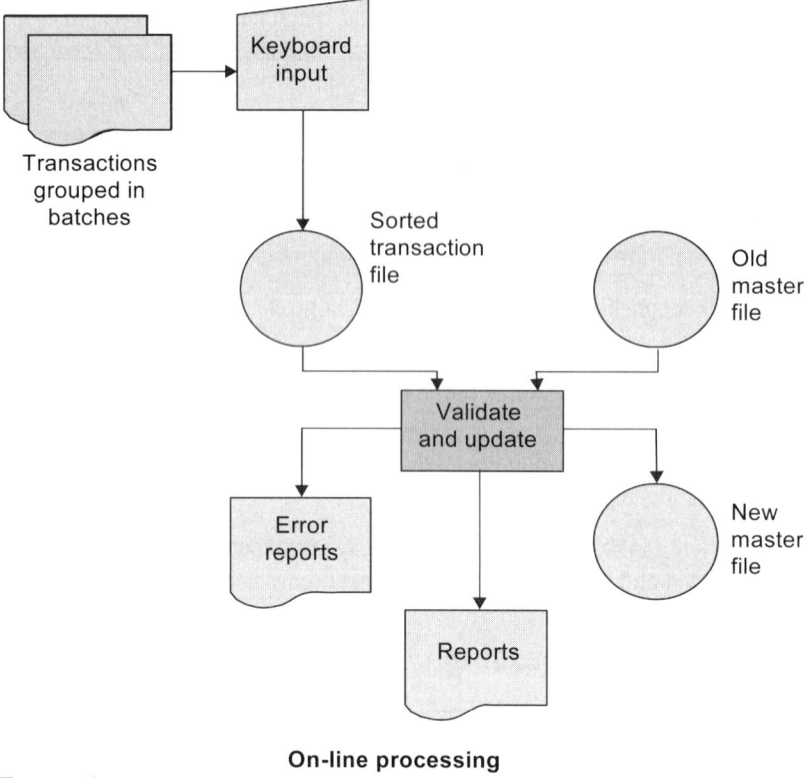

On-line processing

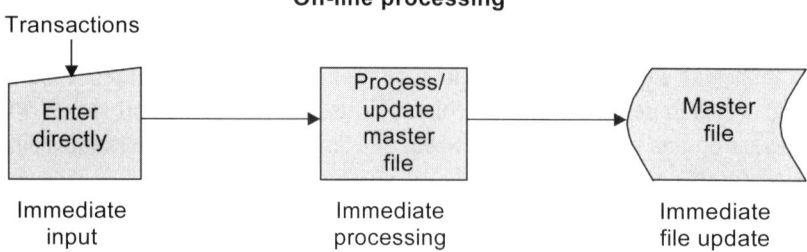

Most modern accounting software packages use real-time processing.

Most computerised ledger systems are fully integrated which means that when one transaction is input on the computer it is recorded in all the relevant accounts and records. For example if a purchase invoice for materials is entered into the computer system an integrated system will automatically make the following entries:

*   Record the purchase in the general ledger accounts
*   Record the invoice in the individual supplier's account in the payables ledger
*   Increase the inventory balance for that type of material in the inventory records

A computerised system can also produce a variety of reports for management including:

*   Inventory records
*   Aged receivables listings
*   Trial balances, income statements and statements of financial position
*   Inventory valuations
*   Payroll analysis

The main advantages of computerised accounting systems are that they are:

*   Quicker than manual systems
*   Generally more accurate, as large numbers of transactions can be processed according to programmed rules
*   Able to provide management with a variety of reports and analyses

Chapter Roundup

- The office in an organisation is a centre for information and administration.

- The most common functions in an office are purchasing, personnel (human resources), general administration, finance and sales and marketing.

- A policy manual should help to ensure that all personnel follow procedures and best practices.

- The main types of transactions that most businesses enter into are sales, purchases, paying expenses, paying employees and purchasing non-current assets.

- In order for management to control the transactions of the business there must be a system of authorisation of transactions in place.

- The basic principle of double entry bookkeeping that for every debit entry there must be a corresponding credit entry.

- Debit entries in ledger accounts are increases in assets or expenses and decreases in liabilities and income.

- Credit entries in ledger accounts are increases in liabilities and income and decreases in assets and expenses.

- Transactions are initially recorded in books of prime entry which are totalled and the totals posted to the ledger accounts.

- An integrated system is one which combines the cost accounting and financial accounting functions in one system of ledger accounts.

- An interlocking system has a cost ledger for the cost accounting function and a financial ledger for the financial accounting function.

- A computerised accounting system will allow much quicker and more accurate entries to the accounting system.

Quick Quiz

1   Which one of the following is a potential disadvantage of centralisation?

    A   Greater control by senior management
    B   Risk reduction in relation to operational decision-making
    C   Local offices are less self sufficient
    D   Consistency of decision-making across the organisation

2   Which one of the following is a potential disadvantage of a policy manual?

    A   It may lead to inflexibility
    B   Personnel follow best practices
    C   Procedures are formalised
    D   It acts as a form of control over activities of employees

3   Which of the following personnel in an organisation would **not** be involved in the sale of goods on credit?

    A   Credit controller
    B   Payables ledger clerk
    C   Sales person
    D   Stores department person

4   What document should normally be completed if a purchase of a non-current asset is required?

    A   A purchase requisition
    B   A despatch note
    C   A goods received note
    D   An invoice

5   What is an accounting equation?

    A   Assets + Liabilities = Capital + profit – drawings
    B   Assets + Liabilities = Capital - profit – drawings
    C   Assets – Liabilities = Capital + profit + drawings
    D   Assets – Liabilities = Capital + profit – drawings

6   What is the double entry for the purchase of materials on credit?

    A   Dr   Materials control   Cr   Payables
    B   Dr   Payables   Cr   Materials control
    C   Dr   Materials control   Cr   Receivables
    D   Dr   Receivables   Cr   Materials control

7   An integrated system combines the cost accounting and financial accounting functions into one system of ledger accounts. Is that true or false?

Answers to Quick Quiz

1   C   Local offices have to rely on head office so are less self-sufficient.

2   A   Although a policy manual is to be recommended, care must be taken that strict adherence to the rules does not create inflexibility and in cases of doubt, a more senior member of staff should be consulted.

3   B   A payables ledger clerk would deal with amounts due to suppliers for purchases and would not usually have any dealings with sales.

4   A   A purchase requisition will need to be completed and as non-current assets are relatively expensive, it will usually have to be authorised by senior management

5   D   Assets – liabilities = Capital + profit – drawings

6   A   Dr   Materials control   Cr   Payables

7   True   This is the definition of an integrated system

Management responsibility and performance measurement

Study guide

1 Introduction

So far we have taken a general look at what management information is, how it is presented and how an accounting system can collect relevant pieces of data and information. We are now going to look at one particular type of management information: measures of management performance.

The managers of a business need to monitor how their particular section of the business is performing; this an important aspect of controlling the activities of the business, but it might also have some bearing on their remuneration.

The performance measures used will depend upon the way in which the business is organised and the type of business, as explained in this chapter.

2 Responsibility centres

FAST FORWARD

> A **responsibility centre** is a function or department of an organisation that is headed by a manager who has direct responsibility for its performance.

Key term

> **Responsibility accounting** is a system of accounting that segregates revenue and costs into areas of personal responsibility in order to monitor and assess the performance of each part of an organisation.

Requirements	Examples of information
What are the manager's resources?	Finance, inventory of raw materials, spare machine capacity, labour availability, the balance of expenditure remaining for a certain budget, target date for completion of a job.
At what rate are the manager's resources being consumed?	How fast is the labour force working, how quickly are the raw materials being used up, how quickly are other expenses being incurred, how quickly is available finance being consumed?
How well are the resources being used?	How well are his objectives being met?

Responsibility centres are usually divided into different categories. Here we shall describe cost centres, profit centres and investment centres.

2.1 Cost centres

FAST FORWARD

> A **cost centre** is any unit of an organisation to which costs can be separately attributed.

A **cost centre** is a production or service location, function, activity or item of equipment for which costs are accumulated.

To collect costs to a cost centre, each cost centre will have a **cost code**. Items of expenditure will be recorded with the appropriate cost code. For example, the equipment maintenance department in a printing factory would be one example of a cost centre. When costs are eventually analysed, there may well be some apportionment of the costs of one cost centre to other cost centres. If this happens:

(a) The costs of those cost centres which receive an apportionment of shared costs should be divided into directly attributable costs (for which the cost centre manager is responsible) and shared costs (for which another cost centre is also directly accountable).

(b) The control system should trace shared costs back to the cost centres from which the costs have been apportioned, so that their managers can be made accountable for the costs incurred.

Information about cost centres might be collected in terms of **total actual costs, total budgeted costs** and **total cost variances** (the differences between actual and budgeted costs). In addition, the information might be analysed in terms of **ratios**, such as the following.

- Cost per unit produced (budget and actual)
- Hours per unit produced (budget and actual)
- Efficiency ratio
- Selling costs per $ of sales (budget and actual)
- Transport costs per tonne/kilometre (budget and actual)

2.2 Profit centres

FAST FORWARD

A **profit centre** is any unit of an organisation to which both revenues and costs are assigned, so that the profitability of the unit may be measured.

Key term

A **profit centre** is part of a business accountable for both costs and revenues.

Profit centre information is needed by managers who are responsible for both revenue and costs. For example, an individual branch of a hairdressing chain would incur costs and generate revenue.

The manager of the profit centre has some influence over both revenues and costs, that is, a say in both sales and production policies.

A profit centre manager is likely to be a fairly senior person within an organisation, and a profit centre is likely to cover quite a large area of operations. A profit centre might be an entire division within the organisation, or there might be a separate profit centre for each product, product range, brand or service that the organisation sells.

In the hierarchy of responsibility centres within an organisation, there are likely to be several cost centres within a profit centre.

2.3 Investment centres

FAST FORWARD

An **investment centre** is a profit centre whose performance is measured by its return on capital employed.

Key term

Investment centres refer to profit centres with additional responsibility for capital investment and possibly for financing, and whose performance is measured by its return on capital employed.

Managers may or may not have the power to make decisions about capital investment – senior management quite often retains control over decisions on high value investments.

Many public sector organisations are required to make a particular level of profit related to their non-current assets (**return on capital**). Some commercial organisations also use investment centres.

Several profit centres might share the same capital items, for example the same buildings, stores or transport fleet, and so investment centres are likely to include several profit centres, and provide a basis for control at a very senior management level.

2.4 Summary

- **Cost centres** collect information on costs
- **Profit centres** collect information on costs, revenues and profits
- **Investment centres** collect information on costs, revenues and profits in relation to the value of non-current assets and working capital

Question

Investment centres

An information system would use investment centres to provide useful information for which of the following.

A   The supervisor of the accounts payable section of the finance department of a large charity.
B   One of three divisional managers for a trading company.
C   The personnel manager of a manufacturing company.
D   A swimming pool manager with authority to buy non-current assets up to $50,000.

Answer

D is the correct answer.

A is a cost centre. This person will have no control over revenue.

B is a profit centre. This person will be responsible for revenue as well as costs for the division. If there were also control over capital expenditure and investment in working capital, investment centres might be used.

C is a cost centre. The personnel department does not earn revenue.

D is the only investment centre. Responsibility will be for costs, revenues and capital expenditure.

3 Performance measures

3.1 Performance measures for cost centres

FAST FORWARD **Performance measurement** aims to establish how well something or somebody is doing in relation to a planned activity.

3.1.1 Productivity

This is the quantity of the product or service produced (**output) in relation to** the resources put in (**input**). For example so many units produced per hour, or per employee, or per tonne of material. It measures **how efficiently resources are being used**.

3.1.2 Cost per unit

FAST FORWARD **Cost per unit** is total costs ÷ number of units produced.

For the manager of a cost centre which is also a production centre one of the most important performance measures will be cost per unit. This is simply the total costs of production divided by the number of units produced in the period.

3.2 Example: cost per unit

The total costs and number of units produced for a production cost centre for the last two months are as follows:

	May	June
Production costs	$128,600	$143,200
Units produced	12,000	13,500
Cost per unit	$\dfrac{\$128,600}{12,000}$	$\dfrac{\$143,200}{13,500}$
	= $10.72	$10.61

3.2.1 Activity

Indices can be used in order to measure activity.

Indices show **how a particular variable has changed relative to a base value**. The base value is usually the level of the variable at an earlier date. The 'variable' may be just one particular item, such as material X, or several items may be incorporated, such as 'raw materials' generally.

In its simplest form an index is calculated as **(current value ÷ base value) × 100%**.

Thus if materials cost $15 per kg in 20X0 and now (20X3) cost $27 per kg the 20X0 value would be expressed in index form as 100 (15/15 × 100) and the 20X3 value as 180 (27/15 × 100). If you find it easier to think of this as a percentage, then do so.

3.3 Example: work standards and indices

Standards for work done in a service department could be expressed as an index. For example, suppose that in a sales department, there is a standard target for sales representatives to make 25 customer visits per month each. The budget for May might be for ten sales representatives to make 250 customer visits in total. Actual results in May might be that nine sales representatives made 234 visits in total. Performance could then be measured as:

Budget	100	(Standard = index 100)
Actual	104	(234 ÷ (9 × 25)) × 100)

This shows that 'productivity' per sales representative was actually 4% over budget.

3.4 Performance measures for profit centres

FAST FORWARD

Ratios and percentages are useful performance measurement techniques.

The **profit margin** (profit to sales ratio) is calculated as (profit ÷ sales) × 100%.

3.4.1 Profit margin

Key term

The **profit margin** (profit to sales ratio) is calculated as (profit ÷ sales) × 100%.

The profit margin provides a simple measure of performance for profit centres. Investigation of unsatisfactory profit margins enables control action to be taken, either by reducing excessive costs or by raising selling prices.

Profit margin is usually calculated using operating profit.

The **operating profit** is the difference between the value of sales (excluding sales tax) and the costs incurred during operations (total operating expenses).

3.5 Example: the profit to sales ratio

A company compares its year 2 results with year 1 results as follows.

	Year 2 $	Year 1 $
Sales	160,000	120,000
Cost of sales		
Direct materials	40,000	20,000
Direct labour	40,000	30,000
Production overhead	22,000	20,000
Marketing overhead	42,000	35,000
	144,000	105,000
Operating profit	16,000	15,000
Profit to sales ratio	$\left(\dfrac{16,000}{160,000}\right) \times 100\%$	10%
	$\left(\dfrac{15,000}{120,000}\right) \times 100\%$	12½%

The above information shows that there is a decline in profitability in spite of the $1,000 increase in profit, because the profit margin is less in year 2 than year 1.

3.6 Gross profit margin

The **gross profit margin** is calculated as gross profit ÷ sales × 100%

Gross profit is the difference between the value of sales (excluding sales tax) and the cost of the goods sold.

The profit to sales ratio above was based on a profit figure which included non-production overheads. The gross profit margin calculates how efficiently a business is using its materials, labour and production overhead in the production process. It is calculated as (gross profit = turnover) ×100%.

For the company in Paragraph 3.5 the gross profit margin would be:

Year 2: $\left(\dfrac{(16,000 + 42,000)}{160,000}\right) \times 100\% = 36.25\%$

Year 1: $\left(\dfrac{(15,000 + 35,000)}{120,000}\right) \times 100\% = 41.67\%$

3.7 Cost/sales ratios

When target profits are not met, further ratios may be used to shed some light on the problem.

- Production cost of sales ÷ sales
- Distribution and marketing costs ÷ sales
- Administrative costs ÷ sales

Subsidiary ratios can be used to examine problem areas in greater depth. For example, for production costs the following ratios might be used.

- Material costs ÷ sales value of production
- Works labour costs ÷ sales value of production
- Production overheads ÷ sales value of production

3.8 Example: cost/sales ratios

Look back to the example in Paragraph 3.5. A more detailed analysis would show that higher direct materials are the probable cause of the decline in profitability.

	Year 2	Year 1
Material costs/sales	$\left(\dfrac{40,000}{160,000}\right) \times 100\%$	25%
	$\left(\dfrac{20,000}{120,000}\right) \times 100\%$	16.7%

Other cost/sales ratios have remained the same or improved.

Question   Profit margins

Use the following summary income statement to answer the questions below

	$
Sales	3,000
Cost of sales	1,800
	1,200
Manufacturing expenses	300
Administrative expenses	200
Operating profit	700

1   The profit margin is

    A   60%
    B   40%
    C   30%
    D   23%

2   The gross profit margin is

    A   60%
    B   40%
    C   30%
    D   23%

Answer

1   D $\dfrac{700}{3,000} \times 100\% = 23\%$

    The profit margin usually refers to operating profit / sales.

2   B $\dfrac{1,200}{3,000} \times 100\% = 40\%$

    The gross profit margin takes the gross profit/sales.

3.8.1 Resources

Traditional measures for materials compare actual costs with expected costs, looking at differences (or variances) in price and usage. Many traditional systems also analyse **wastage**. Measures used in **modern manufacturing environments** include the number of **rejects** in materials supplied, and the **timing and reliability of deliveries** of materials.

Labour costs are traditionally measured by comparing actual costs with expected costs, looking at rate and efficiency **variances**.

Qualitative measures of labour performance concentrate on matters such as **ability to communicate, interpersonal relationships** with colleagues, **customers' impressions** and **levels of skills** attained.

Managers can expect to be judged to some extent by the performance of their staff. High profitability or tight cost control are not the only indicators of managerial performance!

For variable overheads, differences between actual and budgeted costs (ie variances) are traditional measures. Various time based measures are also available, such as:

(a) **Machine down time: total machine hours**. This ratio provides a measure of machine usage and efficiency.

(b) **Value added time: production cycle time**. Value added time is the direct production time during which the product is being made. The production cycle time includes non-value-added times such as set-up time, downtime, idle time and so on. The 'perfect' ratio is 100%, but in practice this optimum will not be achieved. A high ratio means non-value-added activities are being kept to a minimum.

3.8.2 Measures of performance using the standard hour

FAST FORWARD

> Performance measures for **materials** and **labour** include differences between actual and expected (budgeted) performance. Performance can also be measured using the **standard hour**.

Sam Ltd manufactures plates, mugs and eggcups. Production during the first two quarters of 20X5 was as follows.

	Quarter 1	Quarter 2
Plates	1,000	800
Mugs	1,200	1,500
Eggcups	800	900

The fact that 3,000 products were produced in quarter 1 and 3,200 in quarter 2 does not tell us anything about Sam Ltd's performance over the two periods because plates, mugs and eggcups are so different. The fact that the production mix has changed is not revealed by considering the total number of units produced. The problem of how to **measure output when a number of dissimilar products are manufactured** can be overcome, however, by the **use of the standard hour**.

The standard hour (or standard minute) is the **quantity of work achievable at standard performance, expressed in terms of a standard unit of work done in a standard period of time.**

The standard time allowed to produce one unit of each of Sam Ltd's products is as follows.

	Standard time
Plate	$\frac{1}{2}$ hour
Mug	$\frac{1}{3}$ hour
Eggcup	$\frac{1}{4}$ hour

By measuring the standard hours of output in each quarter, a more useful output measure is obtained.

Product	Standard hours per unit	Quarter 1 Production	Quarter 2 Standard hours	Production	Standard hours
Plate	1/2	1,000	500	800	400
Mug	1/3	1,200	400	1,500	500
Eggcup	1/4	800	200	900	225
			1,100		1,125

The output level in the two quarters was therefore very similar.

3.9 Efficiency, capacity utilisation and production volume

Standard hours are useful in computing levels of **efficiency, capacity and production (or activity) volume**. Any management accounting reports involving budgets and variance analysis should incorporate control ratios. The three main control ratios are the **efficiency**, **capacity** and **production volume** ratios.

(a)   The efficiency ratio measures the efficiency of the labour force by comparing equivalent standard hours for work produced and actual hours worked.

(b)   The capacity utilisation ratio compares actual hours worked and budgeted hours, and measures the extent to which planned utilisation has been achieved.

(c)   The production volume ratio compares the number of standard hours equivalent to the actual work produced and budgeted hours.

3.10 Example: ratios and standard hours

Given the following information about Sam Ltd for quarter 1 of 20X5, calculate an efficiency ratio, capacity utilisation ratio and a production volume ratio and explain their meaning.

Budgeted hours	1,100 standard hours
Standard hours produced	1,125 standard hours
Actual hours worked	1,200

Solution

$$\text{Efficiency ratio} = \frac{\text{Standard hours produced}}{\text{Actual hours worked}} \times 100\% = \frac{1,125}{1,200} \times 100\% = 93.8\%$$

The labour force worked 6.2% below standard levels of efficiency (as 93.8 is 100-6.2)

$$\text{Capacity utilisation ratio} = \frac{\text{Actual hours worked}}{\text{Budgeted hours}} \times 100\% = \frac{1,200}{1,100} \times 100\% = 109.1\%$$

$$\text{Production volume ratio} = \frac{\text{Standard hours produced}}{\text{Budgeted hours}} \times 100\% = \frac{1,125}{1,100} \times 100\% = 102.3\%$$

These ratios show that a 9.1% increase in capacity resulted in a 2.3% increase in production.

The capacity ratio multiplied by the efficiency ratio gives us the activity or production volume ratio: 109.1% × 93.8% = 102.3%

Question   Ratios

If   X = Actual hours worked
       Y = Budgeted hours
       Z = Standard hours produced

What is $\frac{Z}{Y}$?

A   Capacity ratio
B   Production volume ratio
C   Efficiency ratio
D   Standard hours produced ratio

Answer

B

3.11 Performance measures for investment centres

Return on capital employed (ROCE) or **return on investment (ROI))** shows how much profit has been made in relation to the amount of resources invested.

3.11.1 Return on capital employed (ROCE)

Key term

Return on capital employed (ROCE) (also called **Return on investment (ROI)**) is calculated as (profit/capital employed) × 100% and shows how much profit has been made in relation to the amount of resources invested.

ROCE is generally used for measuring the performance of investment centres; profits alone do not show whether the return is sufficient when different values of assets are used. Thus if company A and company B have the following results, company B would have the better performance.

	A	B
	$	$
Profit	5,000	5,000
Sales	100,000	100,000
Capital employed	50,000	25,000
ROCE	10%	20%

The profit of each company is the same but company B only invested $25,000 to achieve that profit whereas company A invested $50,000.

ROCE may be calculated in a number of ways, but **profit before interest and tax** (that is, net profit) is usually used.

Similarly **all assets of a non-operational nature** (for example trade investments and intangible assets such as goodwill) **should be excluded** from capital employed.

Profits should be related to average capital employed. In practice many companies calculate the ratio **using year-end assets**. This can be misleading. If a new investment is undertaken near to the year end, the capital employed will rise but profits will only have a month or two of the new investment's contribution.

What does the ROCE tell us? What should we be looking for? There are **two principal comparisons** that can be made.

*   The change in ROCE from one year to the next
*   The ROCE being earned by other entities

3.12 Residual income (RI)

Residual income (RI) is an alternative way of measuring the performance of an investment centre. It is a measure of the centre's profits after deducting a notional or imputed interest cost.

An alternative way of measuring the performance of an investment centre, instead of using ROCE, is residual income (RI). **Residual income** is a **measure of the centre's profits after deducting a notional or imputed interest cost** (calculated on the whole of the capital employed - **not** just on borrowed funds).

Key term

Residual income (RI) is pretax profits less a notional interest charge for invested capital.

Question

A division with capital employed of $400,000 currently earns a ROCE of 22%. It can make an additional investment of $50,000 for a 5 year life with nil residual value. The average net profit from this investment would be $12,000. A notional interest charge amounting to 14% of the amount invested is to be charged to the division each year.

The residual income of the division after the investment, will be

A $5,000
B $32,000
C $37,000
D $39,000

Answer

	$
Divisional profit after investment ((400,000 × 22%) + 12,000))	100,000
Notional interest (450,000 × 0.14)	(63,000)
Residual income	37,000

3.13 Asset turnover

FAST FORWARD ▶ Asset turnover measures how efficiently the assets of the business are being used.

Key term

Asset turnover is a measure of how well the assets of a business are being used to generate sales. It is calculated as (sales ÷ capital employed).

Suppose that two companies both have capital employed of $100,000. However Company A has sales revenue for the year of $150,000 and Company B has sales revenue for the year of $250,000. The asset turnover figure shows how much revenue is being earned for every $1 of capital employed:

$$\text{Company A} = \frac{\$150,000}{\$100,000} = 1.5$$

$$\text{Company B} = \frac{\$250,000}{\$100,000} = 2.5$$

This shows that Company B is earning $2.50 of sales revenue for every $1 invested compared to only $1.50 of sales revenue for Company A.

Note that the asset turnover figure is an absolute figure and not a percentage.

Asset turnover is an important figure in its own right as it shows how efficiently the assets or capital of the business is being used to create sales revenue. However, it is also important as it is one of the elements that make up return on capital employed.

Return on capital employed = Asset turnover × Net profit margin

$$\frac{\text{Net profit}}{\text{Capital employed}} = \frac{\text{Sales revenue}}{\text{Capital employed}} \times \frac{\text{Net profit}}{\text{Sales revenue}}$$

3.14 Example: return on capital employed, asset turnover and net profit margin

A company has the following figures:

	$
Sales revenue	540,000
Net profit	50,000
Capital employed	300,000

$$\text{Return on capital employed} = \frac{\$50,000}{\$300,000} \times 100 = 16.67\%$$

$$\text{Asset turnover} = \frac{\$540,000}{\$300,000} = 1.8$$

$$\text{Net profit margin} = \frac{\$50,000}{\$540,000} \times 100 = 9.26\%$$

Return on capital employed	= Asset turnover	×	Net profit margin
16.67%	= 1.8	×	9.26%

This is an important relationship as it means that any changes in return on capital employed can be accounted for by changes in the profitability measured by net profit margin and in the efficiency of the use of the net assets measured by asset turnover.

Exam focus point

One or more questions on any of these performance measures is likely in this exam.

Chapter Roundup

- A **responsibility centre** is a function or department of an organisation that is headed by a manager who has direct responsibility for its performance.

- A **cost centre** is any unit of an organisation to which costs can be separately attributed.

- A **profit centre** is any unit of an organisation to which both revenues and costs are assigned, so that the profitability of the unit may be measured.

- An **investment centre** is a profit centre whose performance is measured by its return on capital employed.

- **Performance measurement** aims to establish how well something or somebody is doing in relation to a planned activity.

- **Ratios** and **percentages** are useful performance measurement techniques.

- **Cost per unit** is total costs ÷ number of units produced.

- The **profit margin** (profit to sales ratio) is calculated as (profit ÷ sales) × 100%.

- **Return on capital employed (ROCE)** or **return on investment (ROI)** shows how much profit has been made in relation to the amount of resources invested.

- **Residual income (RI)** is an alternative way of measuring the performance of an investment centre. It is a measure of the centre's profits after deducting a notional or imputed interest cost.

- Asset turnover measures how efficiently the assets of the business are being used.

- Performance measures for **materials** and **labour** include differences between actual and expected (budgeted) performance. Performance can also be measured using the **standard hour**.

- The **gross profit margin** is calculated as gross profit ÷ sales × 100%

1   A function or department of an organisation that is headed by a manager who has direct responsibility for its performance is called:

    A   A profit centre

    B   An investment centre

    C   A cost centre

    D   A responsibility centre

2   What is the main aim of performance measurement?

    A   To obtain evidence in order to dismiss someone

    B   To establish how well something or somebody is doing in relation to a planned activity

    C   To collect information on costs

    D   To award bonuses

3   Quantitative measures are expressed in numbers whereas qualitative measure are not. Is this true or false?

4   Place the correct letters in the boxes.

$$\text{ROCE} = \frac{\boxed{}}{\boxed{}} \times 100\% \qquad\qquad \text{Profit margin} = \frac{\boxed{}}{\boxed{}} \times 100\%$$

    A   Profit

    B   Profit

    C   Capital employed

    D   Sales

5   Which one of the following is the correct formula for asset turnover?

    A   Sales ÷ capital employed

    B   Net profit ÷ sales

    C   Capital employed ÷ sales

    D   Sales ÷ net profit

Answers to Quick Quiz

1   D   This is the definition of a responsibility centre.

2   B   Note that the question said 'the **main** aim'. Performance measurement may well be used to decide on bonus levels but this is not the main aim.

3   True   This is how quantitative and qualitative performance measures differ.

4   $\text{ROCE} = \dfrac{A}{C} \times 100\%$ $\text{Profit margin} = \dfrac{B}{D} \times 100\%$

5   A   Asset turnover = sales ÷ capital employed. Net profit margin = net profit ÷ sales revenue

Cost units, cost classification and profit reporting

Study guide

			Syllabus reference
7	(a)	Explain and illustrate the concept of cost units.	4(d)
	(b)	Describe the variety of cost classifications used for different purposes in a cost accounting system, including by responsibility, function, behaviour, direct/indirect.	4(d)
	(c)	Describe and illustrate the nature of variable, fixed and mixed (semi-variable, stepped-fixed) costs.	4(d)
	(d)	Describe and illustrate the classification of material and labour costs.	4(d)
	(e)	Prepare and explain the nature and purpose of profit statements in absorption and marginal costing formats.	4(d)
	(f)	Calculate the cost of a product or service.	4(d)

1 Introduction

Let us suppose that in your hand you have a red biro which you bought in the newsagent's down the road for 50c. Why does the newsagent charge 50c for it? In other words what does that 50c represent?

From the newsagent's point of view the cost can be split into two.

Price paid by newsagent to wholesaler	Z
Newsagent's 'mark-up'	Y
	50 c

If the newsagent did not charge more for the biro than he paid for it (Y) there would be no point in him selling it. The mark-up itself can be split into further categories.

Pure profit	X
Amount paid to shop assistants	X
Expenses of owning and operating a shop (rent, electricity, cleaning and so on)	X
	Y

The newsagent's **profit** is the amount he personally needs to live: it is like your salary. Different newsagents have different ideas about this: this is why you might pay 60c for an identical biro if you went into another newsagent's. The shop expenses are amounts that have to be paid, whether or not the newsagent sells you a biro, simply to keep the shop going. Again, if other newsagents have to pay higher rent than our newsagent, this might be reflected in the price of biros.

The amount paid to the wholesaler can be split in a similar way: there will be a profit element and amounts to cover the costs of running a wholesaling business. There might also be a cost for getting the biro from the wholesaler's premises to the shop and, of course, there will be the amount paid to the manufacturer.

In this chapter we will look in more detail at the type of costs that are incurred in the manufacture of goods, such as the biro in the example above, including different ways of classifying those costs.

2 Cost units

 **FAST FORWARD**

A **cost unit** is a unit of product which has costs attached to it.

2.1 Cost units

Key term

A **cost unit** is a unit of product or service to which costs can be related.

One factor that may cause things to become slightly more complicated is that a cost unit is not always a single item. It might be a batch of 1,000 if that is how the individual items are made. In fact, a cost per 1,000 (or whatever) is often more meaningful information.

Examples of cost units include the following.

- Room (in a hotel)
- Value of a construction contract
- Batch of 1,000 shoes
- Patient night (the cost of a patient staying in a hospital for a night)

A possible cost unit for a hospital might be 'cost per patient'. This however, is not particularly useful for control purposes as different patients will spend different amounts of time in hospital. The patient per night cost unit is much more useful. Notice that this is made up of **two parts**, the patient and the night. These two-part cost units are known as **composite cost units** and they are used most often in service organisations.

FAST FORWARD

Cost information is needed to aid price setting, decision making, planning and budgeting,   control and reporting.

Managers need to know what resources are used and what costs are incurred in the production of a cost unit. This information may be used in a number of ways – such as the situations described below.

(a)   **Setting a selling price** that covers the cost of manufacture and makes a profit.
(b)   **Decision-making**. For example, whether to sell product A or B, which will depend upon how much profit each product makes, for which we need to know the cost.
(c)   **Planning and budgeting** future activities relies on knowing production quantities and costs so that we know what resources we will need, how much this will cost and whether we can afford it.
(d)   **Control** of resources and costs of production is possible if we know what the quantities and costs ought to be. If costs are higher, or if more time is needed to make the cost units than was expected, then this would need investigation so that any problems can be ironed out.
(d)   **Reporting** the results of the business relies on knowing the costs incurred and the value of inventory of the manufactured goods.

2.2 Production costs

Look at your biro (pen) and consider what it consists of. There is probably a red plastic cap and a little red thing that fits into the end, and perhaps a yellow plastic sheath. There is an opaque plastic ink holder with red ink inside it. At the tip there is a gold plastic part holding a metal nib with a roller ball.

Let us suppose that the manufacturer sells biros to wholesalers for 20c each. How much does the little ball cost? What share of the 20c is taken up by the little red thing in the end of the biro? How much did somebody earn for putting it there?

To elaborate still further, the manufacturer probably has machines to mould the plastic and do some of the assembly. How much does it cost, per biro, to run the machines: to set them up so that they produce the right shape of moulded plastic? How much are the production line workers' wages per biro?

Any of these separate production costs could be calculated and recorded on a unit cost card which records how the total cost of a unit (in this instance, a biro) is arrived at.

A unit cost card is shown on the following page.

BIRO – UNIT COST CARD		
Direct materials	$	$
Yellow plastic	X	
Red plastic	X	
Opaque plastic	X	
Gold plastic	X	
Ink	X	
Metal	X̲	
		X
Direct labour		
Machine operators' wages	X	
Manual assembly staff wages	X̲	
		X
		X
Direct expenses		X
Total direct cost (or prime cost)		X
Overheads (production)		X
Production cost (or factory cost)		X
Overheads (administration, distribution and selling)		X̲
Total cost		X̲

3 Direct and indirect costs

 **FAST FORWARD**

Costs can be divided into three elements, **materials, labour** and **expenses.**

The cost card above separates out the three main elements of the cost unit.

- Materials
- Labour
- Expenses

For manufacturers it is useful to further subdivide costs into direct and indirect costs.

FAST FORWARD

Costs can be classified as **direct** or **indirect**.

Key term

> **Direct costs** can be traced specifically to a cost unit.

- **Direct materials** – which form part of the end product
- **Direct labour** – involved directly in making the product
- **Direct expenses** – it is rare for expenses to be directly traceable to the product

The factory will also have **indirect costs** or **factory overheads** which are not directly traceable to the product but are still part of the cost of making it.

- **Indirect materials** – such as lubricants for machinery
- **Indirect labour** – such as supervisors and maintenance workers
- **Indirect expenses** – such as heating and lighting for the factory

There are also **non-manufacturing overheads** in a manufacturing business. These are not included in the production cost of goods or for inventory valuation purposes. An appropriate portion of these overheads is sometimes included on the cost card so that an appropriate price can be set.

Examples include

- The accountant's salary (a non-manufacturing labour cost)
- The office rates (non-manufacturing expenses)

Question

Canine Ltd makes dog leads. It buys in leather, thread and metal clips to make them, employs people to operate stitching machines and assemble the finished leads and has various running costs (overheads) for the rented factory space it uses.

Which of the following activities would be classified as indirect labour?

A   Dog lead clip
B   Factory rent
C   Wages for machine operator
D   Wages for factory manager

Answer

D   The factory manager's wages are a production cost, but are not directly traceable to each cost unit. The wages are therefore classified as indirect labour. A is direct materials, B is an indirect expense and C is direct labour.

Exam focus point

An exam question might well ask you to classify a cost as direct or indirect or determine which costs are direct or indirect.

4 Cost behaviour

FAST FORWARD

Cost behaviour patterns demonstrate the way in which costs are affected by changes in the level of activity.

Instead of categorising materials, labour and expenses costs into direct and indirect costs, it can sometimes be very useful to use a different system, one that is based on cost behaviour.

Key term

Cost behaviour is the way that costs change as the level of activity changes.

4.1 Level of activity

Key term

The **level of activity** refers to the amount of work done, or the volume of production.

The basic principle of cost behaviour is that **as the level of activity rises, costs will usually rise**. It will cost more to produce 2,000 units of output than it will cost to produce 1,000 units; it will usually cost more to make five telephone calls than to make one call and so on. However, this system identifies several types of cost which respond differently to a change in activity level.

4.2 Fixed costs

A fixed cost is a cost which tends to be unaffected by increases or decreases in the volume of output. Fixed costs are a period charge, in that they relate to a span of time; as the time span increases, so too will the fixed costs (which are sometimes referred to as period costs for this reason).

A sketch graph of a fixed cost would look like this.

Graph of fixed cost

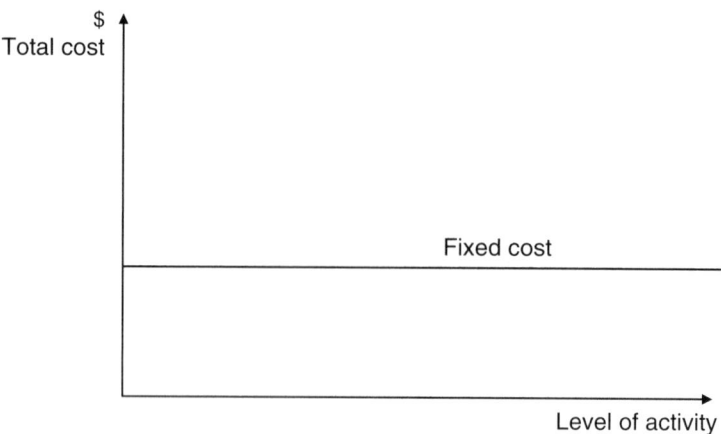

The following are fixed costs.

(a) The salary of the managing director (per month or per annum)
(b) The rent of a single factory building (per month or per annum)
(c) Straight line depreciation of a single machine (per month or per annum)

Because the total fixed costs remain the same for all levels of activity, if you calculate the fixed cost per unit, this will decrease as more units are produced.

Graph of fixed cost per unit

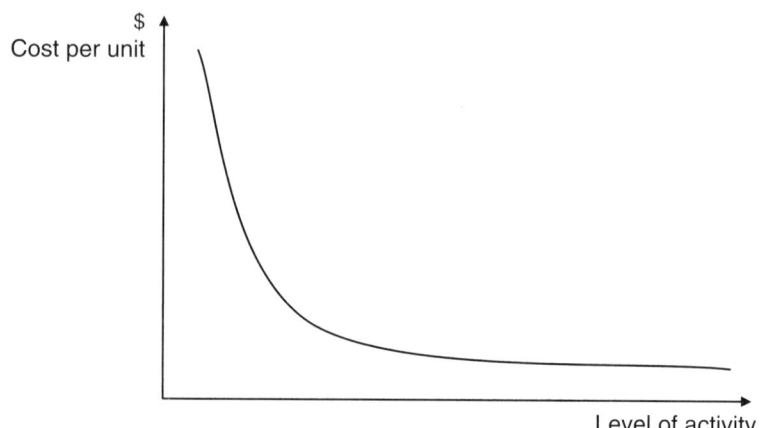

4.3 Stepped-fixed costs

Stepped-fixed costs are costs which are fixed in nature within certain levels of activity.

Many items of cost are a fixed cost in nature within certain levels of activity. For example the depreciation of a machine may be fixed if production remains below 1,000 units per month, but if production exceeds 1,000 units, a second machine may be required, and the cost of depreciation (on two machines) would go up a step. A sketch graph of a stepped-fixed cost would look like this.

Graph of stepped-fixed cost

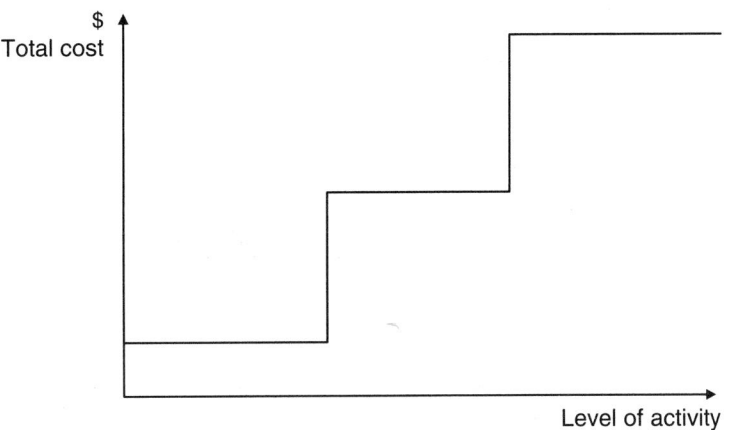

Other examples of step costs are as follows.

(a) **Rent**, where accommodation requirements increase as output levels get higher.

(b) **Basic wages**. Basic pay of employees is nowadays usually fixed, but as output rises, more employees (direct workers, supervisors, managers etc) are required.

4.4 Variable costs

A variable cost is a cost which tends to vary directly with the volume of output. The variable cost per unit is the same amount for each unit produced whereas *total* variable cost increases as volume of output increases. A sketch graph of a variable cost would look like this.

Graph of variable cost

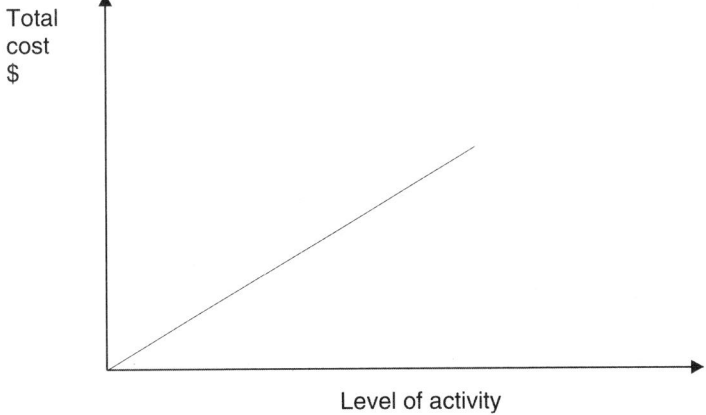

The cost will be the same for each unit produced giving the following graph for variable cost per unit.

Graph of variable cost per unit

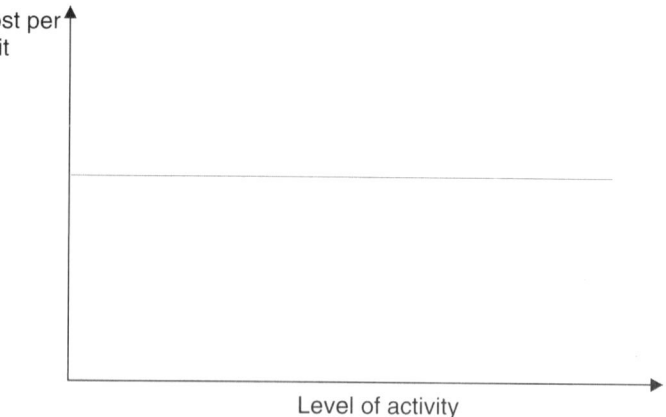

A constant variable cost per unit implies that the purchase price per unit of material purchased or cost per labour hour worked and so on is constant, and that the rate of material usage/labour productivity is also constant. In other words, **constant rate and efficiency levels are implied in variable costs.**

(a)   The most important variable cost is the cost of raw materials (where there is no discount for bulk purchasing. Bulk purchase discounts reduce the cost of purchases).

(b)   Direct labour costs are, for very important reasons, classed as a variable cost even though basic wages are usually fixed.

(c)   Sales commission is variable in relation to the volume or value of sales.

At this point it is important to stress that variable cost is *not* just another name for a direct cost. The distinctions that can be made are as follows.

(a)   **Costs are either variable or fixed, depending upon whether they change when the volume of production changes.**

(b)   **Costs are either direct or indirect, depending upon how easily they can be traced to a specific unit of production.**

4.5 Mixed costs (or semi-variable costs or semi-fixed costs)

FAST FORWARD

Mixed costs (semi-variable/semi-fixed costs) are partly fixed and partly variable, and therefore only partly affected by changes in activity levels.

These are cost items which are **part fixed** and **part variable**, and are therefore partly affected by changes in the level of activity.

Graph of semi-variable cost

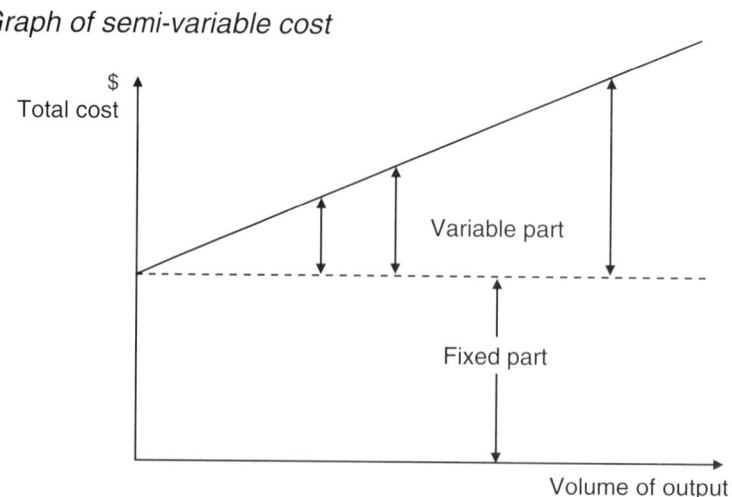

Examples of these costs include electricity and gas bills, both of which are costs where there is normally a standing basic charge plus a variable charge per unit of consumption.

Question

Are each of the following likely to be variable or fixed costs?

(a) Charges for telephone calls made
(b) Charges for rental of telephone
(c) Annual salary of the chief accountant
(d) Managing director's subscription to the Institute of Directors
(e) Cost of materials used to pack 20 units of product X into a box

Answer

(a) Variable
(b) Fixed
(c) Fixed
(d) Fixed
(e) Variable

Exam focus point

The graphs of these cost behaviours are important as a question might give you a graph and ask you to decide which cost behaviour is depicted.

5 Functional costs

FAST FORWARD

Costs can also be analysed according to their **function**. For example, production, distribution and selling, administration and financing costs.

When we talk about functional costs we are not talking about a different **type** of cost from those we have met already, but about a way of grouping costs together according to what aspects of an organisation's operations (what **function**) cause them to be incurred.

A convenient set of functions is the following.

(a) **Production costs**. Materials and labour used and expenses incurred to make things and get them ready for sale.
(b) **Distribution and selling costs**. Costs incurred both to get the finished items to the point where people can buy them and to persuade people to buy them.
(c) **Administration costs**. This is a vague term. You might like to think of these costs as the materials and labour used and the expenses incurred in co-ordinating the activities of the production function and the distribution and selling function.
(d) **Financing costs**. The expenses incurred when a business has to borrow to purchase non-current assets, say, or simply to operate on a day to day basis.

These divisions are not the only ones that could be made, nor are there rigid definitions of what is a production cost, what is an administration cost and so on.

6 Calculating the cost of a product or service

FAST FORWARD

The cost of a product or service can be built up on a **cost card**, which identifies
- Direct costs
- Prime cost
- Production overheads
- Production costs
- Non-production overheads
- Total cost

Returning to the cost card at the start of the chapter, you should now be in a position to understand all the different types of cost referred to. Our next step is to build a cost card up for ourselves.

In practice, this means measuring the amount of materials used and the time taken to perform the tasks. These quantities can then be costed from the cost bookkeeping records.

For overheads, or indirect costs, it is more difficult to ascertain the exact amount that relates to each cost unit, so a method has to be found of sharing out the cost over the cost units made.

In later chapters we will cover how these costs are recorded and calculated in more detail, but for now we will concentrate on producing a cost card and understanding the types of costs involved.

6.1 Example: calculating the cost of a product

Skeggy Limited makes 20,000 Braces per year. Each Brace requires ½ hour of labour at $5 per hour and 3 bought-in components, costing $1.25, $2 and 40c each respectively. The packaging for the Brace costs $16 for 100 boxes. The business incurs fixed production costs of $4,000 per annum, and the cost of selling, administration and distribution works out at 50c per item sold. Calculate the production cost and the total cost of a Brace and record this information on a cost card.

Firstly, it is necessary to decide which costs fall into the different categories that you would use on a cost card.

- Direct materials – components
- Direct labour – labour
- Production overheads – fixed production costs
- Non-production overheads – selling, administration and distribution costs

Then, the amount of each cost per unit of product can be calculated and slotted in to the cost card.

Brace – Unit cost card		$
Direct materials	– components(1.25 +2.00+0.40)	3.65
	– box ($16/100)	0.16
Direct labour (1/2 h @ $5 per h)		2.50
Prime cost		6.31
Production overheads	($4,000 / 20,000 units)	0.20
Production cost		6.51
Non-manufacturing overheads		0.50
Total cost		7.01

Service organisations are those which offer services, for example

- Professional services: accountants and solicitors
- Personal services: hairdressers
- Repairs and maintenance: plumbers and garages.

They will need to cost their cost units in a similar way. A garage will need to cost a standard vehicle service, a hairdresser will cost a cut and blow dry and an accountant will cost an audit and tax service for a particular type of client. In service organisations, the major cost tends to be labour.

Question

Prime cost

A service for a sports car requires 3 hours of a skilled mechanic's time followed by ½ hour of unskilled labour. Rates of pay are

(a)   Skilled: $9 per hour
(b)   Unskilled: $5 per hour

Oil, oil filter, screen wash and spark plugs cost $6.90 in total. Rent and rates for the industrial unit from which the service centre operates, work out at $4 per hour. Administration costs are $2 per service.

The prime cost of the service is

A $29.50
B $36.40
C $50.40
D $52.40

Answer B. Prime cost is the total direct cost. A is the material cost only, C is the service cost and D is the total cost, as shown in the cost card below.

Sports car service cost card

			$
Direct materials			6.90
Direct labour	– skilled	(3h @ $9 per h)	27.00
	– unskilled	(½h @ $5 per h)	2.50
Prime cost			36.40
Production overheads		(3½h @ $4)	14.00
Service cost			50.40
Non-manufacturing overheads			2.00
Total cost			52.40

(Note that the production overheads were shared amongst service jobs on the basis of time taken)

7 Profit reporting

FAST FORWARD

Absorption costing and **marginal costing** are different ways of accounting for costs. If there are changes in inventory levels during a period, marginal costing and absorption costing give different profit figures.

Earlier on, we mentioned that an important reason for finding the cost of cost units produced was so that we could report the profit made and value any closing inventory. For management accounting purposes there are two ways of doing this, which differ in their treatment of fixed costs.

- **Absorption costing**: the cost of the product is the variable production cost plus the fixed production cost.

- **Marginal costing**: the cost of the product is the variable production cost only. Fixed production costs are treated as a period cost rather than a product cost, and are charged to the income statement in full in the period in which they are incurred.

This will lead to different inventory values, and to a different reported profit if inventory quantities rise or fall over the period in question.

Question

Production costs

Which of the following costs is not included as a production cost in marginal costing?

A Direct labour
B Direct materials
C Variable overheads
D Fixed overheads

Answer

Answer D

Direct labour, direct materials and variable overheads are all variable costs and are included as a production cost in marginal costing, so A, B and C are incorrect. Fixed overheads are not a production cost in marginal costing; they are treated as a period cost.

7.1 Example: absorption costing and marginal costing

Robbers Limited makes one product, the Cop. At 1 June, there are 40 Cops in inventories held. Each Cop requires 2 hours of labour and 1kg of raw material. Labour is paid $8 per hour, and raw material costs $12 per kg. Robbers Limited incurs fixed production overheads of $2,000 per month and the factory produces 1,000 Cops each month.

A Cop sells for $35. Sales in June were 1,000 Cops, but in July, sales fell to 900 Cops.

7.2 Absorption costing

The absorption cost of a Cop can be found by drawing-up a unit cost card. The variable costs are found by multiplying the quantity used by the cost. The fixed production cost is spread over the units produced.

Cop – unit cost card (absorption costing)	$
Variable production costs	
Direct material 1kg @ $12 per kg	12.00
Direct labour 2h @ $8 per hour	16.00
Total variable cost	28.00
Fixed production overheads $2,000/1,000	2.00
Total production cost	30.00

A profit statement can now be produced for June and July, using these costs.

	June		July	
	$	$	$	$
Sales		35,000		31,500
Opening inventory (40 × $30)	1,200		1,200	
Production (1,000 × $30)	30,000		30,000	
	31,200		31,200	
Less: closing inventory (40 × $30)	1,200	(140 × $30)	4,200	
Cost of sales		30,000		27,000
Gross Profit		5,000		4,500

Let's now compare these figures with those generated by marginal costing.

7.3 Marginal costing

Cop – unit cost card (marginal costing)	$
Variable production costs	
Direct material 1kg @ $12 per kg	12.00
Direct labour 2h @ $8 per hour	16.00
Total variable cost or marginal cost	28.00

The marginal costing profit statement is a little different. Firstly, the fixed overheads are not included in the product cost, but are brought in to the income statement in full. Secondly, a new sub-heading is needed in marginal costing: **contribution.**

Key term

Contribution is sales less variable, or marginal, costs.

This term can also be used in relation to an individual unit; in this case contribution is the selling price less the variable cost per unit. The term contribution is short for 'contribution towards covering fixed costs and making a profit'.

	June		July	
	$	$	$	$
Sales		35,000		31,500
Opening inventory (40 × $28)	1,120		1,120	
Production (1,000 × $28)	28,000		28,000	
	29,120		29,120	
Less: closing inventory (June 40 × $28; July 140 × $28)	1,120		3,920	
Variable cost of sales		28,000		25,200
Contribution		7,000		6,300
Less: fixed overheads		2,000		2,000
Profit		5,000		4,300

Note: In this example there are no variable non-production costs such as sales and distribution but be aware that contribution is sales less all variable costs (production and non-production).

In June, the absorption costing profit was the same as the marginal costing profit: $5,000. This is because the production quantity was 1,000 units, and the quantity sold was the same, 1,000 units. Therefore, both absorption costing and marginal costing will have charged $2,000 of fixed production overheads against profit.

In July, however, production was 1,000 units but only 900 units were sold; inventory increased by the 100 unsold units, rising from 40 to 140 units. In marginal costing this made no difference to the fixed overheads charged: the full $2,000 was still charged in this period. But under absorption costing, each unit of inventory produced in the period that was still held at the end of the period will include $2 of the fixed overheads incurred in the period. This part of the fixed overheads will be carried forward in the value of closing inventory and charged against profit in a future period.

So, under absorption costing 100 units of inventory will carry $200 of fixed overheads out of this profit statement, which accounts for the $200 additional absorption costing profit compared with the marginal costing profit. Of course, when the inventory is sold, this will 'release' the fixed overheads to be charged against the marginal costing profit. So, in a future period the profit related to these 100 units of inventory will be $200 less under absorption costing than under marginal costing.

Question

Marginal profit vs absorption profit

Which of the following statements is true?

A   In the long term, there will be no difference between marginal costing profits and absorption costing profits

B   Marginal costing profits are always greater than absorption costing profits

C   Absorption costing profits are always greater than marginal costing profits

D   Differences between marginal costing profits and absorption costing profits always reverse in the following period

Answer

Answer A

In general, as inventory levels rise and fall, any differences will tend to reverse. This does not necessarily happen in the following period, so D is incorrect. B and C are incorrect as any differences depend on whether inventory levels are rising or falling.

7.4 Marginal costing and absorption costing compared

Marginal costing and absorption costing are different.

(a) In marginal costing

 (i) Closing inventory is valued at marginal production cost.

 (ii) Fixed costs are charged in full against the profit of the period in which they are incurred.

(b) **In absorption costing** (sometimes referred to as **full costing**):

 (i) Closing inventory is valued at full production cost including a share of fixed production costs.

 (ii) The effect of this is that under absorption costing the cost of sales in a period will include some fixed overhead incurred in a previous period (in opening inventory values). The cost of sales will also exclude some fixed overhead incurred in the current period as this is carried forward in closing inventory values to be charged to a subsequent accounting period.

The difference between the two methods is shown in the following example.

7.5 Example: marginal and absorption costing compared

Two Left Feet Ltd manufactures a single product, the Claud. The following figures relate to the Claud for a one-year period.

	50%	100%
Activity level		
Sales and productions (units)	400	800
	$	$
Sales	8,000	16,000
Production costs:		
variable	3,200	6,400
fixed	1,600	1,600
Sales and distribution costs:		
variable	1,600	3,200
fixed	2,400	2,400

The normal level of activity for the year is 800 units. Fixed costs are incurred evenly throughout the year, and actual fixed costs are the same as budgeted.

There were no inventories of Claud at the beginning of the year.

In the first quarter, 200 units were produced and 160 units sold.

Required

(a) Calculate the fixed production costs absorbed by Clauds in the first quarter if absorption costing is used.

(b) Calculate the profit using absorption costing.

(c) Calculate the profit using marginal costing.

(d) Explain why there is a difference between the answers to (b) and (c).

Solution

(a)

$$\frac{\text{Budgeted fixed production costs (annual)}}{\text{Budgeted output (normal level of activity annual)}} = \frac{\$1,600}{800\,\text{units}}$$

Absorption rate = $2 per unit produced.

During the first quarter, the fixed production overhead absorbed was

200 units × $2 = $400.

(b) **Profit for the quarter, absorption costing**

	$	$
Sales (160 × $20)		3,200
Production costs		
Variable (200 × $8)	1,600	
Fixed (absorbed overhead (200 × $2))	400	
Total (200 × $10)	2,000	
Less closing inventory (40 × $10)	400	
Production cost of sales		1,600
Gross profit		1,600
Less: sales and distribution costs		
variable (160 × $4)	640	
fixed (¼ of $2,400)	600	
		1,240
Net profit		360

(c) **Profit for the quarter, marginal costing**

	$	$
Sales		3,200
Variable production costs	1,600	
Less closing inventory (40 × $8)	320	
Variable production cost of sales	1,280	
Variable sales and distribution costs	640	
Total variable costs of sales		1,920
Total contribution		1,280
Less:		
Fixed production costs incurred	400	
Fixed sales and distribution costs	600	
		1,000
Net profit		280

(d) The difference in profit is due to the different valuations of closing inventory. In absorption costing, the 40 units of closing inventory include absorbed fixed overheads of $80 (40 × $2) , which are therefore costs carried over to the next quarter and not charged against the profit of the current quarter. In marginal costing, all fixed costs incurred in the period are charged against profit.

	$
Absorption costing profit	360
Fixed production costs carried forward in inventory values	80
Marginal costing profit	280

This example demonstrates a number of points.

(a) Under **absorption costing**, both variable and fixed non-production overheads (eg administration, sales and distribution) are deducted from gross profit to give net profit – they aren't included in production costs.

(b) Under **marginal costing** the variable component of non-production overheads (eg administration, sales and distribution) - and the variable component of production costs - are deducted from sales to give the contribution. Fixed costs (both production and non-production) are deducted from contribution to give net profit.

(c) If there are changes in inventory during a period, marginal costing and absorption costing give **different profit** figures.

    (i) **If inventory levels increase absorption costing will report the higher profit** because some of the fixed production overhead incurred during the period will be carried forward in closing inventory (which reduces cost of sales) to be set against sales revenue in the

following period instead of being written off in full against profit in the period concerned (as in the example above).

      (ii)   **If inventory levels decrease, absorption costing will report the lower profit** because as well as the fixed overhead incurred, fixed production overhead which had been brought forward in opening inventory is released and is included in cost of sales.

(d)   If the opening and closing inventory volumes and values are the same, marginal costing and absorption costing will give the **same profit** figure.

(e)   **In the long run, total profit will be the same** whether marginal costing or absorption costing is used. The different accounting methods only affect the profit of individual accounting periods.

7.6 Absorption costing or marginal costing?

Both methods are widely used for costing purposes, but marginal costing has the advantage of being better for decision-making purposes.

Chapter Roundup

- A **cost unit** is a unit of product which has costs attached to it.

- Cost information is needed to aid price setting, decision making, planning and budgeting, control and reporting.

- Costs can be divided into three elements, **materials, labour** and **expenses.**

- Costs can be classified as **direct** or **indirect**.

- **Cost behaviour patterns** demonstrate the way in which costs are affected by changes in the level of activity.

- **Stepped-fixed costs** are costs which are fixed in nature within certain levels of activity.

- **Mixed costs** (semi-variable/semi-fixed costs) are partly fixed and partly variable, and therefore only partly affected by changes in activity levels.

- Costs can also be analysed according to their **function**. For example, production, distribution and selling, administration and financing costs.

- The cost of a product or service can be built up on a **cost card**, which identifies
  - Direct costs
  - Prime cost
  - Production overheads
  - Production costs
  - Non-production overheads
  - Total cost

- **Absorption costing** and **marginal costing** are different ways of accounting for costs. If there are changes in inventory levels during a period, marginal costing and absorption costing give different profit figures.

1   A unit of profit or service to which costs can be related is known as?

    A   A cost centre
    B   A cost unit
    C   A product unit
    D   A service unit

2   Which one of the following cost elements does not form part of the overheads?

    A   Indirect expenses
    B   Indirect labour
    C   Indirect materials
    D   Indirect profit

3   The basic principle of cost behaviour is that as the level of activity rises, costs will usually _____ .
Which is/are the missing word/words?

    A   Fall
    B   Rise
    C   Stay consistent
    D   Fall then rise again

4   A cost which is unaffected by increases and decreases in the volume of output is called?

    A   Stepped-fixed
    B   Variable
    C   Constant
    D   Fixed

5   Which one of the following is an example of a stepped-fixed cost?

    A   Factory rent
    B   Salaries
    C   Electricity bill
    D   Straight line depreciation

6   Costs can be analysed according to their function. Which one of the following is not an example of a functional cost heading?

    A   Production costs
    B   Administration costs
    C   Financing costs
    D   Carriage out costs

Answers to Quick Quiz

1   B   This is the definition of a cost unit.

2   D   Indirect profit.

3   B   The basic principle of cost behaviour is that as the level of activity rises, costs will usually rise.

4   D   The name given to cost unaffected by increases and decreases in the volume of output is fixed costs.

5   C   Electricity usually has a fixed element (the standing charge) and a variable element (the charge per unit of electricity used). Options A, B and D are all usually fixed costs.

6   D   Carriage out costs. These costs would normally come under the functional heading of 'distribution and selling costs'.

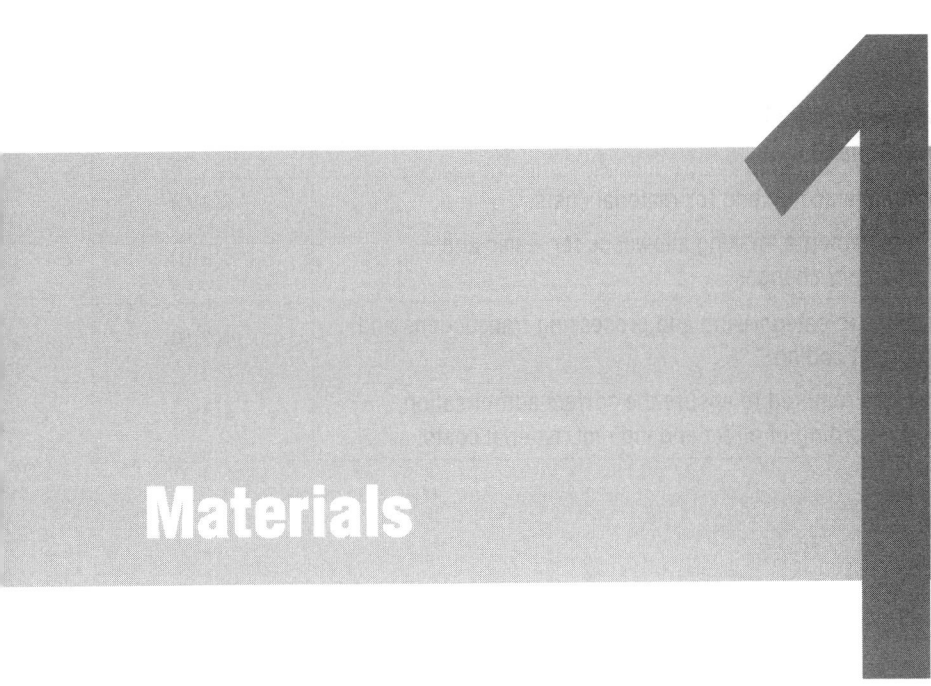

Materials

11

Study guide

			Syllabus reference
7	(d)	Describe and illustrate the classification of material and labour costs (material costs covered here).	4(d)(ii)
8	(a)	Describe and illustrate the accounting for material costs.	4(a)(i)
	(b)	Calculate material requirements, making allowance for sales and product/materials inventory changes.	4(a)(i)
9	(a)	Explain the use of codes In categorising and processing transactions and the importance of correct coding.	4(d)(i)
	(c)	Describe the procedures required to ensure the correct authorisation, coding, analysis and recording of direct and indirect material costs.	4(d)(i)

1 Introduction

There are three main elements of costs for most businesses, these are materials, labour and expenses or overheads. In this chapter we are going to consider the first of the three elements, materials.

We will look at how materials are ordered and received, how they are classified and how they are accounted for. One important element of the recording and accounting for all costs in a business is that of coding. Only if the costs are correctly coded will they be accounted for correctly so we start the chapter with a section on coding in general.

2 Coding

FAST FORWARD

For elements of **cost** and **income** to be correctly analysed, classified and recorded they must initially be correctly coded for entry into the accounting records.

We have discussed the various types of income and expenditure, and the importance of ensuring that these items are recorded accurately so as to ensure accurate management information. We will now look at the practical aspects of ensuring this.

In many organisations, income and expenditure items are **coded** before they are included in the accounting records. Coded means giving something a **code**. What exactly is a code?

Key term

> A **code** is a system of words, letters, figures or symbols used to represent others.

In this chapter we are going to look at the different source documents for materials, the ways in which organisations use **coding lists** to code income and expenditure and the authorisation procedures that must be followed to ensure correct recording of income and expenditure.

Most organisations use computers to record their accounting transactions because they have the following advantages.

- They record and retrieve information quickly and easily
- They are automatically accurate and have built in checking facilities
- They can file a large amount of information in a small space
- They are capable of sorting information in many different ways

Management information is only one part of the organisation's information system, which will be based on **transaction processing** (data processing). Other applications can be built on top of the basic information system, and spreadsheets can be used in conjunction with it for reporting purposes.

The information system will also support the needs of the **financial accounts** which, as we have explained, are subject to **external regulations.** Under UK company law, directors are responsible for ensuring that accounting records do the following.

- Show an analysis of all income and expenditure
- Show the financial position of the company at any particular moment in time
- Record all assets and liabilities of the company (including inventory where applicable)

Accounting records must be retained for future reference.

Some information must be separately identifiable in order to meet other regulatory requirements (for example **sales tax**) or specific accounting requirements (for example **donations** to political causes or charities).

Some computer systems are able to sort information from transaction processing into the correct categories for both financial and management accounting purposes. This avoids the need to enter data more than once.

When data is entered into an accounting system, each item is coded with a specific **code** from a list of accounts.

Codes can be **alphabetical** and/or **numerical**. The length and complexity of a coding system will depend upon the needs and complexity of the organisation.

For financial accounting purposes it is common to use **general ledger codes** which correspond to the different areas of the statement of financial position and income statement.

2.1 Example: numeric codes

Type of account	Code range
Non-current asset	1000 – 1999
Current asset	2000 – 2999
Current liability	3000 – 3999
Revenue	4000 – 4999
Long-term liability	5000 – 5999
Capital	6000 – 6999
Within each section, the codes can be broken down into smaller sections:	
Fixtures and fittings	1000 – 1099
Land and buildings	1100 – 1199
Plant and machinery	1200 – 1299
Motor vehicles	1300 – 1399
and so on. Gaps between the numbers used give scope for breaking the categories down further (for example there could be a separate account for each building) and for adding new categories if necessary.	

Some types of account require **more detail**. For example, each customer needs a separate account, although in the statement of financial position the total 'receivables' will be shown. Suppliers (payables) also need an account each and a total for the statement of financial position.

Alphabetical codes, using part of the company or person's name, are common but, because names can be duplicated, an additional code may be necessary.

2.2 Example: alphabetical codes

Customer	Code
J Miller Ltd	MIL 010
M Miller	MIL 015
A Milton	MIL 025

Some computer systems save time for operators by offering a **'menu'** of accounts when part of the name is typed in.

Some codes can help users to **recognise the items** they describe. For example, a shoe shop could code their inventory by type of shoe, colour, size, style and male or female. A pair of red women's sandals, size 5, style 19 could then become:

Shoe type	Colour	Size	Style	Male/Female
SA	R	5	19	F
BO	B	8	11	M

and the second item would be men's brown boots, size 8, style 11.

We have already stressed the importance of coding costs and revenues correctly for management information (and financial accounting) purposes. The key to achieving this in any organisation is an **understanding** of the coding list and any related guidance in the policy manual.

We have already explained that correct coding requires you to have a good understanding of the **organisation** as well as the **coding list**. You need to know the following.

- The main activities of the organisation
- The main sources of income
- The main items of expenditure
- Details of the organisational structure

In some cases, you may need to ask for **help from other people** in order to code transactions correctly.

An **organisation chart** can help to make sense of the coding structure. Here is a simple one for an accounting firm divided into departments.

Coding errors can happen in a variety of ways, such as errors in keying in the original data and applying the wrong code (because either the transaction or the coding structure have not been understood).

When management information is produced, large errors are often obvious. For example a doubling of sales revenue in one month is rather unlikely unless there has been a sales campaign in that month. It is more likely that a decimal point has been misplaced in a figure or another form of income has been incorrectly coded to sales revenue.

2.3 Example: coding problems

Motor expenses for the three cars belonging to J Miller & Son are all coded to a single expense account and are usually around $1,200 a month. In June the total is almost $15,000. Mr Miller (the firm's owner) asks you to look into the reasons why. You decide to get a print-out of the motor expenses account for June. It looks like this.

Code M057	Motor expenses	$
3.6.X1	Petrol	22.70
5.6.X1	Petrol	18.50
7.6.X1	Repairs to S 657 PNO	235.70

8.6.X1	Petrol	22.00
10.6.X1	Petrol	18.00
12.6.X1	Tyres for R 393 FGH	140.00
15.6.X1	Petrol	24.50
18.6.X1	Petrol	230.00
22.6.X1	Purchase of T 191 PJF	12,950.00
25.6.X1	Petrol	21.50
27.6.X1	Petrol	23.65
29.6.X1	Road tax R 393 FGH	155.00
30.6.X1	Depreciation charge S 657 PNO	290.00
30.6.X1	Depreciation charge R 393 FGH	250.00
30.6.X1	Depreciation charge T 191 PJF	310.00

Total for the month of June $14,711.55

(a) There are two problems which should be fairly obvious:

18/6 $230 seems an unlikely petrol bill

22/6 The purchase of a car has been coded to expenses instead of non-current assets

There are also bills for repairs, tyres and road tax all in one month which is probably not typical. Having spotted these anomalies, you should now act by investigating them, correcting any errors.

(b) (i) The petrol receipt should be checked and the entry corrected.

(ii) The entry for the purchase of the car should be corrected, ie removed from the expense account and re-entered under the appropriate non-current asset code. Any items of expenditure on long-term non-current assets which a company intends to retain for its own use are capital items, not expense items.

(iii) No action is needed for the other motor expenses which are correctly coded.

3 Documents for buying and selling

> **FAST FORWARD**
>
> When goods are required by a business the person requiring the goods must normally complete a **purchase requisition** which must be authorised by an appropriate manager.

The documents involved in buying and selling are prime sources of cost and revenue information. Their number and complexity will depend on the type and size of both the organisation and the purchase. In this section we will look at the typical administrative procedure for the purchase of some desks by Abacus Ltd, a retailer of office furniture.

A **purchase requisition** is be prepared by the person who wants to buy the goods, such as the storekeeper, and then it must be countersigned (**authorised**) by the supervisor or departmental head who is responsible for the department's budget.

> **FAST FORWARD**
>
> The purchase requisition is then passed to the **purchasing department** who will decide on the most appropriate supplier.

The requisition is passed to the buyer (purchasing department) who will find out about suppliers, prices and other details relating to the items that have been requisitioned. If Abacus Ltd has a regular supplier for the goods, then the purchase requisition may show their catalogue number at this stage. Otherwise, it will be filled in later, along with the order number and supplier's name.

```
                    PURCHASE REQUISITION

                                    Number: 62
                                    Date:     21.02.20X1

 Quantity   Description   Suppliers    Purchase    Supplier
                          Catalogue    Order No
                          No

    25      Executive desks   BX 320      489      Desks'x'us



 Signed: ....John Marshall........    Approved: .....Jim Davey.....

 Authorised: ...Mary Great......
```

If an appropriate supplier is not already used by the buying department then they may send out a **letter of enquiry** to several suppliers in order to find out a price, delivery date, delivery charges, discounts available, and terms of payment, for twenty five desks.

FAST FORWARD

The **supplier** may then provide a **quotation** or an **estimate** which may include either trade or cash discounts.

The different suppliers might respond with a catalogue and a price list (for standard goods), a **quotation** (for non-standard goods) or a letter of reply. For services such as building work or repairs, an **estimate** will usually be provided.

The buyer must select an appropriate supplier based on the information received. If **discounts** are offered they may be of two types.

(a)   A **trade discount** is given for large orders or special customers and will be shown as a deduction on the invoice.

(b)   A **cash discount** is usually given for prompt payment within a stated period (for example payment within 7 days gives a 3% discount). It cannot be shown as a deduction until payment has been made.

If **sales tax** is payable, discounts are deducted from the cost of the goods before the **sales tax** is calculated and added to the invoice.

FAST FORWARD

The purchasing department will then send a **purchase order** to the supplier.

Once a supplier has been selected, the buyer will prepare a **purchase order** to ask for the goods to be supplied. Copies of the order are sent to the following.

•   The **supplier** – to ask for the goods.
•   The **accounts department** – for checking against the invoice when it arrives.
•   The **stores section** – for updating the inventory records.
•   The **goods received** section – so that they expect the goods.

The buyer should also retain a copy on file.

BPP
LEARNING MEDIA

PURCHASE ORDER

Abacus Ltd
24 Smith Street
London   Order Number: *489*
SE11 9JT   Date: *1.3.2001*

Tel: 020 7868 9375

To: Desks'r'us
     19 Croydon Road
     Balham
     CR8 6BZ

Please supply

25   *Executive desks*   *Catalogue number Bx320*   *Price each $200*

Delivery by road   Signed ...*Jim Davey*............
To the above address   (Buyer)

> **FAST FORWARD**
>
> The goods will be sent, normally accompanied by a **delivery note**, and when received by the business a **goods received note** will be completed.

The supplier will usually send an **advice note** to say when the goods will be delivered and, if delivering the goods with its own transport, a **delivery note** will be sent with the driver for the customer to sign.

The customer's copy of the delivery note confirms that the goods have been delivered. Another copy of the delivery note is taken by the driver and given to the supplier to confirm that the customer has received the goods. If the supplier does not use its own transport, a **consignment note** will provide the same evidence as the advice note.

When the desks arrive at the goods received section at Abacus Ltd, a **goods received note** is prepared and sent to other departments so that they know that the goods have arrived. Copies of the goods received note are sent to the following.

- The **accounts department** – to check against the invoice
- The **stores section** – for updating inventory records
- The **buyer** – to confirm that the goods ordered have arrived
- The **goods received section** will keep a record on file

> **FAST FORWARD**
>
> Finally, a **purchase invoice** will be received by the business from the supplier detailing the amount that is due to be paid – the net of sales tax amount of the invoice must be coded to ensure that it is correctly recorded in the accounting records as must the sales tax.

The **supplier's sales department** will send the customer an **invoice** detailing the amount that they need to pay for the desks.

```
                          INVOICE

From: Desks'r'us              Number:              1340
      19 Croydon Road         Date/tax point:      10.3.20X1
      Balham                  Sales tax reg number 774 5513 23
      CR8 6BZ

Tel:  020 8775 0679

To:   Abacus Ltd
      24 Smith Street
      London
      SE11 9JT              Your order number:  489


Quantity  Description                              Price       $
  25      Executive desks Catalogue number BX 320  $200 each   5,000.00
                                                   VAT AT 17.5%  875.00
                                                   Total due   5,875.00



                    Terms: Payment in 30 days

                    Delivered on 9.3.20X1
```

The customer (Abacus Ltd) should check the sales invoice carefully. In particular, they should check the following.

(a)   That the goods have been delivered and are in satisfactory condition (check goods received note).

(b)   That the price and terms are as agreed (look at the purchase order).

(c)   That the calculations on the invoice are correct (including **sales tax**).

If the sales invoice is correct, it is passed for entry to the payables ledger. Once it is entered into the payables ledger it is recorded as a purchase and the invoice is paid. If the sales invoice is thought to be incorrect, the supplier is notified of the discrepancies.

If the supplier has made any errors on the sales invoice, he will usually issue a credit note (which is effectively the reverse of an invoice). A credit note may be issued for the whole of the invoice, in order to enable both companies to remove it from their books and replace it with a correct invoice.

If a customer has been overcharged, a **credit note** may be issued to reduce the original sales invoice to its correct value.

Not all organisations will go through these steps in their buying and selling procedures but they must all check that goods and services purchased are properly ordered, received and paid for and that sales revenue is properly recorded. Many **computerised accounting systems** will carry out some of these checks automatically.

The procedures we have described in this section can be summarised as follows.

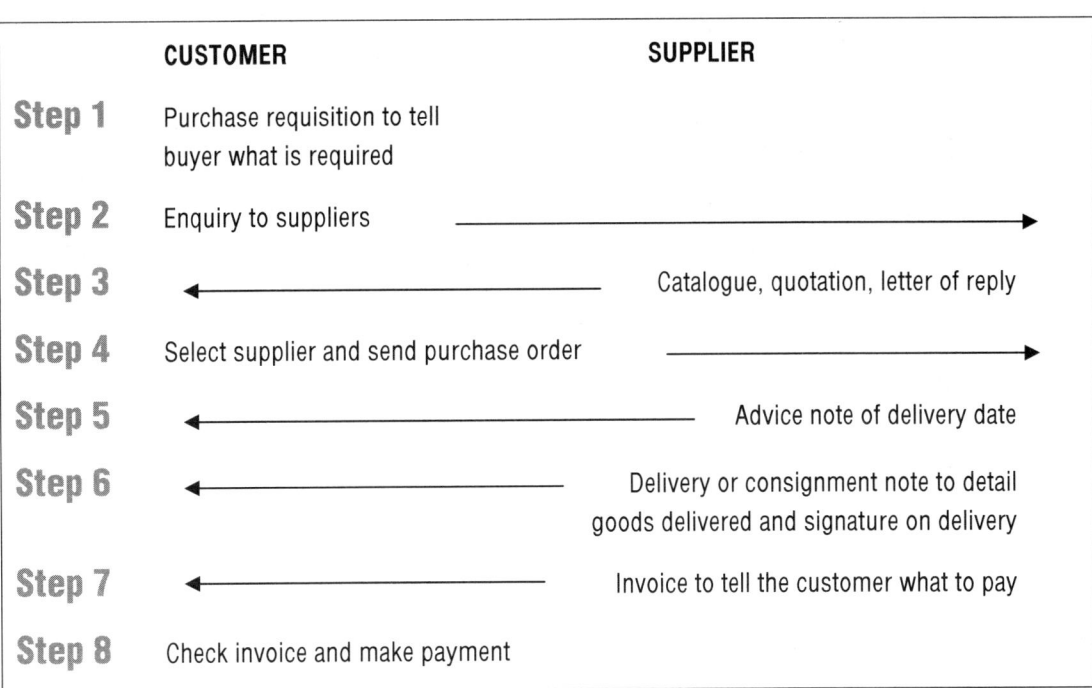

	CUSTOMER	SUPPLIER
Step 1	Purchase requisition to tell buyer what is required	
Step 2	Enquiry to suppliers	————————————————→
Step 3	←————————————————	Catalogue, quotation, letter of reply
Step 4	Select supplier and send purchase order	————————————————→
Step 5	←————————————————	Advice note of delivery date
Step 6	←————————————————	Delivery or consignment note to detail goods delivered and signature on delivery
Step 7	←————————————————	Invoice to tell the customer what to pay
Step 8	Check invoice and make payment	

Exam focus point

The documents involved in the purchasing/selling cycle are important and an exam question could ask you to identify a particular document.

3.1 Coding purchases

Imagine that you work for a firm of gardeners and are sitting at your computer looking at a **purchase order** for fertiliser. Firstly you must check this invoice, secondly, you must enter it into the accounting system, using the principles of double entry. The purchase invoice will create an **account payable** so you need to know how suppliers are coded. It will also be a cost to the firm, but under which category should it be analysed?

Don't forget that the cost to the company will be the **net** cost and **sales tax** will be coded to the **sales tax account** to be set off against **tax on sales**. Coding the net cost will depend on the firm's **policy** for dealing with this type of supply. If the jobs undertaken are mostly large and fertiliser is ordered for particular customers then it will probably be coded so that it can be charged to that **particular job** (ie treated as a direct cost). If, on the other hand it is delivered to the firm in bulk and used as needed it may well be treated as an **overhead** or indirect cost.

Telephone bills are obviously an overhead cost to the business. Depending on the coding structure and the organisational structure, different telephone lines may be charged to different parts of the business. The individual codes give information for different departments, while the code range for telephone expenses will give a total telephone cost for the organisation.

In the same way, details of **motor expenses** may be dealt with in one expense account with different accounts for different types of cost.

- Insurance
- Road fund licence
- Petrol
- Repairs and maintenance

Alternatively details of motor expenses may be analysed by individual vehicles (perhaps using the registration number in the code). In companies with many vehicles, the fleet manager may well want information on costs per vehicle (or type of vehicle) but in small organisations with few vehicles, this may not be necessary.

Question

Extract from code list   **Telephone numbers and locations**

Telephone expenses 5500-5599
5510 General administration
5530 Sales and marketing
5570 Manufacturing

020 7668 9923 Managing director
020 7668 9871 Marketing manager
020 7668 9398 Factory floor
020 7668 9879 Accounts office
0879 6534 Salesperson's mobile

Which telephone lines would you charge to code 5510?

A   Sales persons mobile and the marketing manager
B   Managing director and accounts office
C   Factory floor and accounts office
D   Managing director and marketing manager

Answer

Answer B

The marketing manager's line and the salesperson's mobile would be classed as sales and marketing. The factory floor line would be given a manufacturing code.

Question

Here is a summary of the net value of sales invoices for the month of September and an extract from the coding list of a company that sells cosmetics worldwide. What is the net sales value analysed to code R140 (Europe)?

Invoice No	Net sales value $	Country
8730	10,360.00	Canada
8731	12,750.73	England
8732	5,640.39	Spain
8733	15,530.10	Northern Ireland
8734	3,765.75	South Africa
8735	8,970.22	Kenya
8736	11,820.45	Italy
8737	7,640.00	France
8738	9,560.60	Australia
8739	16,750.85	Germany

Sales revenue codes: R100 – R199

R110	Area 1	UK
R120	Area 2	North America
R130	Area 3	South America
R140	Area 4	Europe
R150	Area 5	Africa
R160	Area 6	Australia

Helping hand. If you are not sure whether the countries listed are in a particular area of the world – find yourself an atlas and look them up.

A $25,100.84
B $41,851.69
C $54,602.42
D $70,132.52

Answer

Answer B

The invoices would be coded as shown below.

Invoice no	Net sales value $	Country	Code
8730	10,360.00	Canada	R120
8731	12,750.73	England	R110
8732	5,640.39	Spain	R140
8733	15,530.10	Northern Ireland	R110
8734	3,765.75	South Africa	R150
8735	8,970.22	Kenya	R150
8736	11,820.45	Italy	R140
8737	7,640.00	France	R140
8738	9,560.60	Australia	R160
8739	16,750.85	Germany	R140

Question
Accounting documents

You work for the accounts department of Abacus Ltd and have received invoice number 1340 from Desks'r'us (see previous paragraphs) for checking. Which documents will you need to check the details of the invoice to?

A   Purchase order and goods received note
B   Goods received note and purchase requisition
C   Delivery note and purchase requisition
D   Advice note and despatch note

Answer

Answer A

Question
Goods received notes

The goods received note relating to invoice 1340 is shown below.

GOODS RECEIVED NOTE

NUMBER 547

SUPPLIER: Desks'r'us
19 Croydon Road
Balham
CR8 6BZ

Date received: 9.3.2001

Quantity	Description	Order number
25	Executive desks	489

Carrier	Received by	Checked by	Location
Desks'r'us	M Smith	B Martin	Bay 5

Condition of goods: 1 desktop badly scratched

Distribution:
accounts ✓
stock control
buyer

Abacus Ltd should now

A   Pay the invoice in full on the due date and request a refund
B   Pay the invoice in full on the due date and request a credit note
C   Wait for a replacement desk before any payment is made
D   Pay the net amount of the invoice and credit note, when received

Answer

Answer D

This is the best course of action. A replacement desk may not be available immediately, so C is incorrect. A is inappropriate as businesses tend to cancel errors on invoices by means of a credit note rather than a refund. B would be pointless as a refund would be required.

4 Documents for recording materials

FAST FORWARD

The physical quantity of each line of inventory will often be recorded on a **bin card** in the stores department and a similar document known as the **stores ledger account** will be kept by the accounts department which also includes inventory values.

An important item purchased by a manufacturing business is materials. These are generally kept in a warehouse or inventory room, which is usually referred to as the stores department. They will keep an eye on the inventory of raw materials, and raise a purchase order when the stores run low.

Most businesses will keep track of the quantities of materials that they have in inventories held by maintaining an inventory record for each type of material held. This will be updated each time material is received into, or issued from, stores, and a new balance of inventories held can be calculated. This is known as a **perpetual inventory system**, and it can be manual or computerised. There are two types of inventory record which may be kept, and sometimes they will both be used. These are **bin cards** and **stores ledger accounts**.

4.1 Bin cards

These are manual records that are written up and kept in the stores department. An example is shown here.

BIN CARD

Description: reels (30 cm diameter)　　　　　　Bin No. 232

Code No: R4089

Stock units: units

Receipts			Issues			Balance
Date	Reference	Quantity	Date	Reference	Quantity	Quantity
2003						
1 May						40
5 May	GRN 0067	200				240
			7 May	MR 296	30	210
			10 May	MR 304	20	190
			11 May	MR 309	50	140
13 May	MRN 127	10				150

The information on the bin card gives all the details the storekeeper needs to know.

(a) Description: of the inventory item for which this is a record.

(b) Inventory code: for unambiguous identification and for ease of updating computerised inventory records, a code is essential.

(c) Inventory units: the units in which the material is measured e.g. metres, kilograms, boxes etc.

(d) Bin number: the location of the items in the store.

(e) Issues to production: date, quantity and a reference to the materials requisition (MR), the document which the production department use to request material from stores.

(f) Receipts: date, quantity and details of the GRN for goods delivered to the business or materials returned note (MRN) for goods returned to inventory when they have not been used in production.

(g) Balance: the quantity of inventory on hand after each inventory movement.

4.2 Stores ledger accounts

The stores ledger accounts are very similar to bin cards. They carry all the information that a bin card does, and they are updated from the same sources: GRNs, MRs and MRNs. But there are two important differences.

1. Cost details are recorded in the stores ledger account, so that the unit cost and total cost of each issue and receipt is shown. The balance of inventory after each inventory movement is also valued. The value is recorded as these accounts form part of the costing bookkeeping records.
2. The stores ledger accounts are written up and kept in the costing department, or in a stores office separate from the stores by a clerk experienced in costing bookkeeping.

Stores ledger accounts are very often computerised, and this would enable the amount of **free stock** to be monitored.

At any point in time the amount of **free stock** can be calculated as inventory on hand plus inventory on order less any inventory that has been scheduled for use.

Key term

Free stock is inventory on hand + inventory on order – inventory that has been scheduled for use.

Sometimes, inventory that is physically present in the stores, or even inventory that has not been received into stores yet, will already be allocated to a job or a department. Of course, it is helpful to take this into account when monitoring inventory levels, as only free stock is free to be issued to other departments or jobs.

Because bin cards and stores ledger accounts are independent, they can be used as a control to check the accuracy of the records. Theoretically, the quantities of inventory recorded should be the same; if they are not, this would have to be investigated and the appropriate adjustment made.

4.3 Materials requisitions

A materials requisition will be completed when materials are needed from stores by the production department. An official from production will sign the form to authorise it, and stores will issue the materials when the form is given to them. It is then used as a source document for:

(a) Updating the bin card in stores;
(b) Updating the stores ledger account in the costing department; and
(c) Charging the job, overhead or department that is using the materials.

The originating department will fill in the requisition as shown below.

MATERIALS REQUISITION				
Material required for: *Job 1478* (job)			No 309	
Department: *Assembly*			Date *11 May 2004*	
Quantity	Description	Code No	Price per unit	$
50	*30 cm diam reels*	*R4089*		
Foreman: *D Jameson*				

The price details and value will be filled in by the cost department prior to updating the stores ledger accounts and charging the relevant job/overhead/department.

A materials returned note will accompany any unused material back to stores. This will contain the same details as the materials requisition, and will be used as the source document to update the same records. This time, though, the material will be a receipt into stock and a deduction from the job originally charged with the material issued.

5 Ordering inventory

FAST FORWARD

When the store keeper places an order for materials the **amount** that will be **ordered** will be dependent upon the sales and or manufacturing plans for the immediate future.

As we have seen, from time to time the stores manager will decide that an order needs to be placed. The manager will also have to determine how many units of the item of inventory to order. In some organisations a set amount will be ordered each time an order is placed. In other organisations the amount of the order will be determined by the future plans for sales and production.

5.1 Example: order amounts – finished goods

A business buys and sells Deltas. At the beginning of June the stores manager realises that there are only 35 Deltas in stock and decides to place an order for more. He ascertains from the sales department that planned sales for the next three months in units are as follows:

	June	July	August
Planned sales	120	150	130

The stores manager feels that at the end of August there should be 50 Deltas remaining in stock.

How many Deltas must he order?

Solution

	Units
Sales (120 + 150 + 130)	400
Less: opening inventory	(35)
Add: closing inventory requirement	50
Order quantity	415

The opening inventory units are deducted as we already have these in stock and therefore do not need to buy them. The closing inventory however is added as we want to have these left over at the end of August after selling the 400 units.

If raw materials that are used in production are being replenished then similar calculations are required but this will be based upon the production plans for the period under consideration.

5.2 Example: order amounts – raw materials

A business makes a product, the Eel, each unit of which requires 4kg of material X. At the end of July the stores manager decides to place an order for more of material X as there are only 220kg in stock at that date. The production plans for the next two months are 400 Eels in August and 500 Eels in September. At the end of September it is planned to have 300kg of material X in stock.

How much of material X should be ordered?

Solution

	Kg
Material X required for production (900 x 4kg)	3,600
Less: opening inventory	(220)
Add: closing inventory requirements	300
Order quantity	3,680

Question

A business sells a product called the Inka and each unit of Inka requires 5.5kg of material K. Inventories of material K are 1,600 kg at the start of August 20X4 and the following production is planned for the next three months.

	August	September	October
Production in units of Inkas	1,000	1,100	1,200

The stores manager is about to place an order for material K and he requires there to be enough closing inventory of material K in order to produce 200 Inkas. What is the size of the order he must place in order to ensure that there is enough material K for the three months of the production and for the closing inventory requirements?

A   16,750 kg
B   17,650 kg
C   18,150 kg
D   18,650 kg

Answer

Answer B

	kg
Material required for production (3,300 x 5.5kg)	18,150
Less: opening inventory	(1,600)
Add: closing inventory(200 x 5.5kg)	1,100
	17,650 kg

6 Accounting for materials

FAST FORWARD

The materials purchased are recorded as a debit in the **materials control account**.

In Chapter 8 we revised the basics of double entry bookkeeping. In this section we will look at the detailed accounting for materials purchased by a business and then issued to production.

FAST FORWARD

Materials issued to production must be classified as either **direct** or **indirect** materials. Direct materials are credited to the materials control account and debited to the work in progress account. Indirect materials are credited to the materials control account and debited to the production overhead account.

A distinction was made in the previous chapter between direct costs and indirect costs. Direct costs are those which can be directly associated to the production of a cost unit whereas indirect costs are those which cannot. This is the case with materials.

Direct materials are those which are part of the cost of making the product. **Indirect materials** are other materials that are part of the production process. Either they are materials such as machine lubricant which cannot be allocated to a specific cost unit or alternatively they are small components in the cost unit which due to their immaterial value are treated as indirect materials such as screws and bolts.

The importance of the distinction between direct and indirect materials is due to their cost accounting treatment. Direct materials are part of the cost of the product or cost unit whereas indirect materials are classified as overheads. This difference in classification affects the accounting treatment.

When direct materials are issued to production the accounting entry is to debit a work in progress account. This is the account which gathers together the costs of production for a period. However when indirect materials are issued to production they are debited instead to the production overhead control account. The treatment of these overheads will be dealt with in Chapter 10.

6.1 Example: accounting for materials costs

A manufacturing business has purchased materials costing $102,000 on credit during the month of July 20X3. At the start of July there were inventories of raw materials of $13,000. During the month $88,000 of direct materials were issued to production and $15,000 of indirect materials.

We will now prepare the accounting entries for the materials for the month of July.

Solution

We must start with entering the opening inventory and the purchases into the materials control account.

MATERIALS CONTROL ACCOUNT

	$		$
Opening inventory	13,000		
Payables	102,000		

The other side of the entry for the purchases will be to the payables account in an integrated system but to the cost ledger control account in an interlocking system.

Now we will deal with the issues of materials to the production process. For both the direct and indirect materials the materials control account will be credited but the debit entries will be different – for the direct materials the debit entry is to the work in progress control account whereas the debit entry for the indirect materials is to the production overhead control account.

MATERIALS CONTROL ACCOUNT

	$		$
Opening inventory	13,000	Work in progress control	88,000
Payables	102,000	Production overhead control	15,000

WORK IN PROGRESS CONTROL

	$		$
Materials control	88,000		

PRODUCTION OVERHEAD CONTROL

	$		$
Materials control	15,000		

Finally the materials control account can be balanced to find the closing balance of materials at the end of July.

MATERIALS CONTROL ACCOUNT

	$		$
Opening inventory	13,000	Work in progress control	88,000
Payables	102,000	Production overhead control	15,000
		Closing inventory	12,000
	115,000		115,000

As you can see the accounting treatment of direct and indirect materials is very different therefore it is important that they are correctly classified. This is done by ensuring that each materials requisition is correctly coded as to whether the materials are direct materials or indirect materials.

We saw earlier in the chapter that sometimes materials are returned from production unused and this is recorded on a materials returns note. Again any return must be correctly coded to ensure that the materials movement is correctly classified as either a movement of direct materials or a movement of indirect materials.

The double entry for any such returns would be as follows:

Direct materials

DEBIT   Materials control
CREDIT   Work in progress control

Indirect materials

DEBIT   Materials control
CREDIT   Production overhead control

Question

Double entry for materials

A manufacturing business has issued $67,400 of direct materials to the production department during the month and $12,600 of indirect materials.

What is the double entry for these issues?

A	DEBIT	Materials control account	$80,000	
	CREDIT	Work in progress control		$67,400
	CREDIT	Production overhead control		$12,600
B	DEBIT	Materials control account	$80,000	
	CREDIT	Work in progress control		$12,600
	CREDIT	Production overhead control		$67,400
C	DEBIT	Work in progress control	$67,400	
	DEBIT	Production overhead control	$12,600	
	CREDIT	Materials control		$80,000
D	DEBIT	Work in progress control	$12,600	
	DEBIT	Production overhead control	$67,400	
	CREDIT	Materials control		$80,000

Answer

Answer C

Exam focus point

The cost accounting double entry for materials is highly examinable.

Chapter Roundup

- For elements of **cost** and **income** to be correctly analysed, classified and recorded they must initially be correctly coded for entry into the accounting records.

- When goods are required by a business the person requiring the goods must normally complete a **purchase requisition** which must be authorised by an appropriate manager.

- The purchase requisition is then passed to the **purchasing department** who will decide on the most appropriate supplier.

- The **supplier** may then provide a **quotation** or an **estimate** which may include either trade or cash discounts.

- The purchasing department will then send a **purchase order** to the supplier.

- The goods will be sent, normally accompanied by a **delivery note**, and when received by the business a **goods received note** will be completed.

- Finally, a **purchase invoice** will be received by the business from the supplier detailing the amount that is due to be paid – the net of sales tax amount of the invoice must be coded to ensure that it is correctly recorded in the accounting records as must the sales tax.

- The physical quantity of each line of inventory will often be recorded on a **bin card** in the stores department and a similar document known as the **stores ledger account** will be kept by the accounts department which also includes inventory values.

- At any point in time the amount of **free stock** can be calculated as inventory on hand plus inventory on order less any inventory that has been scheduled for use.

- When the store keeper places an order for materials the **amount** that will be **ordered** will be dependent upon the sales and or manufacturing plans for the immediate future.

- The materials purchased are recorded as a debit in the **materials control account**.

- Materials issued to production must be classified as either **direct** or **indirect** materials. Direct materials are credited to the materials control account and debited to the work in progress account. Indirect materials are credited to the materials control account and debited to the production overhead account.

1   Which one of the following is **not** one of the three main elements of cost in most businesses?

   A   Selling costs
   B   Materials
   C   Labour
   D   Overheads

2   When materials are received by a business what is the internal document completed by the receiving department?

   A   Purchase requisition
   B   Goods received note
   C   Invoice
   D   Despatch note

3   Statement 1. A cash discount is given for large orders or special customers and will be shown as a deduction on the invoice.

   Statement 2. A trade discount is usually given for prompt payment within a stated period. It cannot be shown as a deduction until payment has been made.

   A   Both statements are false
   B   Both statements are true
   C   Statement 1 is true and statement 2 is false
   D   Statement 1 is false and statement 2 is true

4   The sales tax inclusive amount (rather than the net amount) should be coded on a purchase invoice. Is this true or false?

5   What is the double entry for issues of materials to production?

   A   Dr   Materials control account   Cr   WIP account
   B   Dr   Materials control account   Cr   Payables
   C   Dr   WIP account   Cr   Materials control account
   D   Dr   Payables   Cr   Materials control account

Answers to Quick Quiz

1   A   Selling costs. Selling costs would normally be classed as overheads so are not usually thought of as a main element of cost.

2   B   Goods received note. This is prepared when the goods arrive and it is sent to other departments so that they know that the goods have arrived.

3   A   They are both false because statement 1 describes a trade discount not a cash discount. Statement 2 describes a cash discount, not a trade discount.

4   False   It is the net amount which should be coded on a purchase invoice.

5   C   Dr WIP account   Cr Materials control account. (Remember that indirect materials would be debited to the production overhead)

12

Labour costs

Study guide

			Syllabus reference
7	(d)	Describe and illustrate the classification of material and labour costs (labour costs covered here).	4(a)(ii)
8	(c)	Describe and illustrate the accounting for labour costs (including overtime premium and idle time).	4(a)(ii)
	(d)	Prepare an analysis of gross earnings.	4(a)(ii)
	(e)	Explain and illustrate labour remuneration methods.	4(a)(ii)
	(f)	Calculate the effect of remuneration methods and changes in productivity on unit labour costs.	4(a)(ii)
9	(d)	Describe the procedures and documentation required to ensure the correct coding, analysis and recording of direct and indirect labour costs.	4(d)(ii)

1 Introduction

In this chapter we cover the second element of business costs, labour.

2 Documents for labour costs

FAST FORWARD

> Hourly paid workers are generally paid a **flat rate per hour** with a premium for overtime hours.
>
> The hours worked are often recorded on **clock cards**, **job cards** or **time sheets**.

Labour costs are an important element of **total costs**. Labour costs include **wages** (usually weekly) and salaries (usually monthly) paid to employees, and other payments such as agency workers or contractors who supply labour.

Records showing how each individual's pay has been calculated are known as **payslips**. Records of total labour costs paid to employees are known as the **payroll**.

Some workers earn a **flat rate** per hour or week or month, while others may have a 'normal' **hourly rate** and special **overtime rates**. Workers who are paid hourly often record their hours by using a **clock card** to show the times at which they arrived and left work each day. An example is shown below.

No				Ending	
Name					
	HOURS	RATE	AMOUNT	DEDUCTIONS	
Basic				Income Tax	
O/T				NI	
Others				Other	
Total				Total	
Less: deductions					
Net due					

Time	Day	Basic time	Overtime
0910	M		
1700	M		
0803	T		
1700	T		
0840	W		
1740	W		
0902	Th		
1648	Th		
0848	F		
1622	F		

Signature . . . .

Management will be most interested to know how much individual cost and profit centres spent on wages in a particular period. It is important therefore that the total wages for individual employees are collected to the correct cost centres.

If employees work on different jobs or products that span more than one cost centre, they will need to keep a record of the time spent on each job or product. This can be done by recording wages information on a jobcard such as the one shown below.

JOB CARD

Department	*Machining hours*	Job No	*M 431*
		Operation no	*6*

Time allowance	*2 hours*	Time started	*9.30*
		Time finished	*11.15*
		Hours on job	*1¾*

Description of job	Hours	Rate	Cost
File raw edges	*1¾*	*$4*	*$7*

Employee no	*129*	Certified by	*J Dowson*
Signature	*P Potter*		

2.1 Example: analysing wages costs

A production foreman running two production departments of equal size may have his labour cost shared 50 : 50 between them.

A computer programmer serving various departments within the organisation as required may have his labour cost shared by reference to the time spent in each department.

In many **service organisations**, where labour is a very important part of total costs, **charges** to clients will be based upon the hours worked for them. For example, lawyers, accountants and garage mechanics will keep time sheets to show the hours of work done for individual clients and the charge made to the client will have to cover this, plus an amount for overheads.

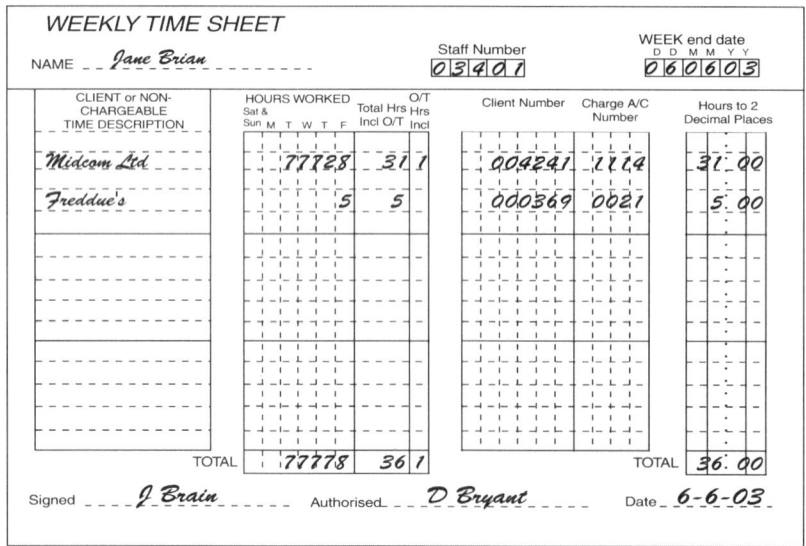

Employees who agree to work shifts, in particular different shifts over a period of time, receive extra wage payments. These extra payments are known as **shift allowances.**

Sometimes, employees may receive wages that are directly related to the output that they produce. This is known as **output related pay.** For example, workers in a widget factory might receive a basic wage rate plus:

- An extra $100 if they produce more than 1,000 widgets per week
- An extra $150 if they produce more than 1,200 widgets per week

Some employees are paid according to the number of units of a product that they produce in a week or month. This is known as **piecework**. In these cases the employees are paid a set amount for each good unit that they produce.

However there are two variations to the system. In some cases there may be a guaranteed weekly minimum payment in case there is not enough work available for the employee. In other cases there may be a differential piecework system whereby a higher unit amount is paid the more the employee produces.

2.2 Example: piecework

FAST FORWARD

An alternative to hourly pay is a **piecework system** where employees are paid according to the number of good units of production.

A business has a piecework system for remuneration of its employees. The system works as follows:

$3.20 per unit for up to 40 units per week
$3.50 per unit for each unit between 41 and 50 units per week
$3.80 per unit for each unit over 51 units per week

There is a guaranteed weekly wage of $120 per week.

One employee has produced the following amounts for the last two weeks:

Week 1   35 units
Week 2   44 units

What is the employee's gross wage for week 1 and week 2?

Solution

	Week 1 $	Week 2 $
35 units × $3.20	112	
40 units × $3.20		128
4 units × $3.50		14
	112	142

In week 1 as the piecework rate is less than the guaranteed weekly minimum the amount to be paid will be the guaranteed amount of $120. In week 2 the employee's earnings are $142.

In other remuneration systems employees are paid a flat hourly rate but are then rewarded for higher productivity by a bonus scheme. Such schemes can be for an individual or on a group basis.

An individual bonus scheme only works where the employee has full control over his own productivity or speed of his work which means that the speed of his work is not dependent upon either the production of other employees or the speed of machinery. Bonus schemes can be set up in many ways but typically under an individual scheme a standard will be set for productivity such as production of 20 units per hour. If the employee exceeds this standard then the value of the time saved or extra production is split between the employer and employee according to some formula so that the employee benefits from a bonus.

In other types of work environment a group bonus scheme may be set up. Under this type of scheme if a group of employees or even the whole factory exceed a certain target then a bonus is payable to all member of the group.

3 Unit labour costs

Some remuneration schemes involve either an individual or group **bonus scheme** in an attempt to improve productivity.

The labour cost is often a large element of the cost of a product and the remuneration method and productivity of the workforce can significantly affect the unit cost of the product.

3.1 Example: change of remuneration method

The **labour cost** can often be a significant element of unit cost and it can change if different remuneration methods are introduced or reduced by an increase in productivity.

A business makes one product which is made individually by each employee. In the past the 10 employees have been paid at an hourly rate of $5 per hour for 38 hours each week and any overtime hours are paid at the rate of time and a half. In a typical week the employees would each work for 6 overtime hours and on average produced 1,000 units of the product each week.

In an attempt to improve productivity the management have decided to change the remuneration package to a piecework system where each employee will be paid at the rate of $2.10 per unit for the first 80 units produced and $2.50 per unit for any units produced over and above 80. It is anticipated that each employee will produce 110 units per week.

What is the unit labour cost under the hourly rate system and under the piecework system?

Solution

Unit labour cost – hourly rate

	$
Labour cost (10 × 38 hours × $5)	1,900
Overtime (10 × 6 × $7.50)	450
Total labour cost	2,350
Cost per unit ($2,350/1,000)	$2.35 per unit

Unit labour cost – piecework

	$
10 × 80 × $2.10	1,680
10 × 30 × $2.50	750
Total labour cost	2,430
Unit labour cost ($2,340/1,100)	$2.21 per unit

3.2 Example: increase in productivity

A business has a factory in which the 40 employees are paid at an hourly rate of $6.80 per hour for a 35 hour week. Any overtime hours are paid at a rate of $9.00 per hour. Each unit of the product takes an average of 2 hours to produce and in an average week each of the employees works 3 hours of overtime.

In an attempt to improve productivity the management are considering investing some new machinery which it is anticipated will reduce the time required for each unit by 15 minutes. It is hoped that there will now be no overtime worked.

What is the effect on the total labour cost and the labour cost per unit of the increase in productivity.

Solution

	$
Labour cost (40 x 35 × $6.80)	9,520
Overtime (40 x 3 × $9.00)	1,080
Total labour cost	10,600

Number of units (40 × 38 hours/2)	760 units
Cost per unit (10,600/760)	$13.95 per unit
Labour cost (40 × 35 × £6.80)	9,520
Number of (40 × 35 hours/1.75)	800 units
Cost per unit (9,520/800)	$11.90 per unit

4 Gross pay and deductions

FAST FORWARD

The employer must **deduct** income tax and employee's National Insurance Contributions from the gross pay before paying the net pay to the employees.

The **total labour cost** for an employer is the gross pay plus the employer's National Insurance Contributions.

Whatever method of remuneration a business chooses the amount due to the employees is known as the **gross pay.** However this is not the amount that the employee will receive as the employer has a statutory duty to deduct income tax (in the form of PAYE in the UK) and also the Employee's National Insurance Contributions. The resulting figure after these deductions is the **net pay** that the employee will receive.

4.1 Example: gross pay to net pay

An employee is paid at an hourly rate of $7.00 for a 35 hour week with any overtime hours paid at time and a half. During week 22 the employee worked for 41 hours.

The income tax to be deducted was $55 and the Employee's National Insurance Contributions for the week were $28.

What is the employee's net pay?

Solution

	$
Gross pay – 41 hours x $7.00	287
6 hours x $3.50	21
Total gross pay	308
Less: Income tax	(55)
National Insurance contributions	(28)
Net pay	225

It is also possible that there may be other deductions from an employee's gross pay as well as income tax and National Insurance. For example if the company runs a contributory pension scheme there may be a further deduction for pension contributions that the employer will put into the pension scheme on the employee's behalf.

As far as the employer is concerned the cost of employment is the gross pay of the employee. This is due to the fact that although the employee is only paid the net amount the employer must also pay the income tax and the Employee's National Insurance Contributions over to the Inland Revenue.

There is also a further cost to the employer as he must also pay Employer's National Insurance Contributions on behalf of each employee.

4.2 Example: labour cost

Returning to the employee from the previous example the Employer's National Insurance Contribution for the week is $31. What is the labour cost to the employer for this employee for the week?

Solution

	$
Gross pay	308
Employer's National Insurance Contribution	31
Total labour cost	339

In some business's there may be an additional cost to the employer for example if the employer's agreement is that he will contribute to the pension scheme on the employee's behalf.

Two payslips for the month of April for advisers working for a financial services firm, and a corresponding extract from the firm's payroll, follow. Examine the two slips and the extract, then answer this question:

What is the total labour cost to the firm of employing these two advisers for the month?

A $2,275.20
B $2,925.00
C $3,025.00
D $3,383.11

PAY ADVICE

Name: *Carol Hathaway*   Employee number: *173*

Month number: 1   Date: **28.4.20X1**   Tax Code: 453L

	$	$
Basic pay		*1,000.00*
Commission		*575.00*
Total gross pay		*1,575.00*
Less pension		*50.00*
Gross taxable pay		*1,525.00*
Deductions:		
Income tax	*233.50*	
National Insurance	*114.70*	
		348.20
Net pay		*1,176.80*

PAY ADVICE

Name: **Mark Greene** Employee number: **174**

Month number: **1** Date: **28.4.20X1** Tax Code: **490L**

	$	$
Basic pay		1,000.00
Commission		450.00
Total gross pay		1,450.00
Less pension		50.00
Gross taxable pay		1,400.00
Deductions:		
Income tax	199.40	
National Insurance	102.20	
		301.60
Net pay		1,098.40

EXTRACT FROM PAYROLL

Employee no	Gross pay	Employee pension	Tax	Employee NI	Net pay	Employer pension	Employer NI
173	1,575.00	50.00	233.50	114.70	1,176.80	50.00	136.49
174	1,450.00	50.00	199.40	102.20	1,098.40	50.00	121.62

Answer

Answer D

The total labour cost for the two employees is made up of gross pay plus employer's contributions to pension and National Insurance. This comes to $3,383.11.

 ## Question

Wage payment schedule

You are the Accounts Assistant at Mark Balding's clothes factory (Mark Balding's Ltd).

It is your first day back in the office after a week's holiday. One of the items on your desk is a memo from a cost centre manager and is shown below.

<table>
<tr><td colspan="2" align="center">**MEMO**</td></tr>
</table>

To:	Accounts Assistant
From:	Cost Centre Manager (Denim range)
Date:	9 May 20X1
Subject:	Missed wage payment

We missed a wage payment for Sandra Bloggs, a sewing machinist (denim range) for the last week of April 20X1. Sandra works four days a week and worked 28 hours at the rate of $6 per hour and then worked on her day off (7 hours at time and a half) so that the order for Alma's Ltd was finished by the end of April.

Please calculate the basic wage payments and employee costs and then pass the details on to the payroll department for the personal deductions and coding. Sandra is entitled to an employer's pension contribution of 5% of basic wage payment and Employer's National Insurance Contributions are 12½% above $84 per week.

Many thanks

Task

Complete the wage payment schedule shown below.

PAYROLL CALCULATION SCHEDULE APRIL 20X1		
NAME:		
DEPARTMENT:		
BASIC RATE:		
HOURS WORKED:		
HOURS FOR OVERTIME PREMIUM:		
	Calculation	Amount $
OVERTIME PREMIUM		
EMPLOYER'S PENSION CONTRIBUTION		
EMPLOYER'S NIC		

PAYROLL CALCULATION SCHEDULE APRIL 20X1		
NAME:	Sandra Bloggs	
DEPARTMENT:	Denim Range	
BASIC RATE:	$6.00 per hour	
HOURS WORKED:	35	
HOURS FOR OVERTIME PREMIUM:	7	
	Calculation	Amount $
	35 hrs × $6	210
OVERTIME PREMIUM	7 hrs × $6 × 0.5	21
EMPLOYER'S PENSION CONTRIBUTION	5% × $210	10.50
EMPLOYER'S NIC	$210 + $21 = $231 $231 − $84 = $147 $147 × 12.5%	18.37

Exam focus point

You need to understand all the costs involved in the total wages cost to the business.

5 Accounting for labour costs

FAST FORWARD

Direct labour costs are the costs of the hours worked by the production workers at the normal hourly rate.

Indirect labour costs include the overtime premium for direct workers and any idle time hours for direct workers as well as the indirect workers employment costs.

In just the same was as for materials the labour costs of a business must be classified as either direct labour costs or indirect labour costs as these will be accounted for differently.

We have already seen that the total labour cost to an employer is the gross pay plus the Employer's National Insurance contribution and any other further payments such as pension contributions that the employer pays on behalf of the employee. Now we must determine how the total labour cost is analysed between direct and indirect costs.

The basic distinction for classification of labour costs is that the labour costs of production workers are direct costs and the labour costs of other workers are indirect costs. However there are two specific areas where the costs of the production workers are often treated as indirect rather than direct.

When overtime is worked by employees they tend to be paid an additional premium over the general hourly rate, known as the **overtime premium.** The overtime premium is generally treated as an indirect cost rather than a direct cost of production. However there is an exception to this – if a customer requests that overtime is worked in order to complete a job earlier then the entire overtime payment will normally be treated as a direct cost of the job.

At some point during the working day it is entirely possible that production workers find that there is no work for them to do. This could be due to factors such as production scheduling problems or machine breakdowns. These hours which are paid for but during which no work is being done are known as **idle time.** The cost of idle time hours tends to be treated as an indirect labour cost.

5.1 Example: overtime and idle time

Given below are the labour costs incurred by a manufacturing business for the week commencing 23 July 20X5.

Direct production workers 1,200 hours @ $6.40 per hour
Direct production workers overtime hours 200 @ $9.40 per hour
Indirect workers 400 hours @ $5.20 per hour
Indirect workers overtime hours 50 @ $8.00 per hour
Of the hours paid to the direct production workers 40 of these were idle time hours.

What is the total for direct labour and indirect labour for the week?

Solution

Direct labour cost

	$
Direct production workers basic hours (1,200 + 200 – 40) @ $6.40	8,704

Indirect labour cost

Direct production workers – overtime premium

	$
200 hours × ($9.40 – 6.40)	600
Idle time hours 40 × $6.40	256
Indirect workers (400 × $5.20)	2,080
Indirect workers – overtime (50 × $8.00)	400
	3,336

Question	Direct and indirect labour cost

During the week ending 30 June 20X3 the direct production workers in a factory worked for 840 hours in total. Of these hours 60 were idle time hours and 100 were overtime hours. The hourly rate of pay is $8.00 with overtime hours being paid at time and a half.

During the same week the indirect workers worked for 120 hours at a rate of $6.00 per hour with no overtime hours.

What is the direct labour cost and the indirect labour cost for the week?

	Direct labour cost	*Indirect labour cost*
A	$5,440	$2,400
B	$6,240	$1,600
C	$6,640	$1,200
D	$6,720	$1,120

Answer

Answer B

	$
Direct labour (840 – 60) × $8.00	6,240

	$
Indirect labour	
Indirect workers 120 × $6.00	720
Direct workers overtime premium	
100 hours × $4	
Direct workers idle time	
60 hours × $8	480
	1,600

Once the distinction between the direct labour and indirect labour costs has been made we can go on to consider the detailed ledger account entries for the labour cost. The main accounting takes place in the wages control account.

5.2 Example: ledger accounting for labour costs

The **gross pay** is **debited** to the **wages control account** and the direct cost element is then transferred to the work in progress account whilst the indirect cost element is transferred to the production overhead control account.

A business paid its employees net pay of $15,000 for week 34. This was after deductions for income tax and National Insurance Contributions (NIC) of $6,000. The direct labour element of this was $18,000 and the indirect labour cost was $3,000.

Write up the ledger accounts to reflect the labour cost.

Solution

The first step is to debit the wages control account with the gross pay which is made up of the net amount paid to the employees and the income tax and NIC. The other sides of the entries are to the bank account for the net pay and to an Inland Revenue creditor account for the income tax and NIC as these amounts must be paid over to the Inland Revenue shortly.

WAGES CONTROL ACCOUNT

	$		$
Bank – net pay	15,000		
Inland Revenue – deductions	6,000		

The direct labour cost is then credited to the wages control account and debited to the work in progress account, as were direct materials, as part of the direct cost of making the products.

The indirect labour cost is credited to the wages control account and debited to the production overhead control account together with any indirect materials used.

WAGES CONTROL ACCOUNT

	$		$
Bank – net pay	15,000	Work in progress	18,000
Inland Revenue – deductions	6,000	Production overhead	3,000
	21,000		21,000

WORK IN PROGRESS

	$		$
Direct materials	50,000		
Wages control	18,000		

PRODUCTION OVERHEAD CONTROL

	$		$
Indirect materials	4,000		
Wages control	3,000		

Question | Labour double entry

A business has incurred direct labour costs of $25,600 and indirect labour costs of $3,800. What is the double entry required to record these?

A	DEBIT	Wages control	$29,400	
	CREDIT	Work in progress		$25,600
	CREDIT	Production overhead		$3,800

B	DEBIT	Wages control	$29,400	
	CREDIT	Work in progress		$3,800
	CREDIT	Production overhead		$25,600
C	DEBIT	Work in progress	$25,600	
	DEBIT	Production overhead	$3,800	
	CREDIT	Wages control		$29,400
D	DEBIT	Work in progress	$3,800	
	DEBIT	Production overhead	$25,600	
	CREDIT	Wages control		$29,400

Answer

Answer C

As we have seen the labour cost is the gross wages or salaries of the employees. It is important that we distinguish between direct labour and indirect labour and this will be done by careful coding of the payroll.

The payroll will consist of a listing for each department of the net pay, deductions and overtime details. These must be coded correctly to ensure that the gross pay is correctly analysed between direct and indirect labour and is collected by the correct cost centre.

Exam focus point

The cost accounting double entry for labour costs is highly examinable.

Chapter Roundup

- Hourly paid workers are generally paid a **flat rate per hour** with a premium for overtime hours.

- The hours worked are often recorded on **clock cards**, **job cards** or **time sheets**.

- An alternative to hourly pay is a **piecework system** where employees are paid according to the number of good units of production.

- Some remuneration schemes involve either an individual or group **bonus scheme** in an attempt to improve productivity.

- The **labour cost** can often be a significant element of unit cost and it can change if different remuneration methods are introduced or reduced by an increase in productivity.

- The employer must **deduct** income tax and employee's National Insurance Contributions from the gross pay before paying the net pay to the employees.

- The **total labour cost** for an employer is the gross pay plus the employer's National Insurance Contributions.

- **Direct labour costs** are the costs of the hours worked by the production workers at the normal hourly rate.

- **Indirect labour costs** include the overtime premium for direct workers and any idle time hours for direct workers as well as the indirect workers employment costs.

- The **gross pay** is **debited** to the **wages control account** and the direct cost element is then transferred to the work in progress account whilst the indirect cost element is transferred to the production overhead control account.

1   What is the name of the amount paid in excess of the normal hourly rate for overtime hours?

    A   Overtime payments
    B   Overtime premium
    C   Overtime excess
    D   Overtime special payment

2   A system where the amount paid per unit increases as the individual's production increases is known as:

    A   Shiftwork
    B   Idle time work
    C   Bonus scheme
    D   Differential piecework

3   If overtime is worked at the request of the customer how is the overtime premium normally treated?

    A   As a direct labour cost
    B   As an indirect labour cost

4   How is the cost of idle time hours usually treated?

    A   As a direct labour cost
    B   As a indirect labour cost
    C   Neither of the above

5   What is the double entry for direct labour costs?

    A   Dr   Wages control   Cr   WIP
    B   Dr   Wages control   Cr   Payables
    C   Dr   WIP   Cr   Wages control
    D   Dr   Payables   Cr   WIP

Answers to Quick Quiz

1   B   Overtime premium. Note that an overtime payment is the total payment made for overtime hours whereas the overtime premium is the amount paid in excess of the normal hourly rate for the overtime hours.

2   D   This is the definition of differential piecework

3   A   At the request of a customer, overtime premium is usually treated as a direct cost. If it's due to general pressures of production then it will be treated as an indirect cost.

4   B   Idle time hours are usually treated as an indirect labour cost

5   C   Debit   Work in progress
        Credit   Wages control

13

Overhead costs

Study guide

			Syllabus reference
8	(g)	Explain and illustrate the process of cost apportionment and absorption for indirect costs (excluding reciprocal services)	4(a)(iii)
9	(e)	Describe the procedures and documentation required to ensure the correct authorisation, coding, analysing and recording of direct and indirect expenses.	4(a)(iii)
	(f)	Describe the procedures and documentation to ensure the correct coding, analysis and recording of sales.	4(c)(ii)

1 Introduction

In this chapter we cover the third element of business costs, expenses. On fairly rare occasions an expense will be classified as a direct expense. For example if a piece of machinery was hired for a particular job then the hire charges are a direct cost of that job. However, in the majority of cases expenses are indirect expenses - such as rent, rates, insurance, heat and light etc.

2 Absorption costing

FAST FORWARD

Overheads are made up of indirect materials, indirect labour and indirect expenses.

Under **absorption costing principles**, the production overheads of a business are absorbed into the cost of each of the products.

Absorption costing is a costing method where the cost of goods sold and the value of closing inventory both include an element of indirect costs or overheads.

Key term

Overheads are made up of indirect materials, indirect labour and indirect expenses.

The overheads of the business, under absorption costing are required to be included in the cost of the products of the business. In this chapter we will consider the process whereby the production overheads are absorbed into the cost of the production units.

In overview, the process is to share out all of overheads amongst the cost centres that incur them and then to share their overheads amongst the products made in the cost centre. However we have to recognise that not all of these cost centres are **production cost centres**, ie cost centres that actually produce goods. Some of the cost centres which incur overheads are **service cost centres**. These are areas of the business that provide necessary services to the production cost centres such as stores, maintenance or a canteen.

The overheads incurred by the service cost centres must in turn be shared amongst the production cost centres until all of the overheads are within the production cost centres. Then finally the total overhead can be shared amongst the units which are made in each of the production cost centres.

3 Allocation and apportionment of overheads

FAST FORWARD

The first stage of the process is the allocation of specific overheads to specific **cost centres** – then joint overheads are apportioned to each cost centre on an **appropriate basis**.

The first stage in the process is to **allocate** any specific overheads to individual cost centres that have incurred them. These will often be items such as indirect materials and indirect labour.

However there will be many expenses of the business such as rent and rates which are shared by a number of different cost centres. These joint expenses must be **apportioned** between the cost centres on some suitable basis. For example rent and rates are often apportioned or shared out between cost centres on the basis of the amount of floor area that each cost centre occupies. The machinery insurance costs might be apportioned on the basis of the value of the machinery in each cost centre.

There is not necessarily any right or wrong basis to use for apportionment, but the basis chosen should be fair.

3.1 Example: allocation and apportionment

A manufacturing business has two production cost centres, assembly and finishing, and two service cost centres, stores and maintenance. The following expenses are expected to be incurred in the forthcoming year.

	$
Indirect materials – assembly	13,500
finishing	8,000
maintenance	2,000
Indirect labour – assembly	14,000
finishing	9,000
stores	28,000
maintenance	36,000
Machinery depreciation	10,000
Rent and rates	60,000
Heat and light	15,000
Power	18,000
Insurance of machinery	8,000

You are also given the following information:

	Assembly	Finishing	Stores	Maintenance	Total
Floor area (sq m)	1,000	500	400	100	2,000
Power usage (%)	55%	35%	5%	5%	100%
Net book value of machinery $000	50	30	15	5	100

We will now allocate and apportion the overheads to the four cost centres.

Solution

	Assembly $	Finishing $	Stores $	Maintenance $	Total $
Indirect materials	13,500	8,000	–	2,000	23,500
Indirect labour	14,000	9,000	28,000	36,000	87,000
Machinery depreciation (net book value)					
(10,000 × 50/100)	5,000				
(10,000 × 30/100)		3,000			
(10,000 × 15/100)			1,500		
(10,000 × 5/100)				500	10,000
Rent and rates – floor area					
(60,000 × 1,000/2,000)	30,000				
(60,000 × 500/2,000)		15,000			
(60,000 × 400/2,000)			12,000		
(60,000 × 100/2,000)				3,000	60,000
Heat and light – floor area					
(15,000 × 1,000/2,000)	7,500				
(15,000 × 500/2,000)		3,750			
(15,000 × 400/2,000)			3,000		
(15,000 x 100/2,000)				750	15,000
Power (% usage)					
(18,000 × 55%)	9,900				
(18,000 × 35%)		6,300			
(18,000 × 5%)			900		
(18,000 × 5%)				900	18,000
Insurance (net book value)					
(8,000 × 50/100)	4,000				
(8,000 × 30/100)		2,400			
(8,000 × 15/100)			1,200		
(8,000 × 5/100)				400	8,000
	83,900	47,450	46,600	43,550	221,500

Question

Cost centres

A business has two production cost centres, A and B, and one service cost centre, the warehouse. The rent and rates expense for the business is anticipated to be $25,000 for the coming year. The floor space occupied by each cost centre in square metres is as follows:

Cost centre A	1,200 sq m
Cost centre B	1,800 sq m
Warehouse	2,000 sq m

How much of the rent and rates expense should be apportioned to cost centre B?

A $6,000
B $9,000
C $10,000
D $25,000

Answer

Answer B

$25,000 × 1,800/5,000 = $9,000

FAST FORWARD ➤➤

The **overheads** of the **service cost centres** must then be reapportioned to the production cost centres on an appropriate basis.

The next stage in the apportionment process is to reapportion the service cost centre overheads to the production cost centres. In order to do this there needs to be an appropriate basis of apportionment usually based upon the use that each production cost centre makes of the service cost centres.

Exam focus point

For exam questions you will need to be able to carry out basic apportionment of overheads.

3.2 Example: reapportionment of service cost centre costs

You now have further information about the use that assembly and finishing make of stores and maintenance:

	Assembly	Finishing
Number of stores requisitions	100	30
Maintenance call outs per annum	30	20

Reapportion the service centre costs to the production cost centres.

Solution

	Assembly $	Finishing $	Stores $	Maintenance $	Total $
	83,900	47,450	46,600	43,550	221,500
Stores (requisitions)					
(46,600 × 100/130)	35,846				
(46,600 × 30/130)		10,754	(46,600)		–
Maintenance (call outs)					
(43,550 × 30/50)	26,130				
(43,550 × 20/50)		17,420		(43,550)	–
	145,876	75,624	–	–	221,500

Question — Reapportionment of service cost centre

The process of allocation and apportionment of overheads has been carried out for a business with the following totals calculated:

	Production cost centres A $	B $	Service canteen $	Cost centres stores $
Allocated and apportioned overhead	24,600	32,400	18,500	8,200

The production cost centres have the following details:

	Production cost centres A	B
Number of employees	100	150
Number of materials requisitions	60	104

What is the total overhead for production cost centre B after reapportionment of the service cost centre overheads?

A $10,400
B $16,300
C $35,000
D $48,700

Answer

Answer D

	$
Allocated and apportioned overhead	32,400
Canteen overhead (18,500 × 150/250)	11,100
Stores overhead (8,200 × 104/164)	5,200
Total overhead	48,700

4 Absorption of overheads

FAST FORWARD

Once all of the overheads have been apportioned to the production cost centres an **overhead absorption rate** is determined normally based upon direct labour hours or machine hours.

The final stage of the process now that all of the overheads have been allocated and apportioned to the production cost centres is to find an absorption rate with which to absorb or include the overhead into the cost of each unit of production. This is done by finding a basis for absorption which will generally tend to be based upon the activity of the department.

4.1 Example: absorption of overheads

The assembly department is a largely machine based department whereas the finishing department is largely labour based. The management of the business have decided that the assembly department overheads should be absorbed on the basis of machine hours and that the finishing department overheads should be absorbed on the basis of labour hours.

The budgeted machine hours in the assembly department is 100,000 whereas the budgeted labour hours for the finishing department is 20,000.

The overhead absorption rate is as follows:

Assembly $\quad \dfrac{\$145,876}{100,000} = \$1.46$ per machine hour

Finishing $\quad \dfrac{\$75,624}{20,000} = \$3.78$ per labour hour

Question

Overhead absorption rate

A business has two production cost centres, manufacturing and packaging. The overheads and other details for these cost centres are as follows:

	Manufacturing	Packaging
Budgeted overhead	$154,000	$89,000
Labour hours	110,000	68,000
Machine hours	35,000	60,000

Management have decided that the overheads are to be absorbed on the basis of labour hours in the manufacturing department and on the basis of machine hours in the packaging department.

What is the overhead absorption rate per hour in each department (to the nearest cent)?

	Manufacturing	Packaging
A	$1.40	$1.31
B	$1.40	$1.48
C	$4.40	$1.31
D	$4.40	$1.48

Answer B

$$\text{Manufacturing} = \frac{\$154,000}{110,000} = \$1.40 \text{ per labour hour}$$

$$\text{Packaging} = \frac{\$89,000}{60,000} = \$1.48 \text{ per machine hour}$$

FAST FORWARD ⟩ The **overhead absorption rate** is then used to cost each product depending upon how many relevant hours each product takes in each production cost centre.

For each product that is produced in the two departments a certain amount of overhead will be included in the cost of the product based upon the number of hours that the product spends in each production cost centre.

4.2 Example: product costs

One of the products of the business is the Powerpuff. This product has direct material costs of $14.30 per unit and direct labour costs of $16.50 per unit. Each unit of the Powerpuff spends 6 machine hours in the assembly department and 3 labour hours in the finishing department.

What is the final unit cost of the Powerpuff?

Solution

	$
Direct materials	14.30
Direct labour	16.50
Assembly overhead (6 hours x $1.46)	8.76
Finishing overhead (3 hours x $3.78)	11.34
Total unit cost	50.90

Question   **Total overhead per product**

A business has two production departments, assembly and polishing. One of the products made in these departments is the Stun. Details for these departments and the Stun are as follows:

	Assembly	Polishing
Budgeted overhead	$94,800	$74,800
Budgeted labour hours	20,000	40,000
Budgeted machine hours	60,000	15,000
Stun – labour hours per unit	3 hours	5 hours
Stun – machine hours per unit	4 hours	2 hours

Overheads in the assembly department are to be absorbed on the basis of machine hours and in the polishing department on the basis of labour hours.

How much overhead in total would be included in the cost of a Stun?

A $3.45
B $8.48
C $10.06
D $15.67

Answer D

$$\text{Assembly overhead absorption rate} = \frac{\$94,800}{60,000} = \$1.58 \text{ per machine hour}$$

$$\text{Polishing overhead absorption rate} = \frac{\$74,800}{40,000} = \$1.87 \text{ per labour hour}$$

	$
Overhead to be absorbed	
Assembly $1.58 x 4 hours	6.32
Polishing $1.87 x 5 hours	9.35
Total overhead	15.67

FAST FORWARD In order for overheads to be initially allocated and apportioned to the correct cost centres all overhead invoices must be carefully coded.

So the process of absorbing overheads into the costs of production starts with the allocation and apportionment of the indirect expenses to the each cost centre. It is therefore important that each individual expense is correctly coded to the correct cost centre.

For items of expense that are to be allocated to a specific cost centre, there will be only one code. These amounts will tend to be indirect materials which will be coded on the materials requisition and indirect labour which will be coded from the payroll. If any invoices are received for expenses for a specific cost centre then the net amount of the invoice must be coded to that cost centre.

For expenses which have to be apportioned between cost centres then the cost accountant will carry out the apportionment on the approved basis of apportionment and the amounts for each cost centre will be coded to that cost centre.

5 Sales income

FAST FORWARD The sales income of the business may be analysed in a number of different ways depending upon the needs of management – whatever analysis is required each sales invoice must be carefully coded.

In the last three chapters we have seen how the cost accountant will analyse, code and record the three elements of cost – materials, labour and overheads. The cost accountant will also need to ensure that sales income is also correctly analysed, coded and accounted for.

The sales of a business may be analysed in a number of different ways for management accounting purposes depending upon the needs of management. The possible ways of analysing sales income include by:

- Product
- Geographical region
- Department
- Division

Whatever analysis is required by management each sales invoice must be coded to ensure that the sales income is correctly recorded. As with expenses it is the net amount of the invoice that must be coded as the sales tax will be recorded separately in the sales tax control account.

When the sales invoices have been coded the double entry will be:

DEBIT   Receivables or bank
CREDIT   Sales

There may be a number of different sales accounts according to the analysis required for example a sales account for each product or for each geographical region.

Chapter Roundup

- **Overheads** are made up of indirect materials, indirect labour and indirect expenses.

- Under **absorption costing principles**, the production overheads of a business are absorbed into the cost of each of the products.

- The first stage of the process is the allocation of specific overheads to specific **cost centres** – then joint overheads are apportioned to each cost centre on an **appropriate basis**.

- The **overheads** of the **service cost centres** must then be reapportioned to the production cost centres on an appropriate basis.

- Once all of the overheads have been apportioned to the production cost centres an **overhead absorption rate** is determined normally based upon direct labour hours or machine hours.

- The **overhead absorption rate** is then used to cost each product depending upon how many relevant hours each product takes in each production cost centre.

- In order for overheads to be initially allocated and apportioned to the correct cost centres all overhead invoices must be carefully coded.

- The sales income of the business may be analysed in a number of different ways depending upon the needs of management – whatever analysis is required each sales invoice must be carefully coded.

Quick Quiz

1   What is the name given to the costing method where the cost of goods sold and the value of closing inventory include an element of indirect costs or overheads?

    A   Absorption costing
    B   Allocation costing
    C   Apportionment costing
    D   Activity-based costing

2   Which one of the following is the formula for calculating an overhead absorption rate?

    A   Actual activity level ÷ budgeted total overhead
    B   Budgeted activity level ÷ budgeted total overhead
    C   Budgeted total overhead ÷ budgeted activity level
    D   Budgeted total overhead ÷ actual activity level

3   Put the following stages of absorption costing into the correct order.

    A   Reapportionment
    B   Allocation
    C   Absorption
    D   Apportionment

4   The net amount of the sales invoice must be coded, rather than the sales tax inclusive amount. Is this true of false?

5   What is the double entry for sales on credit?

A	Dr	Sales	Cr	Payables
B	Dr	Sales	Cr	Receivables
C	Dr	Payables	Cr	Sales
D	Dr	Receivables	Cr	Sales

1 A This is absorption costing. Absorption costing involves allocating specific overheads and apportioning any joint expenses.

2 C Budgeted total overhead ÷ budgeted activity level. Remember that overhead absorption rates are calculated before the actual figures are known so they must use 'budgeted' figures.

3 1B, 2D, 3A, 4C. Specific overheads are first allocated to cost centres. Then joint overheads are apportioned to each cost centre on an appropriate basis. The overheads of service cost centres are then reapportioned to production cost centres. Once all of the overheads have been apportioned an overhead absorption rate can be determined and overheads can be absorbed.

4 True As with expenses, it is the net amount of the invoice that must be coded as the sales tax will be recorded separately in the sales tax control account.

5 D Debit   Receivables

Credit Sales

14

Information for comparison

Study guide

			Syllabus reference
10	(a)	Explain the purpose of making comparisons.	5(a)
	(b)	Identify relevant bases for comparison: previous period data, corresponding period data, forecast/budget data.	5(a)
	(d)	Explain the concept of flexible budgets.	5(a)
	(e)	Use appropriate income and expenditure data for comparison.	5(a)

1 Introduction

We saw in Chapter 6 that management information helps managers plan, control and make decisions. We have also discussed how managers obtain actual data for the current period.

We now go on to discuss how managers make comparisons between actual data and other data. In doing so they can assess the **significance** of the actual data for the period. Comparing current results with other data can make the information more useful. Comparisons may also help to show up any errors that have occurred.

2 Types of comparison

FAST FORWARD

Comparing actual results with **other information** helps to put them in context and may show up errors.

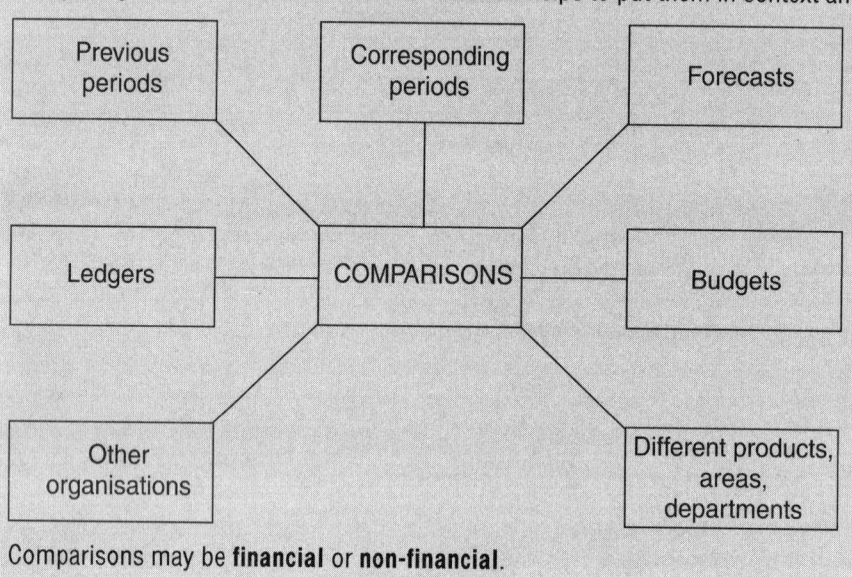

Comparisons may be **financial** or **non-financial**.

Many types of comparison are possible. The ones chosen depend on the needs of the individual and the organisation.

FAST FORWARD

Choice of the comparison to make depends on the **characteristics** of the organisation, the **individual** and the **activity** being reported.

Common comparisons include the following.

2.1 Comparisons with previous periods

The most common comparison of a previous period is when **one year's final figures** are **compared** with the **previous year's**. A business's statutory financial accounts contain comparative figures for the previous year as well as the figures for the actual year. As financial accounts are sent to shareholders, this comparison is obviously of great interest to them.

Some companies' financial accounts contain figures for the last five years. Comparing the figures for five years may be more valuable than comparing the figures for two years. **Long-term trends** become more apparent over five years. If the comparison is only over two years, one or other year might be unusual for various reasons. This will distort the comparison.

For management accounting purposes year-on-year comparisons are insufficient by themselves. Management will wish to pick up problems a lot sooner than the end of the financial year. Hence comparisons are often made for management accounting purposes **month-by-month** or **quarter-by-quarter** (three months-by-three months).

2.2 Comparisons with corresponding periods

Making comparisons month-by-month or quarter-by-quarter is most useful when you expect figures to be reasonably even over time. However demand for many products fluctuates **season-by-season**.

2.3 Example: seasonal fluctuations

A company making Christmas decorations had sales for the quarter ended 31 December that were considerably greater than sales for the previous quarter ended 30 September. For the quarter ended the following 31 March its sales decreased significantly again. Should its managers be concerned?

Based on the information given, we cannot tell. All the information tells us is that most people buy Christmas decorations in the three months leading up to Christmas. Comparing the December quarter's sales with the quarters either side is not very useful, because we are not comparing like with like. People are far more likely to buy Christmas decorations in the December quarter.

A far more meaningful comparison would therefore be to compare the December quarter's sales with those of the December quarter of the previous year, since the demand conditions would be similar.

This example demonstrates where comparisons with corresponding periods can be very useful, in businesses where the trade is **seasonal** (you would expect significant variations between adjacent periods).

Another example is heating bills. If the heating bill for the summer quarter is less than that for the winter quarter, the difference does not tell you anything about organisational performance, only about the weather.

2.4 Comparisons with forecasts

Businesses make forecasts for a number of purposes. A very common type of forecast is a **cash flow forecast**.

2.5 Example: cash flow forecast

GEORGE LIMITED: CASH FLOW FORECAST FOR FIRST QUARTER

	Jan $	Feb $	Mar $
Estimated cash receipts			
From credit customers	14,000	16,500	17,000
From cash sales	3,000	4,000	4,500
Proceeds on disposal of non-current assets	–	2,200	–
Total cash receipts	17,000	22,700	21,500

Estimated cash payments

To suppliers of goods	8,000	7,800	10,500
To employees (wages)	3,000	3,500	3,500
Purchase of non-current assets	–	12,500	–
Rent and rates	–	–	1,000
Other overheads	1,200	1,200	1,200
Repayment of loan	2,500	–	–
	14,700	25,000	16,200
Net surplus/(deficit) for month	2,300	(2,300)	5,300
Opening cash balance	1,200	3,500	1,200
Closing cash balance	3,500	1,200	6,500

The purpose of making this forecast is for the business to be able to see how likely it is to have problems **maintaining** a **positive cash balance**. If the cash balance becomes negative, the business will have to obtain a loan or overdraft and have to pay interest costs.

At the end of the period management will **compare** the **actual figures** with the **forecast figures**, and try to assess why they differ. Differences are likely to be a sign that some of the **assumptions** made when drawing up the original forecast were **incorrect**. Hence management, when making forecasts for future periods, may wish to change the assumptions that are made.

Comparisons within organisations

Organisations may wish to compare the performance of departments and different sales regions.

2.6 Example: analysis of results by sales area

PANDA LIMITED: ANALYSIS OF RESULTS BY SALES AREA

	Area 1 $'000	Area 2 $'000	Area 3 $'000	Total $'000
Sales (A)	600	500	150	1,250
Direct costs by areas:				
Cost of goods sold	320	250	60	630
Transport & outside warehousing	60	35	15	110
Regional office expenses	40	45	28	113
Sales people's expenses	30	25	11	66
Other regional expenses	20	15	8	43
Total direct cost by areas (B)	470	370	122	962
Gross profit (A – B)	130	130	28	288

Alternatively comparisons may be on a product by product basis.

2.7 Example: analysis of results by product

TEDDY LIMITED: ANALYSIS OF RESULTS BY PRODUCT

	Product A $'000	Product B $'000	Product C $'000	Total $'000
Sales	200	350	250	800
Variable costs of goods sold	95	175	90	360
Gross contribution	105	175	160	440
Variable marketing costs:				
Transport and warehousing	5	26	37	68
Office expenses	8	20	7	35
Sales salaries	15	44	25	84
Other expenses	2	7	6	15
Total variable marketing costs	30	97	75	202
Contribution	75	78	85	238

We shall discuss the importance of contribution in the final chapter.

2.8 Non-financial comparisons

As well as being made in **financial terms** (costs and revenues), you may make comparisons in other ways. For example you may compare units produced or sold. Other possible comparisons include measures of quality/customer satisfaction, time taken for various processes etc.

2.9 Example: a hospital casualty department

A hospital casualty department will aim to deal with incoming patients quickly, efficiently and effectively but numbers and types of patients are hard to predict. Comparing waiting times or cases dealt with per day will be misleading if one day includes the victims of a serious train crash and another covers only minor injuries. Long term comparisons might give a clearer picture and help to identify usage patterns (for example busy Saturday nights). Comparisons with other casualty departments might be even more revealing.

Question	Useful comparisons

Which of the comparisons given to the following individuals are the right ones to help them to assess the performance of their work teams?

(a)   Daily output in units compared with the same day, for the previous week, for a shift supervisor in a car factory

(b)   December sales value compared with the previous month for the sales manager of a firm trading in Christmas decorations

(c)   This year's examination results compared with last year for a secondary school headteacher

A   (a) only
B   (b) only
C   (a) and (c)
D   None of them

Answer

In (a) the information is not precise enough, in (b) you are not comparing like with like and in (c) other comparisons are needed.

(a)   Daily figures will not help the supervisor to judge the performance of his particular shift (there are other shifts during the day).

(b)   You would expect December sales to be the highest for the year so comparison with December last year and the year-to-date with last year might be more meaningful.

(c)   Exam results only measure one aspect of a school's objectives and will be affected by the quality of pupils as well as teachers.

2.10 Comparison with budgets

Most organisations have long-term goals which can be divided into:

*   **Objectives** (measurable steps towards achieving their goals)
*   **Action plans** (detailed steps for achieving their objectives)

The action plans are often expressed in money and provide:

*   An overall view for management
*   Assurance that different departments' plans co-ordinate with each other

The financial plan is usually called a **budget**.

> A **budget** is an organisation's plan for a forthcoming period, expressed in monetary terms.

> Budget comparisons are popular because they show whether budget holders are **achieving** their **targets**.
>
> Budget reports may be **combined** with **other information** such as non-financial information, ratios etc.

Budgets, like forecasts, represent a view of the future. However the two are not identical. Forecasts represent a prediction of what is **likely to happen**, the most likely scenario. Budgets may be a **target** rather than a prediction. The target may be a very stiff one and it may be far more likely that the business fails to reach the target than that it does achieve the target. However management may feel that setting a stiff target may keep staff 'on their toes'.

You can use budgets to check that the organisation's financial plan is working by **comparing** the **planned results** for the day, week, month or year to date **with** the **actual results**. Differences between these are known as **variances**.

The ways in which managers use budgets is a part of a continuous process of planning, monitoring performance and taking action on variances. This is sometimes called the **control cycle** and can be illustrated as follows.

2.11 The control cycle

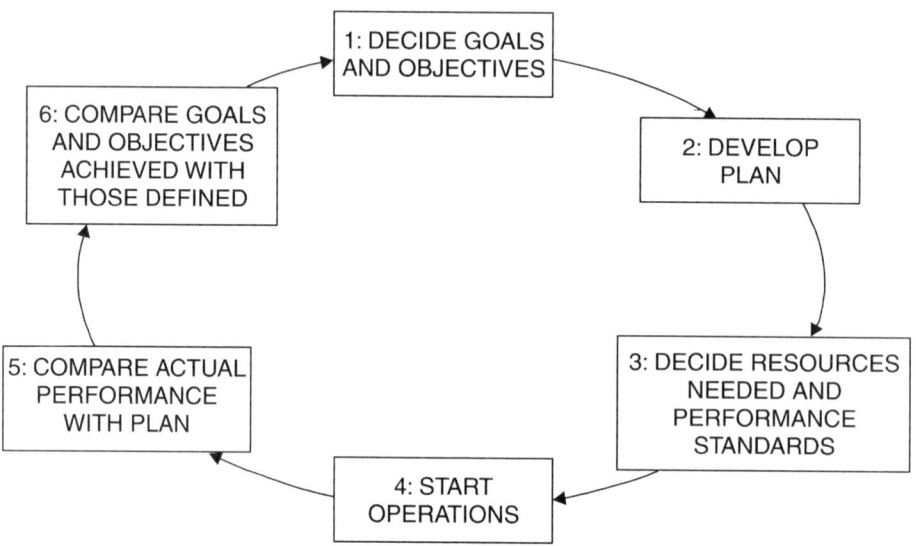

Stages of the control cycle is what we are looking at here.

3 Identifying differences

3.1 Variances and flexible budgets

> Variances can be calculated by comparing the fixed budget with the actual results (total variance) or comparing the flexed budget with the actual results (activity or price variance).
>
> You should report differences in such a way that managers can **understand them** and pick out **vital information easily**. Comparisons should not be cluttered with irrelevant information or too much detail.

There are two ways of looking at variances. The first way is to compare the budget figures to the actual figures achieved and this is called a total cost variance (or total sales variance).

For example, XYZ Ltd produces a product M. The following information is available for June.

	Budget	*Actual*	*Variance*
Material Cost	$5,000	$7,000	$2,000 (adverse)

The total cost variance comparing budget to actual cost is $2,000 adverse.

The problem with this type of variance calculation is that the volume of production may be different from the budgeted volume. This means that variance may not be very helpful for management making decisions on the product M.

In the example 3.2, more was spent on materials than we budgeted for so we have an adverse variance. At first sight this may seem like a bad thing and management may decide product M is costing too much. However, it turns out that there was such a large demand for product M in June that twice as many units of M were produced and sold. The materials were brought from an alternative supplier and cost only 35c per units instead of 50c per unit. This means that XYZ Ltd produced and sold more units and paid less per unit for the materials than budgeted. This is a good thing!

To make a useful comparison between the actual and budgeted figures we can use the second type of variance calculation. We can **adjust** or **flex** the budget to reflect the same production levels as was actually achieved. The new budget, flexed to the actual production level is known as the **flexible budget.** These variances are called the activity variance and the price variance.

FAST FORWARD
Flexible budgets should be used for comparison if the actual level of production is different from the original budget.

3.2 Example: flexible budget

Here is a production cost report for week 32 for the department making cartons.

	Actual	Budget	Variance	
Production (units)	5,000	4,800		
	$	$	$	
Direct materials	1,874	1,850	24	Adverse
Direct labour	825	810	15	Adverse
Prime cost	2,699	2,660	39	Adverse
Fixed overheads	826	840	14	Favourable
TOTAL COST	3,525	3,500	25	Adverse

Required

Prepare a flexible budget for week 32 for the department making cartons.

Solution

The figures above illustrate how easy it is to gain a misleading picture of performance if like is not compared with like. At first glance, it would seem that the results are generally worse than expected. An adverse difference, or variance, indicates that the actual cost was more than expected, and this was the case for direct costs, and the overall cost.

But if you were reminded that the budget was for a production level of 4,800 units, whilst 5,000 units were actually produced, this would change the picture. We might now suspect that the performance was better than expected, but to quantify and confirm that suspicion, we need to flex the original budget and make a new comparison.

All variable costs, such as direct materials and direct labour, will change in line with the change in production level, but fixed costs will remain the same.

	Actual	Flexed budget		Variance	
Production (units)	5,000	5,000			
	$	$		$	
Direct materials	1,874	1,927	$\left(\dfrac{1,850\times5,000}{4,800}\right)$	53	Favourable
Direct labour	825	844	$\left(\dfrac{810\times5,000}{4,800}\right)$	19	Favourable
Prime cost	2,699	2,771		72	Favourable
Fixed overheads	826	840		14	Favourable
Total cost	3,525	3,611		86	Favourable

Comparisons with budget are an extremely important aspect of management accounting, and need to be considered in more detail. This is done in the next chapter.

Question

Flexible budgets

Here is a production cost report for MWR Ltd for the three month period January-March 20X5.

	Actual	Budget
Production and sales (units)	3,000	2,000
	$	$
Sales revenue	30,000	20,000
Direct materials	8,500	6,000
Direct labour	4,500	4,000
Fixed overheads		
– Depreciation	2,200	2,000
– Rent and rates	1,600	1,500
Total cost	16,800	13,500
Profit	13,200	6,500

Required

Prepare a flexible budget for MWR Ltd for the three month period January-March 20X5.

Answer

FLEXIBLE BUDGET MWR LTD JANUARY-MARCH 2005

	Actual	Flexed budget	Variance	
Production and sales (units)	3,000	3,000		
	$	$	$	
Sales revenue	30,000	30,000		
Direct materials (W1)	8,500	9,000	500	Favourable
Direct labour (W2)	4,500	6,000	1,500	Favourable
Fixed overheads (W3)				
– Depreciation	2,200	2,000	200	Adverse
– Rent and rates	1,600	1,500	100	Adverse
Total cost	16,800	18,500	1,700	Favourable
Profit	13,200	11,500	1,700	Favourable

Workings

(1) **Direct materials**

Cost per unit = $\dfrac{\$6,000}{2,000\,\text{units}}$ = $3 per unit

Therefore 3,000 units = 3,000 × $3 = 9,000

(2) **Direct labour**

$$\text{Cost per unit} = \frac{\$4,000}{2,000\,\text{units}} = \$2 \text{ per unit}$$

Therefore 3,000 units = 3,000 × \$2 = \$6,000

(3) **Fixed overheads**

The flexed budget for fixed overheads will be the same as the original budget as overheads are **fixed costs**.

3.3 Other uses of comparisons with budgets

Businesses obviously need to be **co-ordinated**. For example you cannot increase sales if you do not have the goods available, or increase stocks if you don't have the money to pay for them. Variance reporting is important in alerting management to unplanned changes in one area of the business which may affect another. For example an unplanned decrease in production will affect future sales unless it can be made up.

Chapter Roundup

- Comparing actual results with other information helps to put them in context and may show up errors.

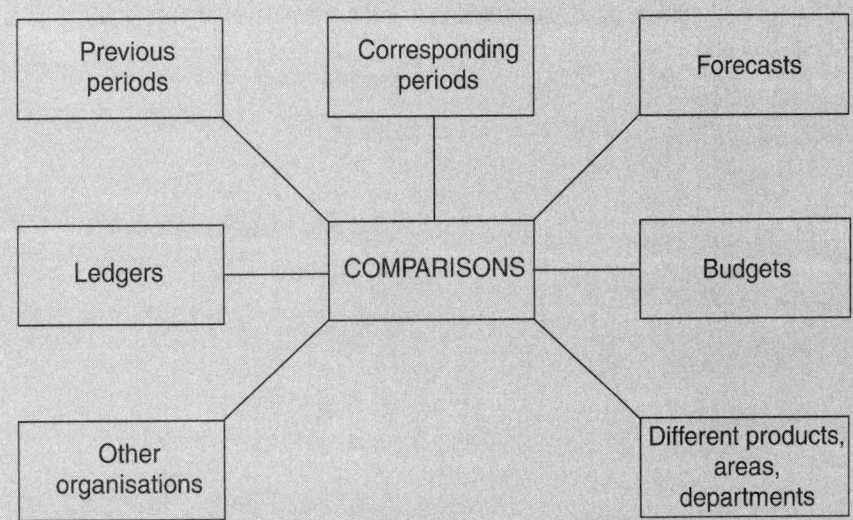

- Comparisons may be financial or non-financial.

- Choice of the comparison to make depends on the characteristics of the organisation, the individual and the activity being reported.

- Variances can be calculated by comparing the fixed budget with the actual results (total variance) or comparing the flexed budget with the actual results (activity or price variance).

- You should report differences in such a way that managers can understand them and pick out vital information easily. Comparisons should not be cluttered with irrelevant information or too much detail.

- Flexible budgets should be used for comparison if the actual level of production is different from the original budget.

- Budget comparisons are popular because they show whether budget holders are achieving their targets.

- Budget reports may be combined with other information such as non-financial information, ratios etc.

1   Which one of the following options is a financial comparison?

    A   Number of units produced compared to last year
    B   Number of units sold compared to last year
    C   Profit compared to last month
    D   Customer satisfaction compared to last month

2   A budget is expressed in monetary terms. Is this true or false?

3   When are flexible budgets used?

    A   When the actual level of production is different from the original budget
    B   When the actual level of production is the same as the original budget
    C   When the budgeted level of production is met exactly
    D   None of the above.

Answers to Quick Quiz

1   C   Comparisons made in financial terms (costs and revenues) are financial comparisons. Options A, B and D are non-financial comparisons. Sometimes these are more difficult to compare, for example customer satisfaction may be hard to measure.

2   True   A budget is an organisation's plan, expressed in monetary terms.

3   A   Flexible budgets should be used for comparison if the actual level of production is different from the original budget.

15

Variances

Study guide

			Syllabus reference
10	(c)	Explain the forecasting/budgeting process and the concept of feedforward and feedback control.	5(a)(iii)
11	(a)	Explain the concept of exception reporting.	5(b)(ii)
	(b)	Calculate variances between current actual and historical/forecast data.	5(b)
	(c)	Identify whether variances are favourable or adverse.	5(b)(i)
	(d)	Identify possible causes of variances.	5(b)(iii)
	(e)	Explain factors affecting the decision whether to investigate variances.	5(b)

1 Introduction

We stated in the last chapter that budgets can be used to check whether management's action plan is working. You compare the planned results for the day, week, month or year-to-date with actual results. Differences between actual figures and the budget are called **variances**.

Key term

> **Variance reporting** is the reporting of differences between budgeted and actual performance.

2 Calculating variances

FAST FORWARD

> **Variance reports** help budget holders to perform their function of **control**. The reports are especially useful if they separate controllable from non-controllable variances.

It is worth repeating the point made in the last chapter that a **total variance** compares the **fixed** budget and the **actual** results and the **activity variance** and **price variance** compare the **flexed** budget with the **actual** results. Once this has been done, it is merely a case of calculating the difference between actual and budget, and deciding whether the variance is favourable or adverse.

Variances are:

- **Favourable** if the business has more money as a result
- **Adverse** if the business has less money as a result

Favourable variances are not always good for the organisation. For example failure to recruit necessary staff will result in a favourable variance (less wages). It may, however, mean that business does not reach its production targets.

Reporting variances to the appropriate person draws attention to areas which are not running according to plan.

2.1 Example: Calculation of variances as a percentage

Here is an extract from a monthly cost report for a residential care home.

	Budgeted $	Actual $	Variance $	Variance %
Laundry	1,000	1,045	45 (A)	4.5
Heat and light	1,500	1,420	80 (F)	5.3
Catering	8,500	8,895	395 (A)	4.6
Nursing staff	7,000	6,400	600 (F)	8.6
Ancillary staff	10,600	10,950	350 (A)	3.3

$$\text{Variance \%} = \frac{\text{Actual costs} - \text{Budgeted costs}}{\text{Budgeted costs}} \times 100\%$$

3 Sales revenue variance calculations

FAST FORWARD

There are three types of sales revenue variance. These are the total sales revenue variance, the activity (or volume) variance and the selling price variance.

3.1 Introduction

Total sales revenue variance = activity variance + selling price variance.

Now we will look at the variance calculations using fixed and flexed budgets.

3.2 Total sales revenue variance

The total sales revenue variance measures the combined effect of the following.

* The actual selling price being different to standard selling price
* The actual sales volume being different to budgeted sales volume

The following example will illustrate how the total sales revenue variance is calculated.

3.3 Example

The following budgeted cost and selling price data relate to SM Limited's single product.

	$ per unit	$ per unit
Selling price		21.00
Direct cost	12.25	
Overhead cost	1.75	
		14.00
Budgeted profit		7.00

Data for last period were as follows.

Budgeted sales units	740
Actual sales units	795
Actual sales revenue	$16,200

Solution

	$
Sales revenue should have been (740 × $21)	15,540
Sales revenue actually was	16,200
	660 (F)

Question

Total sales revenue variance

Jasper Ltd has the following budget and actual figures for 20X4.

	Budget	Actual
Sales units	600	620
Selling price per unit	$30	$29

Budgeted full cost of production = $28 per unit.

Calculate the total sales revenue variance.

		$
Sales revenue should have been (600 × $30)		18,000
Sales revenue actually was (620 × $29)		17,980
Total sales revenue variance		20 (A)

3.4 Activity (or volume) variance

As mentioned in 3.2, the total sales revenue variance measures the combined effect of a difference in selling price and a difference in quantity sold. The activity (or volume) variance looks at the difference in quantity sold.

3.5 Example

The budgeted sales of SM Ltd were 740 units at a selling price of $21. The actual sales were 795 units at a total sales revenue of $16,200. What is the activity variance?

Solution

	Units
Budgeted sales volume	740
Actual sales volume	795
Activity variance in units	55 (F)
× Budgeted sales price per unit	× $21
Activity variance	$1,155 (F)

Activity variance

Jasper Ltd has the following budget and actual figures for 20X4.

	Budget	Actual
Sales units	600	620
Selling price per unit	$30	$29

Calculate the activity (or volume) variance.

	Units
Budgeted sales volume	600
Actual sales volume	620
Activity variance in units	20 (F)
× Budgeted sales price per unit	× $30
Activity variance	$600 (F)

3.6 Selling price variance

The selling price variance is shown in the example in 3.7. Note that the total sales revenue variance is the activity variance added to the selling price variance.

3.7 Example

The budgeted sales of SM Ltd were 740 units at a selling price of $21 per unit. The actual sales were 795 units at a total sales revenue of $16,200.

What was the selling price variance?

Solution

	$
Sales revenue from 795 units should have been (× $21)	16,695
But was	16,200
Selling price variance	495 (A)

The total sales revenue variance calculated in example 3.3 was $660 favourable. The activity (quantity) variance calculated in example 3.5 was $1,155 favourable. The selling price variance calculated in example 3.7 was $495 adverse.

Note that $660 F =$1,155 F+ $495 A

Question	Selling price variance

Jasper Ltd has the following budget and actual figures for 20X4.

	Budget	Actual
Sales units	600	620
Selling price per unit	$30	$29

Calculate the selling price variance.

Answer

	$
Sales revenue from 620 units should have been (× $30)	18,600
But was	17,980
Selling price variance	620 (A)

4 Cost variance calculations

4.1 Total direct cost variance

There are three types of cost variance. These are the total direct cost variance, the activity variance and the purchase price/efficiency of usage variance.

There are three types of cost variance. These are the total direct cost variance, the activity variance and the purchase price/efficiency of usage variance.

Total direct cost variance = activity variance + purchase price/efficiency of usage variance

The total direct cost variance measures the combined effect of the following

- The actual quantity produced being different to budgeted production volume
- The actual cost price being different to budgeted cost price
- The actual efficiency in which resources are used being different to budgeted efficiency.

4.2 Example

The budgeted materials for CTF Ltd were 800 units at a cost of $20 each. Actual material costs for the month were $17,600.

Solution

	$
Materials should have cost (800 × $20)	16,000
But did cost	17,600
Total direct cost variance	1,600 (A)

Total cost variance

The budgeted materials for HMF Ltd were 500 units at a cost of $15 each. Actual material costs for the month were $5,000.

Calculate the total direct cost variance.

Answer

	$
Materials should have cost (500 × $15)	7,500
But did cost	5,000
Total direct cost variance	2,500 (F)

4.3 Activity (or volume) variance

The activity (or volume) variance looks at the difference in the quantity produced.

4.4 Example

The budgeted materials for CTF were 800 units at a cost of $20 each. Actual materials costs for the month were $17,600 and 820 units were produced.

Solution

	Units
Budgeted production volume	800
Actual production volume	820
Activity variance in units	20 (A)
× Budgeted cost per unit	× $20
Activity variance	$400 (A)

Question Volume variance

The budgeted materials for HMF Ltd were 500 units at a cost of $15 each. Actual material costs for the month were $5,000 and 550 units were produced.

Calculate the activity variance

Answer

	Unit
Budgeted production volume	500
Actual production volume	550
Activity variance in units	50 (A)
× Budgeted cost per unit	× $15
Activity variance	$750 (A)

4.5 Purchase price/efficiency of usage variance

This variance is shown in example 4.6. Note that the total cost variance is the activity variance added to the purchase price/efficiency of usage variance.

4.6 Example

The budgeted materials for CTF Ltd were 800 units at a cost of $20 each. Actual materials costs for the month were $17,600 and 820 units were produced.

Solution

	$
Production of 820 units should have cost ($\times$ $20)	16,400
But did cost	17,600
Purchase price variance	1,200 (A)

Question   Purchase price variance

The budgeted materials for HMF Ltd were 500 units at a cost of $15 each. Actual material costs for the month were $5,000 and 550 units were produced.

Calculate the purchase price variance.

Answer

	$
Production of 550 units should have cost ($\times$ $15)	8,250
But did cost	5,000
Purchase price variance	3,250 (F)

Note that:

Total direct cost variance = Activity variance + purchase price/efficiency of usage variance.

Using examples 4.2, 4.4 and 4.6, the variances are $1,600 adverse , $400 adverse and $1,200 adverse.

$1600A = $400A + $1200A

5 Investigating variances

FAST FORWARD **Exception reporting** highlights variances which might need investigating.

Budgets are also used to allocate financial responsibility to individual managers. For example, the training manager will be responsible for expenditure on training. These responsible people are called **budget holders** and will have to decide what action to take if costs are higher or revenues lower than forecast. Reporting to them is sometimes called **responsibility accounting**.

Budget holders need to be informed of any variances that require investigation. They need not be pestered with immaterial variances, but they will need to look at larger variances, or variances which are showing a worrying trend. For this reason, many businesses operate a system of **exception reporting**.

Key term   **Exception reporting** is the reporting only of those variances which exceed a certain amount or %.

It is like a central heating thermostat with the budget as the temperature setting. Thermostats allow small variations around the setting but if the variation gets larger, they will take appropriate action (switch the boiler on or off) to control the temperature.

The decision to investigate a variance can also depend on whether it is **controllable** or **non-controllable**.

- **Controllable**: can be rectified by managers
- **Non-controllable:** are due to external factors beyond the managers' control

Budget holders may be required to explain why either type of variance has occurred and should take whatever action is needed. If the variance is controllable, management can take action to rectify problems. If the variance is non-controllable, management may wish to revise their plan. Either way budget holders are not necessarily to **blame** for the variance.

Finally, a variance will only be investigated if the cost of the investigation is to be outweighed by the benefits.

5.1 Example: investigation of variances

A manufacturer of copper pipes has budgeted for expenditure of $25,000 on copper in month 6 but actual expenditure is $28,000. Possible reasons for this $3,000 adverse variance include:

(a) **Price increase** by supplier. This may be controllable. The purchasing officer should try alternative suppliers.

(b) **World price rise** for copper. This is non-controllable. The budget may need revising for the rest of the year.

(c) **Higher factory rejection rate** of finished pipes. This is probably controllable but needs investigation. Is the raw material quality satisfactory? (if not, is this due to supplier, purchasing, warehousing?) Is the factory process at fault? (if so why? Poor supervision? Inadequate training? Machinery wearing out? – find out from the factory supervisors/managers).

You can see that reporting variances puts managers on the alert but only gives clues as to where the real problems lie.

FAST FORWARD

Variances can be interdependent.

It is important to understand that variances can be **interdependent**, with a single factor affecting more than one variance. Two examples are given below.

- Buying a better quality of material may increase the cost of materials due to its higher price, but usage of the material may be improved as there is less wastage. It could also decrease the labour cost for a given level of production as fewer hours may be needed to process the material if it is easier to work with, or fewer rejects are produced.

- Using unskilled labour rather than skilled labour for a particular task may cut the cost of labour in terms of rate of pay, but they may take longer to complete the job which will increase the labour cost again. Unskilled workers may also use more material than skilled labour, causing an adverse material variance.

To summarise, significant variances will be reported to the manager responsible who will then investigate the cause of the variance and act by either correcting an operational problem if the variance is controllable, or adjusting the budget if it is non-controllable and expected to continue. This system is known as **feedback control**.

Sometimes, if a variance is foreseen, the manager might take corrective action in advance of the problem in order to avoid a variance. This is known as **feedforward control**.

Question

A hospital decides to cut costs by reducing the number of cleaners employed by 10%. This results in a favourable variance in the budget reports. Is it good for the hospital?

Helping hand. Think of any other impacts a drop in a number of cleaners might have.

Answer

Helping hand. This illustrates not only the importance of non-financial objectives, but also how failure to meet non-financial objectives may impact upon financial objectives.

This is only good if the necessary standards of cleanliness can be maintained. If they can be, then there were probably too many cleaners before. If standards fall, there will be other effects (like more patient infections) which will cost more in the long term and damage the chief goal of improving health.

Question

Controllable and non-controllable variances

Here is an extract from a sales report for Region 3 in month 4 of the budget year.

		$ actual	$ budgeted
Salesperson	Green	8,500	8,000
	Brown	7,600	8,000

Brown is more junior than Green, and has attended fewer training courses. The more 'difficult' customers are shared between the two salespeople.

Brown's variance for month 4 is

A   Favourable and controllable
B   Adverse and controllable
C   Favourable and non-controllable
D   Adverse and non-controllable

Answer

Answer B

Brown's actual sales were $400 less than the budget which is an adverse variance. The information in the question leads us to the conclusion that the variance is controllable as he has been given the same target as the more experienced salesperson. Brown could be sent on more training courses.

Question

Controllable costs

A ward sister in a private hospital has the following changes in ward costs reported as exceptional.

	Actual $	Budget $	Variance $	
Nursing salaries	4,500	4,750	250	Favourable
Drugs and dressings	237	370	133	Favourable

Which of these costs do you think the sister can control?

A   Nursing salaries
B   Drugs
C   Dressings
D   None of the costs

Helping hand. The key to this activity is determining who makes the decisions about which costs.

(a) Nursing salaries would probably be centrally controlled by the hospital and influenced by NHS salaries. Drugs would be determined by a doctor and administered by a nurse. Dressings are probably the only item the ward sister has any control over.

(b) The $300 drugs cost for March looks quite different from the normal pattern of cost. You should look at the ledger account and purchase documents to see if it is correct.

(c) Combining drugs and dressings costs does not seem helpful in a ward report since only one is likely to be a controllable cost for the ward sister.

Question

Performance reports

A company produces the following performance report.

PERFORMANCE REPORT

PRODUCTION COST CENTRES

TOTAL COSTS – APRIL 20X1

	YEAR TO DATE 30.04.X1	
	Actual	**Budget (flexed)**
	$	$
Materials	39,038	35,000
Labour	89,022	85,000
Expenses	18,781	15,000

Which direct cost variances would be brought to the attention of the production managers responsible, if the company reports by exception any variances that vary by more than 10% from budget?

A Materials only
B Materials and labour
C Expenses only
D Expenses and materials

VARIANCE REPORT

PRODUCTION COST CENTRES

APRIL 20X1

	Year to 30 April 20X1
	$
Materials	4,038 (A)
Labour	4,022 (A)
Expenses	3,781 (A)

Comment

The significant variances which are more than 10% from budget are:

- Materials $4,038 (A) = 11.5% $\left(\dfrac{4,038}{35,000} \right)$

- Expenses $3,781 (A) = 25.2% $\left(\dfrac{3,781}{15,000} \right)$

The labour variance is not more than 10% from budget.

- Labour $4,022 (A) = 4.7% $\left(\dfrac{4,022}{85,000} \right)$

Chapter Roundup

- **Variance reports** help budget holders to perform their function of **control**. The reports are especially useful if they separate controllable from non-controllable variances.

- **Exception reporting** highlights variances which might need investigating.

- **Variances** can be **interdependent**.

- There are three types of revenue variance. These are the total sales revenue variance, the activity variance and the selling price variance.

- There are three types of cost variance. These are the total direct cost variance, the activity variance and the purchase price/efficiency of usage variance.

1   A difference between planned and actual results which results in the organisation having less money than forecast is called:

   A   A favourable variance
   B   An adverse variance
   C   A loss
   D   A profit

2   Statement 1   An adverse variance is always good for the business
     Statement 2   An adverse variance is always bad for the business

   A   Both statements are false
   B   Both statements are true
   C   Statement 1 is true but statement 2 is false
   D   Statement 1 is false but statement 2 is true

3   Which of the following statements about exception reporting is false?

   A   It avoids information overload
   B   It makes it easier for managers to spot important variances
   C   It reports variances which exceed a certain amount or %
   D   All variances highlighted should be investigated

4   What is the name given when a variance is foreseen and the manager takes corrective action in advance of the problem to avoid a variance?

   A   Feedforward control
   B   Feedback control
   C   Neither of the above

5   Which of the following options describes an activity variance?

   A   The actual efficiency in which resources are used being different to budgeted efficiency
   B   The actual quantity produced being different to budgeted production volume
   C   The actual cost pricing being different to budgeted cost price
   D   The budgeted efficiency in which resources are used being different to actual efficiency.

Answers to Quick Quiz

1   B   This is an adverse variance.

2   A   An adverse variance is not always good or bad. Whether it is good or bad depends on the reasons for the variance. For example, recruiting extra staff may result in an adverse labour variance but may mean that increased demand required higher levels of production (and higher revenue).

3   D   Not all variances should necessarily be investigated. For example a variance should only be investigated if the cost of the investigation is to be outweighed by the benefits.

4   A   Feedforward control (Feedback control involves acting after the cause of the variance has been investigated.)

5   B   The activity (or volume) variance looks at the difference in the quantity produced.

16

Marginal costing and decision making

Study guide

			Syllabus reference
12	(a)	Explain and illustrate the concept of contribution.	6(a)(i)
	(b)	Calculate and utilise contribution per unit, per £ of sales and per unit of limiting factor.	6(b)(ii)
	(c)	Explain and calculate the break-even point and the margin of safety.	6(a)
	(d)	Analyse the effect on break-even point and margin of safety of changes in selling price and cost.	6(b)(ii)
	(e)	Describe the assumptions, uses and limitations of marginal costing and break-even analysis.	6(a)

1 Introduction

In previous chapters we have covered:

- **Collection** of management information
- **Presentation** of management information
- **Comparisons** with different periods or budgets

This chapter returns to the subject of **marginal costing**, showing how management can use the information that you provide in **decision making**.

2 Making decisions

FAST FORWARD

Management use **management information** to help them make a variety of business **decisions**.

You will always need to know what information is relevant to the decision being made.

When providing management information for decision making, you must work out which costs and revenues are **relevant** to the decision. If in doubt, always clarify this with the person asking for the information.

The manager of a factory making two products believes that one of them is much more profitable than the other and asks for a profit statement to compare them.

Profit statement

	Product A $'000	Product B $'000	Total $'000
Sale revenue	100	120	220
Less: direct (variable) costs	(40)	(70)	(110)
Less: fixed production overheads	(20)	(20)	(40)
Gross profit	40	30	70
Less: other fixed expenses	(20)	(40)	(60)
Net profit/(loss)	20	(10)	10

Do you think the company should stop making product B?

The important idea here is that products can contribute towards paying the fixed costs of the business provided their:

Sales revenue is greater than variable costs.

So for example if 1,000 units of a product are sold at $40 per unit and the actual cost of making those units is $25 per unit, then the excess of revenue over costs = 1,000 (40 – 25) = $15,000. This $15,000 is available as a **contribution** to help pay for fixed costs such as insurance.

The idea of products contributing towards fixed costs is very useful for many decisions and, as we have already said, it is an important concept within a system of marginal costing.

Marginal costing, that is assessing the **contribution** which units sold make towards fixed cost, is one useful technique for assessing options for action.

In the example above a **marginal cost statement** would have made it clear that dropping Product B would decrease profits. The statement would look like this.

MARGINAL COST STATEMENT

	Product A $'000	Product B $'000	Total $'000
Sales revenue	100	120	220
Less: variable costs	(40)	(70)	(110)
Contribution to fixed costs	60	50	110
Fixed production costs			(40)
Other fixed costs			(60)
Net profit			10

In the example, Product B is making a $50,000 contribution to the total fixed costs of $100,000.

The general rule is that, if there are no restrictions on the quantity that can be produced or sold, it is always worth producing products that make a contribution. But what happens if there are limitations on production?

We need to be able to pick the products that lead to the largest profit for the business, which means looking at the contribution each product makes for the amount of the limited resource used. We then rank the products and use up the limited resources on the products that yield the most contribution.

Contribution per unit of a **limiting factor** should be used to decide between products if there is a constraint on production.

2.1 Example: restricted resources

Compass Ltd makes four products, the details of which are given below.

	East $	West $	North $	South $
Selling price	10.00	8.00	8.00	5.00
Direct labour @ $2 per hour	2.00	1.00	3.00	2.00
Direct materials @ $0.50 per kg	4.00	2.00	1.00	0.50
Total variable cost	6.00	3.00	4.00	2.50
Contribution per unit	4.00	5.00	4.00	2.50
Maximum sales quantity	100	200	100	150

In the coming period, Compass Ltd can only get hold of 1,502kg of material. What production plan will maximise the profit of the company?

First we must check that the materials restriction is a limiting factor by determining the material usage if the maximum sales demand were met.

East 100 × 8g	800
West 200 × 4g	800
North 100 × 2g	200
South 150 × 1g	150
	1,950g

So the restriction on materials quantity is a limiting factor.

West seems to have the highest contribution per unit, but it uses more material than the other products, so we have to calculate the contribution per kg of material to ensure that we use the material to earn the highest contribution, and therefore profit.

	East	West	North	South
Contribution per unit	$4.00	$5.00	$4.00	$2.50
Kg material per unit	8	4	2	1
Contribution per kg material	$0.50	$1.25	$2	$2.50
Ranking	4	3	2	1

The production plan that maximises profit will be:

	Material used kg	Contribution $
150 units of South	150	375
100 units of North	200	400
200 units of West	800	1,000
44 units of East (352/8)	352	176
	1502	1,951

Question   Labour hour restriction

Using the information in the example above, which product would rank first if there were no restrictions on the quantity of material available, but labour hours were restricted?

A   East
B   West
C   North
D   South

Answer

Answer B

	East	West	North	South
Contribution per unit	$4.00	$5.00	$4.00	$2.50
Labour hours per unit	1	0.5	1.5	1
Contribution per labour hour	$4	$10	$2.7	$2.5
Ranking	2	1	3	4

Exam focus point

A simple exam question on restricted resources is highly likely.

2.2 Example: decision making

Axle Ltd makes canned dog food for supermarkets to sell as 'own brand'. Each can costs 30c in direct materials and labour and sells for 40c. Axle Ltd's fixed costs for next year are estimated at $50,000. By calculating the contribution from each can, we are able to answer some of the questions which management accountants might encounter.

(a)   If forecast sales are 750,000 cans, what will budgeted profit be?

(b)   If these sales leave some spare production capacity in the factory, should Axle accept a special order for 20,000 cans at 35c per can?

Solution

	$
Selling price	0.40
Less: variable cost – direct materials	0.30
Contribution	0.10

(a) If we have forecast sales of 750,000 cans, we can find out what profit we will make by means of a simple calculation which recognises that profit is what is left over after we have contributed sufficient to cover fixed costs.

   Profit = Contribution – Fixed costs
   = (750,000 × $0.10) – $50,000
   = $25,000

(b) Should the special order be accepted? At a selling price of 35c per can, the contribution per can will be 5c. So the special contract will contribute an extra $1,000 (5c x 20,000) towards profits. The answer is therefore yes, as long as

   (i)   There is spare capacity so that we are not losing production of cans that contribute 10c each to make the cans that only contribute 5c each

   (ii) Existing customers are not upset and demand a reduced price on the cans for which they pay 40c.

 Question   Contribution

Climber Ltd makes climbing ropes which it sell to retailers for $51.60. Each rope uses direct materials costing $8.30 and direct labour costing $2.10. Variable production overheads amount to $1.20 per rope, and the business incurs fixed overheads of $80,000 per year.

How many ropes will Climber Ltd need to sell to make a profit of $50,000?

A   3,250
B   3,156
C   2,000
D   1,942

Answer

Answer A

		$
Selling price		51.60
Less: variable cost – Direct materials	8.30	
– Direct labour	2.10	
– Variable overheads	1.20	
		11.60
Contribution per unit		40.00

Profit = Contribution – fixed costs

$50,000 = (Quantity sold × $40) – $80,000

Quantity sold = $130,000 / $40
= 3,250

If you answered B, you did not include the variable overheads in the variable costs of production. If you answered C, your sales quantity only produced sufficient contribution to cover fixed costs. If you answered D, you excluded variable overheads and the profit required.

3 Breakeven analysis

The **margin of safety** gives a measure of the degree to which sales have to fall before **breakeven point** is reached.

> **Breakeven analysis**, or **cost/volume/profit (CVP) analysis** is the study of the interrelationships between costs, volume and profit at various levels of activity.

Let's return to the example we have just been looking at. Supposing Axle Ltd asked a third question: How many cans does the company need to sell in order to cover its fixed costs of $50,000?

To answer this, you have to consider that each can sold will contribute 10c towards those fixed costs. So the company has to sell enough cans so that those 10c s amount to $50,000. We can express this as:

Quantity sold × 10c = $50,000, or

$$\text{Quantity sold} = \frac{\$50,000}{\$0.10}$$

$$= 500,000 \text{ cans}$$

If the business makes sufficient cans to cover fixed costs only, then it is making neither a profit nor a loss, so the business will **break even**.

> **Breakeven point** is the level of sales where **total contribution = total fixed costs**. At this level the contribution is just enough to cover fixed costs and the company will make neither a profit nor a loss.

Using the same method as above we can find the quantity we need to sell in order to break even for any situation.

$$\text{Breakeven sales quantity} = \frac{\text{Fixed costs}}{\text{Contribution per unit}}$$

The breakeven sales in terms of revenue, rather than quantity can also be calculated.

Breakeven sales revenue = Breakeven sales quantity × selling price per unit

$$\text{Or} = \frac{\text{Fixed costs} \times \text{selling price per unit}}{\text{Contribution per unit}}$$

$$\text{Or} = \frac{\text{Fixed costs}}{\text{Contribution to sales ratio}}$$

> The **contribution to sales** or **C/S ratio** can be found by two means:
> - Total contribution /Total sales
> - Contribution per unit / Selling price per unit

The C/S ratio is useful as it enables you to calculate the breakeven point (in terms of sales revenue) when you don't know the contribution per unit, which can often happen in exam questions! It can also be used when there is a mixture of products, as long as the sales mixture remains the same.

3.1 Example: C/S ratio

	Product G	Product H	Total
Sales volume	2,000	4,000	
Selling price per unit	$8	$9	
Variable cost per unit	$4	$3	
Contribution	$4	$6	
Fixed costs			$20,000

16: Marginal costing and decision making | Part B Management information

Total contribution = $(2{,}000 \times \$4) + (4{,}000 \times \$6) = \$32{,}000$

Total sales = $(2{,}000 \times \$8) + (4{,}000 \times \$9) = \$52{,}000$

$$\text{C/S ratio} = \frac{32{,}000}{52{,}000} = 0.615$$

$$\text{Breakeven revenue} = \frac{\$20{,}000}{0.615} = \$32{,}520$$

The conclusion in this example is that the business will break even if sales total $32,520, and the products are sold in the ratio of 1 G to every 2 Hs.

Question · Breakeven quantity

Product K

C/S ratio	0.4
Selling price per unit	$5
Fixed costs	$4,000

The breakeven quantity is:

A 320
B 1,600
C 2,000
D 10,000

Answer

Answer C

$$\text{Breakeven revenue} = \frac{\text{Fixed costs}}{\text{C/S ratio}} = \frac{\$4{,}000}{0.4} = \$10{,}000$$

$$\text{Breakeven quantity} = \frac{\text{Breakeven revenue}}{\text{Selling price per unit}} = \frac{\$10{,}000}{\$5} = 2{,}000 \text{ units}$$

Alternative calculation

Contribution per unit = C/S ratio × selling price = 0.4 x $5 = $2 per unit

$$\text{Breakeven quantity} = \frac{\text{Fixed costs}}{\text{Contribution}} = \frac{\$4{,}000}{\$2} = 2{,}000 \text{ units}$$

If you answered D, you calculated the breakeven revenue. If you answered B, you multiplied fixed costs by the C/S ratio rather than dividing by it, and stopped there. If you answered A, you multiplied the breakeven revenue by the selling price rather than dividing by it.

One way in which management use breakeven information is to assess how safe the business is from making a loss.

Key term

> **Margin of safety** = $\dfrac{\text{Actual sales} - \text{Breakeven sales}}{\text{Actual sales}} \times 100\%$

The calculation of the margin of safety provides a comparison between the sales needed to cover costs and the expected sales. In the example Axle Ltd breakeven sales can be calculated as follows:

$$\text{Breakeven sales quantity} = \frac{\text{Fixed costs}}{\text{Contribution per unit}}$$

$$= \frac{\$50,000}{\$0.10}$$

$$= 500,000 \text{ units}$$

As the margin of safety is a percentage, it can either be calculated using units sold or $ sales. Axle Ltd's budgeted sales were 750,000, therefore:

$$\text{Margin of safety} = \frac{750,000 - 500,000}{750,000} \times 100\% = 33.3\%$$

Put another way the safety volume of sales is 250,000 units. Axle Ltd will have to sell 250,000 less units before making a loss. The safety margin of 33.3% or 1/3 is quite large.

A 1c rise in costs would affect Axle Ltd's breakeven point and margin of safety as follows:

Contribution = (0.40 – 0.31) = $0.09

$$\text{Breakeven quantity} = \frac{\text{Fixed costs}}{\text{Contribution}} = \frac{\$50,000}{\$0.09} = 555,556 \text{ units}$$

$$\text{Margin of safety} = \frac{750,000 - 555,556}{750,000} \times 100\% = 25.9\%$$

Axle Ltd still has a fairly large margin of safety; the safety volume of sales has reduced from 250,000 to 194,444 (750,000 – 555,556).

<table>
<tr><td>**Exam focus point**</td><td>You need to be confident in calculating a break even point and a margin of safety.</td></tr>
</table>

3.2 The advantages and limitations of breakeven analysis

FAST FORWARD

Do not forget that breakeven analysis does have **limitations**: it is only valid within a 'relevant range' of output volumes; it measures profitability, but does not consider the volume of capital employed to achieve such profits; and it is subject to the other limitations described in this chapter.

3.2.1 Limitations of breakeven analysis (sometimes referred to as CVP analysis)

(a)   It is **assumed** that **fixed costs are the same in total** and **variable costs are the same per unit at all levels of output**. This is a simplification that is only correct within the relevant range of output.

   (i)   Fixed costs will change if output falls or increases substantially (most fixed costs are step costs).

   (ii) The variable cost per unit will decrease where economies of scale are made at higher output volumes, and the variable cost per unit will also eventually rise where diseconomies of scale begin to appear at higher volumes of output (for example the extra cost of labour in overtime working).

(b)   It is **assumed that sales prices will be constant at all levels of activity**. This may not be true, especially at higher volumes of output, where the price may have to be reduced to win the extra sales.

(c)   **Production and sales are assumed to be the same**, therefore the consequences of any increase in inventory levels (when production volumes exceed sales) or 'de-stocking' (when sales volumes exceed production levels) are ignored.

(d)   **Uncertainty** in the estimates of fixed costs and unit variable costs is often **ignored** in breakeven analysis, and some costs (for example mixed costs and step costs) are not always easily categorised or divided into fixed and variable.

3.2.2 The advantages of breakeven analysis

In spite of limitations, breakeven analysis is a **useful technique** for managers in planning sales prices, the desired sales mix, and profitability.

Breakeven analysis should be used with a full awareness of its limitations, but can usefully be applied to **provide simple and quick estimates of breakeven volumes or profitability given variations** in sales price, variable and fixed costs within a 'relevant range' of output/sales volumes.

Breakeven analysis and margin of safety can be useful if the company is expecting to experience increasing costs, or has to reduce selling prices in order to remain competitive. The effect on breakeven point and margin of safety can be examined.

Question
Breakeven point and margin of safety

If Axle Ltd has to decrease the selling price of a can by 2c, the effect will be to

A   Increase the breakeven point and increase the margin of safety
B   Decrease the breakeven point and increase the margin of safety
C   Increase the breakeven point and decrease the margin of safety
D   Decrease the breakeven point and decrease the margin of safety

Answer

Answer C

The effect will be the same as an increase in costs.

Contribution = (0.38 − 0.30) = $0.08

$$\text{Breakeven quantity} = \frac{\text{Fixed costs}}{\text{Contribution}} \times \frac{\$50,000}{\$0.08} = 625,000 \text{ units}$$

$$\text{Margin of safety} = \frac{750,000 - 625,000}{750,000} \times 100\% = 16.7\%$$

Chapter Roundup

- Management use **management information** to help them make a variety of business **decisions**.

- You will always need to know what information is relevant to the decision being made.

- **Marginal costing**, that is assessing the **contribution** which units sold make towards fixed cost, is one useful technique for assessing options for action.

- Contribution per unit of a **limiting factor** should be used to decide between products if there is a constraint on production.

- The **margin of safety** gives a measure of the degree to which sales have to fall before **breakeven point** is reached.

- Do not forget that breakeven analysis does have **limitations**: it is only valid within a 'relevant range' of output volumes; it measures profitability, but does not consider the volume of capital employed to achieve such profits; and it is subject to the other limitations described in this chapter.

1   Which one of the following should be used to decide between products if there is a constraint on production?

    A   Contribution per unit
    B   Contribution per unit of limiting factor
    C   Profit per unit
    D   Profit per unit of limiting factor

2   The level of sales at which total contribution = total fixed costs is known as:

    A   Margin of safety
    B   Contribution
    C   Breakeven point
    D   C/S ratio

3   Product H

C/S ratio	0.5
Selling price per unit	$10
Fixed costs	$6,000

    The breakeven quantity is:

    A   600
    B   1,200
    C   3,000
    D   12,000

4   What is the margin of safety?

    A   Total contribution/Total sales
    B   Fixed costs/Contribution to sales ratio
    C   The product of breakeven sales quantity and selling price per unit
    D   The difference between breakeven point and forecast or actual sales

5   Two statements follow about breakeven analysis.

    1.   It assumes that fixed costs are constant at all levels of output.
    2.   It assumes that variable costs are the same per unit at all levels of output.

    Are the statements true or false?

    A   Both statements are false
    B   Both statements are true
    C   Statement 1 is false but statement 2 is true
    D   Statement 1 is true but statement 2 is false

1   B   Contribution per unit of a limiting factor should be used to decide between products if there is a constraint in production .

2   C   Breakeven point. At this level the contribution is just enough to cover fixed costs and the company will make neither a profit nor a loss.

3   B   Contribution per unit = C/S ratio × selling price = 0.5 × $10 = $5

$$\text{Breakeven quantity} = \frac{\text{Fixed costs}}{\text{Contribution}} = \frac{\$6,000}{\$5} = 1,200 \text{ units}$$

4   D   Option A is the C/S ratio. Options B and C both give the breakeven sales revenue.

5   B   Both statements are true. These are two of the limitations of breakeven analysis.

Pilot paper exam question and answer bank

Information for Management Control

ACCA CERTIFIED ACCOUNTING TECHNICIAN EXAMINATION

INTRODUCTORY LEVEL

PILOT PAPER – JUNE 2004

QUESTION PAPER

Time allowed **2 hours**

ALL FIFTY questions are compulsory and MUST be answered using the answer sheet provided

Do not open this paper until instructed by the supervisor

This question paper must not be removed from the examination hall

The Association of Chartered Certified Accountants

ALL FIFTY questions are compulsory and must be attempted

Please use the candidate Registration Sheet provided to indicate your chosen answer to each multiple choice question.
Each question carries two marks

1   Which of the following is an example of computer hardware?

    A   Compiler

    B   Internal modem

    C   Operating system

    D   Spreadsheet

2   Two statements follow about the purpose of a computer's mouse:
    1.   The purpose of a mouse is to control the cursor on the computer screen.
    2.   The purpose of a mouse is to let people play computer games quickly and cheaply.

    Are the above statements true or false?

    A   Both statements are false

    B   Both statements are true

    C   Statement 1 is false but Statement 2 is true

    D   Statement 1 is true but Statement 2 is false

3   The main piece of computer equipment is called the central processing unit (CPU).

    What is the best definition of a central processing unit?

    A   It contains all the computer programmes

    B   It is created by a computer programmer

    C   It is a programmed computer unit

    D   It is the piece of computer equipment for processing data

4   The date of birth of each employee is held on a computer system.

    Of what is 'date of birth' an example?

    A   A database

    B   A field

    C   A file

    D   A record

5   Which correctly states the maximum amount of data (approximately) that can be stored on the computer storage devices?

    A   3½" floppy 5Gb: CD-ROM 650Mb: DVD 1.44Mb

    B   3½" floppy 1.44Mb: CD-ROM 5Gb: DVD 650Mb

    C   3½" floppy 650Mb: CD-ROM 1.44Mb: DVD 5Gb

    D   3½" floppy 1.44Mb: CD-ROM 650Mb: DVD 5Gb

2

6 Why is it necessary to switch off your computer before going home at the end of the day?

    A   For confidentiality and security reasons

    B   To reduce fire hazards

    C   For both of the above reasons

    D   For neither of the above reasons

7 What is **NOT** now a common method of security when using computer databases?

    A   Identify names

    B   Key for the lock on the computer

    C   Passwords

    D   Restrictions on access rights

8 Why are **PINs** used?

    A   To ensure employees perform their work correctly

    B   To increase the capacity of the computer

    C   To restrict access by unauthorised personnel

    D   None of the above reasons

9 A networked PC system is backed up each evening and the minimum size of the backed-up data is 80Mb.

   What is the most likely back-up medium?

    A   A floppy disk

    B   A high speed printer

    C   A separate part of the file server's hard disk

    D   A zip disk cartridge

10 What term is applied to the practice of retaining computer files no longer required on a daily basis in their original form for storage elsewhere?

    A   Archiving

    B   Microfiching

    C   Microfilming

    D   Shredding

11 You work in your firm's computerised payroll section. Back-ups of confidential and important computer master files containing payroll information need to be securely stored within the office.

   Where should such files be kept?

    A   Box file on the office shelf

    B   Fire-proof locked cabinet

    C   Locked filing cabinet

    D   Payroll clerk's desktop drawer

12 An employee believes that incorrect information held about himself on his company's human resources system has contributed to him not being promoted. The company has acknowledged that the information was incorrect and has now corrected it. However, the employee is now seeking compensation for the loss of income that he feels this error has caused him over the years.

Under what legislation could the employee seek such compensation?

A   Computer Misuse Act

B   Computer Protection Act

C   Data Misuse Act

D   Data Protection Act

13 **What is the scientific term for facts, figures and information?**

A   Consultancy

B   Data

C   Referencing

D   Statistics

14 **Which is true of management information?**

A   It is the same as operating information

B   It must be produced by a computer

C   It should be completely accurate, regardless of cost

D   It should be produced if its cost is less than the increased revenue it leads to

15 **Which is NOT an attribute of effective communication?**

A   Clarity

B   Completeness

C   Complexity

D   Relevance

16 **Which is an example of internal information for the wages department of a large company?**

A   A Code of Practice issued by the Institute of Directors

B   A new national minimum wage

C   Changes to tax coding arrangements issued by the Inland Revenue

D   The company's employees' schedule of hours worked

17 **Which would be included in the financial accounts, but may be excluded from the cost accounts?**

A   Bank interest and charges

B   Depreciation of storeroom handling equipment

C   Direct material costs

D   Factory manager's salary

4

18 **What term is applied to the systematic arrangement of numerical data in order to provide a logical account of analytical results?**

   A   Computerisation

   B   Pictorialisation

   C   Quantification

   D   Tabulation

19 The phrase 'Laura bought a loaf of bred' is contained in a word processed document. It contains a mistake because bred should really read bread.

   What is the most likely way of the author finding this error?

   A   Ask a colleague to carefully proof-read the document and indicate any mistakes

   B   Check the document with the grammar checker in the word processing software

   C   Check the document with the spell checker in the word processing software

   D   Use a document imaging system to identify incorrectly used words

20 **When communicating information, which of the following determine the choice of method used?**

   1.   Comparative cost
   2.   Degree of confidentiality
   3.   Speed of delivery

   A   1 only

   B   3 only

   C   1 and 2 only

   D   1, 2 and 3

21 Two statements follow about the purpose of an e-mail system:
   1.   The purpose of an e-mail system is to send and receive data a computer can work with.
   2.   The purpose of an e-mail system is to send and receive messages quickly and cheaply.

   Are the statements true or false?

   A   Both statements are false

   B   Both statements are true

   C   Statement 1 is false and Statement 2 is true

   D   Statement 1 is true and Statement 2 is false

22 **What is the most appropriate definition of an office?**

   A   A centre for exchanging information between businesses

   B   A centre for information and administration

   C   A place where information is stored

   D   A room where many people using IT work

23 Which is a disadvantage of office manuals?

    A   Strict interpretation of instructions creates inflexibility

    B   The quality of service received from suppliers is reduced

    C   They create bureaucracy and demotivate staff

    D   They do not facilitate the induction and training of new staff

24 Which function is **LEAST** likely to be carried out by an Accounts Department?

    A   Arrangement of payment of creditors

    B   Calculation of wages and salaries to be paid

    C   Despatch of customer orders

    D   Preparation of company financial records

25 What is the main purpose of prime entry records?

    A   Calculate the cash received and spent by a business

    B   Prevent a large volume of unnecessary detail in the ledgers

    C   Provide a monthly check on the double-entry bookkeeping

    D   Separate the taxable and exempt VAT transactions

26 The following relate to the use of order processing software in a company:
1. Legislative changes may be incorporated automatically in periodic updates.
2. Rival companies will be able to use the same software.
3. The company controls development of the software.
4. There may be a large user group to share experiences.

What are advantages to the company of implementing a software package solution to manage order processing?

    A   1 and 3 only

    B   1 and 4 only

    C   2 and 4 only

    D   1, 3 and 4 only

27 The following relate to batch processing or to real-time processing of data:
1. Audit trails are easily made since the processing of data occurs at pre-determined times.
2. Customer queries can be responded to immediately.
3. Processing can be performed during the evening when the computer is not being used interactively.
4. The data is always up-to-date.

What are advantages of real-time processing?

    A   1 and 2 only

    B   1 and 3 only

    C   2 and 4 only

    D   1, 3 and 4 only

6

28 Which of the departments listed is **NOT** a service cost centre in a manufacturing company?

A   Accounting

B   Assembly

C   Maintenance

D   Personnel

29 A company operates a retail supermarket chain selling a range of grocery and household products. It has branches throughout the country and is reviewing the range of goods to be stocked in each of these branches.

How might the company best analyse its profitability for this purpose?

A   By area of the country

B   By contract with each supplier

C   By customer payment method

D   By product line stocked

30 A large hotel has bars, restaurants and banqueting. They are used by hotel residents and outside users. The manager of the hotel is responsible for encouraging residents to use the hotel's catering facilities.

Which report will show how effective the manager has been in achieving this objective?

A   A report analysing the utilisation of hotel services per room occupied

B   A report showing the amount of money spent in the hotel's catering facilities

C   A report showing the number of residents in the hotel at any given time

D   A report showing the occupancy of the various catering facilities

31

Cost per unit (£)

Activity level

Which description best fits the above cost curve?

A   Direct labour cost per unit

B   Direct material cost per unit

C   Fixed production cost per unit

D   Variable production cost per unit

32 Which item would most likely be treated as an indirect cost by a furniture manufacturer?

   A   Fabric to cover the seat of a chair

   B   Metal used for the legs of a chair

   C   Staples to fit the fabric to the seat of a chair

   D   Wood used to make the frame of a chair

33 A company employs 20 direct production operatives and 10 indirect staff in its manufacturing department. The normal operating hours for all employees is 38 hours per week and all staff are paid a basic rate of £5 per hour. Overtime hours are paid at the basic rate + 50%. During a particular week all employees worked for 44 hours to meet the company's general production requirements.

   What amount would be charged to production overhead?

   A   £300

   B   £450

   C   £2,350

   D   £2,650

34 With which costs is absorption costing concerned?

   A   Direct labour costs only

   B   Direct material costs only

   C   Fixed costs only

   D   Variable and fixed costs

35 How is total contribution calculated?

   A   Total revenue less fixed costs

   B   Total revenue less production costs

   C   Total revenue less total costs

   D   Total revenue less variable costs

36 Aspects of payroll include:
   1. Employer's national insurance contribution
   2. Employee's national insurance contribution
   3. Income Tax (PAYE)
   4. Salaries

   Which of the above are costs to an employer?

   A   1 and 4 only

   B   2 and 4 only

   C   2, 3 and 4 only

   D   1, 2, 3 and 4

37 An employee is paid on a piecework basis. The scheme is as follows:

1 – 100 units per day	£0·20 per unit
101 – 200 units per day	£0·30 per unit
> 200 units per day	£0·40 per unit

Only the additional units qualify for the higher rates. Rejected units do not qualify for payment. An employee produced 210 units in a day of which 17 were rejected as faulty.

What did the employee earn for the day?

A   £47.90

B   £54.00

C   £57.90

D   £84.00

38 It is possible for an item of overhead expenditure to be shared amongst several cost centres. It is also possible that an item of overhead expenditure may relate to just one specific cost centre.

What term is used to describe charging an item of overhead to just one specific cost centre?

A   Absorption

B   Allocation

C   Apportionment

D   Re-apportionment

39 **What would be the most appropriate basis for apportioning machinery insurance costs to cost centres within a factory?**

A   Floor area occupied by the machinery

B   Number of machines

C   Operating hours of machinery

D   Value of machinery

40 A firm uses a unique code to identify each customer: the first four letters of each name are followed by four digits.

Which will appear first when customers are sorted into descending order?

A   ADAM0001

B   ADAA0099

C   ADDA0100

D   ABAB0999

41 A firm maintains a stock control database.

What is most likely to occur when suppliers cannot deliver goods on time?

A   Customer demand will rise accordingly

B   Customer orders will not be satisfied

C   Stock levels will become too high

D   Suppliers' delivery quantities will be lowered

42 What is the sequential flow of documents to complete the purchase of goods on credit?

A   Goods received note, purchase order, cheque requisition, invoice, delivery note

B   Purchase order, delivery note, goods received note, invoice, cheque requisition

C   Purchase order, goods received note, delivery note, cheque requisition, invoice

D   Purchase order, invoice, goods received note, cheque requisition, delivery note

43 Which member of staff is most likely to raise a goods received note?

A   Delivery driver

B   Finance director

C   Sales ledger clerk

D   Store clerk

44 The following statements relate to the application of feedback and feedforward control:
    1. Feedback and feedforward are both applied in budgetary planning and control.
    2. Feedback is used in the analysis of variances.
    3. Feedforward enables budgeted data for a period to be amended for the next period.
    4. Feedforward relates to the setting of performance standards.

    Which of the above statements are true?

    A   1 and 2 only

    B   3 and 4 only

    C   1, 2 and 4 only

    D   1, 3 and 4 only

45 Which is the correct description of a flexible budget?

    A   A budget that can be changed according to circumstances

    B   A budget that is adjusted according to actual activity

    C   A budget that is open to negotiation

    D   A budget that is used for planning purposes only

46 A product has a budgeted direct material cost of £5 per unit. In a period production of the product was:

    Budget   9,000 units
    Actual   8,800 units

    £44,380 was incurred on direct materials for the period's production.

    What was the direct material variance, comparing actual with the flexed budget?

    A   £380 Adverse

    B   £380 Favourable

    C   £620 Adverse

    D   £620 Favourable

47 Which of the following is **NOT** a factor that should affect a decision whether to investigate a variance?

    A   Controllability of variance

    B   Cost of investigation

    C   Personnel involved

    D   Trend of variance

48 A company has sold 11,300 units of its single product for a total sales revenue of £88,140. Variable costs and fixed costs are £4.29 and £2.73 per unit respectively.

    What is the contribution sales ratio?

    A   10%

    B   45%

    C   55%

    D   65%

49 Which of the following is **NOT** an assumption used in break-even analysis?

A   Selling price depends upon quantity sold

B   Total variable costs increase in proportion to activity

C   Unit fixed costs increase with a decrease in activity

D   Unit variable costs are a constant

50 The following information is available:

Sales	£103,200	(@ £12 per unit)
Variable costs	£54,180	
Fixed costs	£38,000	

    What level of sales is required to break-even?

    A   6,032 units

    B   8,600 units

    C   £72,381

    D   £80,000

End of Question Paper

11

1	B	A compiler is a special type of software tool used to help write programs. Of the four options, only a modem is hardware.
2	D	The main purpose of a mouse is not to play games!
3	D	The CPU processes instructions and data.
4	B	'Date of birth' would be a field in a database record.
5	D	
6	C	Both reasons are valid.
7	B	Modern computers don't tend to require keys to be 'unlocked'.
8	C	
9	D	A Zip disk would be a better back-up option than part of the server, as it could be stored off site.
10	A	
11	B	A fire proof locked cabinet is the best option within the office.
12	D	Personal information is covered by the Data Protection Act.
13	B	
14	D	All information should bring greater benefits than the cost of producing it – otherwise it is not wroth producing.
15	C	Effective communication should be as simple as possible – complete ideas should be explained clearly.
16	D	Only this option refers to internal information.
17	A	
18	D	

19	A	The spell checker would not pick up 'bred' as it is a valid word. Grammar checkers are unreliable.
20	D	All three items are important.
21	B	
22	B	
23	A	
24	C	
25	B	
26	B	Only items 1 and 4 are valid advantages to the company of implementing the software.
27	C	Real-time systems are updated immediately, so are always up to date.
28	B	
29	D	
30	A	
31	C	The other three are variable costs and therefore would be constant amounts per unit as activity increases whereas the fixed costs remain constant in total but fall per unit as activity levels increase
32	C	Small consumables such as staples are often treated as indirect costs

33 D

		£
Indirect workers –	38 hours × £5 × 10	1,900
	6 hours × £7.50 × 10	450
Direct workers – over time premium 6 hours × £2.50 × 20		300
		2,650

34	D	
35	D	
36	A	The employee's national insurance contributions and PAYE are deducted from the employees' gross pay and paid over to the Inland Revenue and are therefore not a cost to the employer
37	A	Total good production 210 – 17 = 193

	£
100 @ £0.20	20.00
93 @ £0.30	27.90
	47.90

38	B	
39	D	The insurance cost will be based upon the value of the machinery rather than floor area occupied, number of machines or operating hours.
40	C	
41	B	
42	B	
43	D	
44	A	
45	B	

			£
46	A		
		8,800 units should have cost	44,000
		But did cost	44,380
			380 Adverse

47   C

48   B

		£
Selling price £88,140/11,300		7.80
Variable cost		4.29
Contribution		3.51

Contribution to sales ratio $\dfrac{3.51}{7.80} \times 100 = 45\%$

49   A

50   D

Number of units sold	=	£103,200/£12
	=	8,600 units
Variable cost per unit	=	£54,180/8,600
	=	£6.30
Contribution per unit	=	£12.00 – 6.30
	=	£5.70
Break even in units	=	£38,000/5.70
	=	6,666.667
Break even in sales value	=	6,666.667 × £12 = £80,000

List of key terms and index

List of key terms

REVIEW FORM & FREE PRIZE DRAW

All original review forms from the entire BPP range, completed with genuine comments, will be entered into one of two draws on 31 January 2009 and 31 July 2009. The names on the first four forms picked out on each occasion will be sent a cheque for £50.

Name: _____   Address: _____
_____
_____

How have you used this Interactive Text?
(Tick one box only)
☐ Home study (book only)
☐ On a course: college _____
☐ With 'correspondence' package
☐ Other _____

Why did you decide to purchase this Interactive Text? *(Tick one box only)*
☐ Have used BPP Texts in the past
☐ Recommendation by friend/colleague
☐ Recommendation by a lecturer at college
☐ Saw advertising
☐ Other _____

Which BPP products have you used?
☑ Text ☐ Kit ☐ i-Pass ☐ i-Learn

During the past six months do you recall seeing/receiving any of the following?
(Tick as many boxes as are relevant)
☐ Our advertisement in *ACCA Student Accountant*
☐ Other advertisement _____
☐ Our brochure with a letter through the post
☐ Our website www.bpp.com

Which (if any) aspects of our advertising do you find useful?
(Tick as many boxes as are relevant)
☐ Prices and publication dates of new editions
☐ Information on Interactive Text content
☐ Facility to order books off-the-page
☐ None of the above

Your ratings, comments and suggestions would be appreciated on the following areas

	Very useful	Useful	Not useful
Introductory section (How to use this Interactive Text)	☐	☐	☐
Key terms	☐	☐	☐
Examples	☐	☐	☐
Questions and answers	☐	☐	☐
Key learning points	☐	☐	☐
Quick quizzes	☐	☐	☐
Exam alerts	☐	☐	☐
Question Bank	☐	☐	☐
Answer Bank	☐	☐	☐
List of key terms and index	☐	☐	☐
Structure and presentation	☐	☐	☐
Icons	☐	☐	☐

	Excellent	Good	Adequate	Poor
Overall opinion of this Interactive Text	☐	☐	☐	☐

Do you intend to continue using BPP products?   ☐ Yes ☐ No

Please note any further comments and suggestions/errors on the reverse of this page. The BPP author of this edition can be emailed at heatherfreer@bpp.com

Please return this form to: Mary Maclean, CAT Range Manager, BPP Learning Media, FREEPOST, London, W12 8BR

REVIEW FORM & FREE PRIZE DRAW (continued)

Please note any further comments and suggestions/errors below

FREE PRIZE DRAW RULES

1 Closing date for 31 January 2009 draw is 31 December 2008. Closing date for 31 July 2009 draw is 30 June 2009.

2 No purchase necessary. Entry forms are available upon request from BPP Learning Media. No more than one entry per title, per person. Draw restricted to persons aged 16 and over.

3 Winners will be notified by post and receive their cheques not later than 6 weeks after the relevant draw date.

4   The decision of the promoter in all matters is final and binding. No correspondence will be entered into.